Selected Poems and Related Prose

F. T. Marinetti

Selected Poems and

Related Prose

Selected by Luce Marinetti

Translated from the French by Elizabeth R. Napier

and Barbara R. Studholme

With an essay by Paolo Valesio

YALE UNIVERSITY PRESS   NEW HAVEN AND LONDON

To M and D

−E and B

And to D

−E

Designed by James J. Johnson and set in Joanna Roman type by The Composing Room of Michigan, Inc.
Printed in the United States of America by Vail-Ballou Press, Binghamton, New York.

Library of Congress Cataloging-in-Publication Data

Marinetti, Filippo Tommaso, 1876–1944.
[Selections. English. 1996]
Selected poems and related prose / F.T. Marinetti : selected by Luce Marinetti ; translated by Elizabeth R. Napier and Barbara R. Studholme ; with an essay by Paolo Valesio.
p.   cm.
Works translated from the French and Italian.
ISBN 0-300-04103-9

I. Marinetti, Luce.
II. Napier, Elizabeth R., 1950–
III. Studholme, Barbara R. (Barbara Ryder), 1952–
IV. Title
PQ4829.A78A255   1996
841'.912—dc20
                96–11140

A catalogue record for this book is available from the British Library.

The paper in this book meets the guidelines for permanence and durability of the Committee on Production Guidelines for Book Longevity of the Council on Library Resources.

10 9 8 7 6 5 4 3 2 1

Contents

Preface

Luce Marinetti

Although Filippo Tommaso Marinetti (1876–1944) was a prolific essayist, critic, and journalist, he considered himself above all a poet, and it is with his poetic output that this book is concerned. I hope that this brief account of my father's career, from his early association with the Symbolist poets to his formulation of a new kind of poetry liberated from traditional subject matter, syntax, and meter, will give readers a clearer understanding of his achievement.

"Poetry," Marinetti said to me, "is the expression of our intuitions in human language; hence from the beginning it has been both simple and intuitive. Every human being has sensations caused by states of mind. When these sensations are expressed in words, the result is poetry. . . . Poetry is the highest expression of rare, difficult, and complex emotions and intuitions, an expression in which the deepest thoughts are wedded to simple perceptions. This union stirs a wide variety of new poetic emotions. The strongest and most sharply defined of these emotions are imbued with the universal desire for a better world."

From his earliest poems, Marinetti exhorts us to replace the gray ashes of the past with the incandescent lava of the future. His poetry extols the possibilities of a new man-poet, begotten by scientific civilization, and celebrates the machine. "A racecar . . . is more beautiful than the *Victory of Samothrace*," he wrote provocatively in the first Futurist manifesto (1909). If we examine the new beauty invoked by Marinetti, his poetic theory becomes clear and the whole of contemporary literature and art can be understood on the deepest level.

Marinetti strove to be ahead of his time, to demolish the notion that artistic ideals and everyday life are incompatible, and to find poetry in their unity. This is why poetry, like the visual arts, must not merely pique the interest of dilettantes but give voice to vital emotions: for Marinetti, poetry was not an escape from but an exaltation of life.

Born in Egypt to Italian parents, Marinetti was educated in French, first in Alexandria and then in Paris. Possessed of a passionate and venturesome intellect, he established bases in both Milan and Paris, combining a volatile Mediterranean temperament with a modern cosmopolitanism. In April 1899, at age twenty-two, he gained notoriety in Paris when the great actress Sarah Bernhardt recited one of his first poems, "Les Vieux Marins" (The old sailors). The poem won first prize at the "Samedis populaires," a poetry contest organized by the Parnassian Catulle Mendès and the Symbolist Gustave Kahn.

In 1904 Marinetti founded the international

magazine *Poesia* (Poetry) to show the need for literary change. Among its contributors were some of the leading writers of the day: Algernon Charles Swinburne, William Butler Yeats, Emile Verhaeren, Henri de Régnier, and Alfred Jarry. Marinetti wanted above all to publish the most avant-garde of the young European poets. *Poesia* thus became a kind of training ground for the Futurists. The Futurist movement itself was launched on February 20, 1909 with the publication on the front page of the Paris newspaper *Le Figaro* of Marinetti's first brash Futurist manifesto. Beginning as a literary phenomenon, the revolution soon spread to the realms of painting, music, theater, architecture, graphic art, and daily life.

The present anthology of Marinetti's French writings exhibits the wide range of his linguistic experimentation, from free verse to what he eventually called "words in freedom." It was Kahn, with his *Palais nomades* (Nomadic palaces, 1887), who introduced free verse to French literature. Far from repudiating rhyme, Kahn elaborated on it within the strict academic tradition of French verse. Marinetti, on the other hand, heeded only his own poetic imperatives. His first three books—*La Conquête des Etoiles* (The conquest of the stars, 1902), *Destruction* (1904), and *La Ville charnelle* (The sensual city, 1908)—heralded a metrical revolution that was considerably more far-reaching than Kahn's. Despite the poems' apparent classicism and linguistic discipline, Marinetti's exuberance follows no set rules. His characteristic meters, already present in his earliest poems, and his attempts to reinvent verse spring from an emotional impulse that prefigures his visualization of poetic forms. Indeed, Marinetti's poetic evolution can be defined as a quest to liberate verse from theories and mechanical limitations, to place it under the command of its own dynamic spirit, and above all to harmonize it onomatopoeically with the linguistic value of the word.

In *La Conquête des Etoiles*, Marinetti attempted,

with the audacity of youth, to pry open the oyster of the poetic world with the knife of romanticism. The influence of his French Symbolist masters, however, remains clear. He dedicated the book to Kahn, the "veteran" poet, in the following lines:

> The Oracle-Song of the Waves
> "Hey-ho! Hey-ho! Hey-hey!
> O ancient Waves, O Veterans of the Sovereign Sea
> . . . ."

The war of elements rages through *La Conquête des Etoiles* in a steady crescendo: the Veterans of the Sea (the great traditional poets), the huge waves, typhoons, cyclones, and arrogant waterspouts defy the heavens until the celestial forces succumb to the hellish assault and the last star fades:

> Dying Star, alas! half-naked and flexuous,
> its damp flesh turning green!
> Its amethyst face, veiled with slow tears,
> glistened in the seaweed's hair.

In the end, Marinetti's dramatic romanticism remains torn between inner turmoil and contemplation:

> It drenched me with its tears of love,
> the inconsolable Star of my Dream!

Reading the lines of *La Conquête des Etoiles*, with their exuberant flow of extreme images, it is impossible to overlook the sublimity and authenticity of the poem's epic tone. Marinetti manipulates his poetic muse masterfully, immersing the reader in the idealistic meaning of his first epic in verse.

In *Destruction*, Marinetti leaves the romantic limbo of *La Conquête des Etoiles* and adopts a firmer, more virile style. No longer does he find it necessary to seek poetry in the violence of nature; he casts his deepest feelings in a new lyrical language, a language expressive of the full range of human emotions. The poet is now defiant:

You are infinite and divine, O Sea, I know it
by the oath on your foaming lips,
by your oath that attentive Echoes like watchmen
repeat from shore to shore . . . .

now playful:

The scholars have come to your promontories,
prancing like puppets, dangling
from the tangled strings of autumnal rains,
to explore you, O Sea! . . .

now sensual:

O Eastern dancer with your leaping belly
and breasts red with shipwrecks' blood! . .

now gentle:

Later, when I came back home,
a quiet family evening had begun,
beneath the lamp that stretched its neck of flame
and curled its wings of light across the table,
to brood the impassioned desires of my soul
in the fluttering of its silky rays . . .
—like a hen with giant magic golden eggs . . .

now bitterly aware of the sea's ironic derision:

My heart? . . . I wound it in your nocturnal locks
. . .

My heart? . . . I dragged it breathless
through your foaming waves, toothed
like cruel silver saws! . . .

In *Destruction*, Marinetti's wealth of imagery and
analogies is at its most profound and exuberant. Hav-
ing freed poetry from the confines of conventional
subject matter, syntax, and meter, he expresses the col-
ors and sensibilities of his inner life, which vibrates and
responds to every thrill of his creative spirit.

The profound intensity of Marinetti's poetry is
apparent throughout *La Ville charnelle*:

To catch the Night at sleep in the plains,
I crossed the enormous mountain range,
I crushed the Night with my echoing steps,
the honey Night sickening with heat,
envenomed by the climbing moon.

Each stanza of the poem represents the zenith
of his poetic achievement. In this third collection of
verse, Marinetti forsakes his impetuous modernity and
depicts the sensual beauty of a tropical city, the silky
murmur of the African sea, the mosques capped with
yearning spires, the dunes rising like the knees of a
beautiful woman, blanketed with dazzling white
chalk. Gone is the agile, driving rhythm of *Destruction*;
in its place are jewels of oriental rhymes and transpar-
ent echoes of alexandrines. In this flood of images, the
poetic turbulence calms without loss of force, as in the
following lines:

O, opulent City of feminine curves
whose sensual whiteness tempts my mouth,
on your fragrant couch of drowsy trees
blooming with jasmine, black currant, and mint.

Still more ethereal and fantastical is the group
of poems in *La Ville charnelle* called "petits drames de lu-
mières" (Little light plays). Stretching the pathetic fal-
lacy to the extreme limits of pantheism, Marinetti cre-
ates miniature scenes out of the interplay of plants,
elements, and human inventions. All such inventions
arise from an impulse born of desperation and de-
sire—a desire woven into the complex fabric of our ul-
tramodern society. The very titles of these delicate po-
ems reflect their lyrical beauty: "Les Vignes folles et la
levrette du firmament" (The mad vines and the grey-
hound of the firmament), "La Vie des voiles" (The life
of the sails), and "La Mort des Forteresses" (The death
of the fortresses), which includes the poems "Les
Carènes coquettes" (The coy hulls), "L'Inutile Sagesse"
(Useless wisdom), and "La Victoire de l'Aurore" (The

dawn's victory). From the group of "little light plays," I have selected "La Mort des Forteresses" for the present anthology.

In 1911–1912, Marinetti's dynamic poetic sensibility found release again in epic poetry. *Le Monoplan du Pape* (The pope's monoplane) was published in Paris in 1912 but written in 1911 in the trenches of Sidi-Messri, near Tripoli, during the Italo-Turkish War. *Le Monoplan du Pape* reflects the political and social drama of the European crisis. It glorifies the anticlericalism of the time, culminating in a graphic description of Marinetti's beloved Italy and presaging the outbreak of World War I. Marinetti's verse in this volume is transformed into a subtle, impalpable, and potentially mysterious Symbolist music. Through its imagery the poet discovers the secret relationship between external reality and his own inner nature. The sometimes deafening music is not meant to detract from the mystery; rather, it is aimed at grasping the truth of reality. Through such poetry—and later, programmatically, through words in freedom—Marinetti addressed the new needs of civilization in the crowded modern city, with its machines and excitement. To encompass this world poetically, he embarked on a continuous quest for linguistic and visual sensations. For Marinetti, mystery, in short, had to be shattered: nothing could be permitted to intervene between human beings and the real world. In order to achieve this goal, Marinetti glorified the *word*, filled it with sound, and carried it to the most exasperating extremes. As he would declare in "La splendeur géometrique et mécanique" (Geometric and mechanical splendor), first written in 1914 and revised for *Les Mots en liberté futuristes* (Futurist words in freedom), 1919,

> Today from the chaos of new sensibilities we bring forth a new beauty to replace the first. . . . Its elements are...the perishable, the ephemeral, bridled power, speed, light, will . . . ; the instinct

of man multiplied by the machine; the sense of the big city; . . . the wireless imagination, ubiquity, the succinctness and simultaneity of tourism, big business, and journalism; . . . enthusiastic imitation of electricity and the machine, essential brevity and synthesis; the happy precision of lubricated gears and thoughts; the concurrence of energies converging in a single trajectory.

Marinetti was the opposite of Verhaeren, the prisoner of the city. Marinetti's poetry is liberating: its message is that the machine and the city must not enslave human beings, nor vice versa; instead, they should complement each other. The word—what Marinetti called the "essential word"—was the instrument of his quest. The real reason for destroying conventional syntax was to realize a purer rhythmic context. Words in freedom, stripped of their old rhythmic and syntactic connections, cling more tenaciously to reality so that they may establish broader analogies. The object, Marinetti argued, must be directly joined to the image it recalls, producing a totality, a synthesis that can be created only by an essential word:

> I proclaim that lyricism is the very rare *ability to be intoxicated with life and to intoxicate it with ourselves;* the ability to turn into wine the troubled waters of life that surround us and run through us; the ability to paint the world with the special colors of our changing self. Let's suppose that a friend endowed with this lyrical gift finds himself in a zone of intense life (revolution, war, shipwreck, earthquake, etc.) and immediately afterwards comes to tell you his impressions. Do you know what this friend will instinctively do as he begins his story? He will brutally destroy syntax as he speaks, will . . . abolish punctuation and word order, and will bombard your nerves with all his visual, auditory, and olfactory sensations, as their mad gallop takes

him. . . . Thus you will have fistfuls of essential words in no conventional order, your friend being concerned with nothing but the expression of all the vibrations of his self. If this lyrical speaker also has a mind rich in general ideas, he will involuntarily and constantly link these last sensations with all that he has known of the universe, experimentally or intuitively. He will cast great nets of analogies over the world, thus rendering the analogical and essential core of life telegraphically. . . .

This need for succinctness is a response not only to the laws of speed by which we are governed but also to the age-old relationship of the poet and his public. This relationship is much like the intimacy of two old friends who can communicate with a single word, a single glance. This is how and why the poet's imagination must link distant things without *conducting wires*, using instead essential words absolutely *in freedom*. ("Les mots en liberté" [Words in freedom], 1913; revised for *Les Mots en liberté futuristes*, 1919)

The struggle for increasing freedom of expression characterizes all literatures. Words in freedom represent the front line of this struggle—a line that may never be crossed. They arose from Marinetti's desire to express the welter of impressions that besiege the poet in a moment of intense lyricism. He conceived the idea in Tripoli and perfected it in Adrianople, amid the tumult and anxiety of battle. Words in freedom upset the rules of syntax, displaced adjectives and nouns, advocated the infinitive verb, and employed onomatopoeia, synoptic tables, and unconventional spelling. Numbers and other mathematical symbols were inserted in the text as indicators of poetic intensity, and graphic and typographic experiments also became a measure of that intensity. Later, the Futurist poets used words in freedom to express diverse sensibilities: decadence and sophistication, innocence and savagery, drama and irony. Thereafter Marinetti created "motsfondus" ("fusedwords"), explaining that in combining and fusing words, the rhythm and imagery of verse are accelerated.

The first book of words in freedom was *Zang toumb toumb*, written in French in 1912–1913 and published in Italian in 1914. The achievement of *La Ville charnelle* lies in the way the images are interwoven as in a cobweb, one springing from the other. In *Zang toumb toumb*, by contrast, the images fall apart. Words are reduced to essences, spaces become concrete, sounds are heard and even attain visual reality. In his novel *Mafarka le futuriste* (Mafarka the Futurist, 1909), Marinetti had expressed the idea that human beings should control the world they have created; in *Zang toumb toumb* this ideal is proposed as a new religion of life centered on everyday heroism. For Marinetti, the machine meant speed and speed meant conflict. Even so, human beings must be masters rather than slaves. And so poetry was transformed into a festival of sounds: in "Bombardement" (Bombardment), the poet becomes an orchestra conductor, confronted by the deadly machinery of war.

Zang toumb toumb was also the first Futurist visual book. Marinetti devised a new vocabulary of mathematical signs, numbers, capitals, and empty spaces (to allude, for example, to the silence between bomb explosions) in order to make the pathos of battle more resonant. In the section "Ballon captif turc" (Turkish captive balloon) from "Hadirlik quartier général turc" (Hadirlik Turkish headquarters), for instance, the balloon is depicted in graphic characters as an observation post connected telegraphically to the ground. (The French term for radio, T.S.F., stands for *télégraphie sans fils*, or wireless telegraphy.) In the poem "Pont" (Bridge), eight lines have to be read synchronically to evoke eight states of mind, and a plane flying over a reservist is described with two sounds, HHRRRAAAaaa . . . hrrrrrrr, separated by a blank space that is intended not as a phonetic pause but as an interpretation of the sky as a plastic element.

Thus, Marinetti's literary revolution was also a typographic revolution. He was aware that he was standing at a turning point in the history of poetry: the times demanded his discoveries and innovations. Marinetti believed that even material elements had a function in poetry, and Futurist poets immersed themselves in the objects described in their poetry, expressing them sonorously in words. Sound was extremely significant to the Futurists; they even treated the body as an esthetic instrument. In "Simultanéité—Tables synoptiques de valeurs lyriques" (Simultaneity—synoptic tables of lyrical values), first published in 1914 and revised for *Les Mots en liberté futuristes*, Marinetti declared: "These energies of accent, voice, and gesticulation now find their natural expression in the distorted words and typographic disproportions that correspond to grimaces and the chiseling force of gestures. Words in freedom thus become the lyrical, transfigured extension of our animal magnetism."

Marinetti trumpeted this new esthetic theory to the literary avant-garde of Europe. He published the latest words-in-freedom tables in *Les Mots en liberté futuristes*, a book that became the exemplar of his revolution. In 1920 he dedicated his publishing house, Poesia, to all Futurists who wanted to publish words in freedom but whose work had been rejected by conventional editors.

Marinetti's greatest ambition was to establish a mythology of the industrial age. Its protagonists were the absolute "I" as representation of an anarchic-individualistic ideology and the machine as deity, or at least totem, in a Futurist theology of speed. He created a complex network of poetic ideologies in appreciation of the diverse characters acting within an organic co

existence of opposing analogies and emotions. Thus the sea is "infinie et divine" (infinite and divine), "majestueuse" (majestic), "formidable épée à pourfendre les Astres" (a mighty sword to cleave the Stars), but also "menaçante" (menacing). The stars, by contrast, are described in predominantly negative terms: "obscène," "cruelle," "une folle" (obscene, cruel, a lunatic).

Marinetti's poetry is built around linkages between "I" (or "my spirit") and symbols (that is, representations of principles, ideas, forces, and so on). The poet is motivated by a desire to organize a system of abstract and concrete images signifying the unity of reality and conception, a desire to realize the concept and to conceptualize the real, to superimpose temporal planes, to present an uninterrupted series of equations between the environment and the interior world, to fuse existence and imagination. Like every epic poet, Marinetti articulates his verse around certain key images, whether they be characters or emblems. His early Symbolist writings often invest reality with ideological meaning; his Futurist writings, through the use of words in freedom, translate ideological motives into reality.

In Marinetti's poetry, the influence of tradition is marked by his constant crossing of the literary and linguistic boundaries between French and Italian. Marinetti was caught between the Symbolist legacy of his traditional French education on the one hand, and his native language and culture on the other. The resulting tension was a source of his creativity, as well as of great psychic distress. A capable linguist, Marinetti experimented repeatedly with French and Italian, translating and analyzing the sound effects of words. In the 1925 anthology of Futurist poets, *I nuovi poeti futuristi*, he presented his texts in both languages, and it is extremely interesting to analyze the relationship he established between the two. What emerges clearly is the importance of his Symbolist experience. The thread that winds from the earlier Symbolist poetry through words in freedom and fusedwords constitutes, as it were, an autobiography of the author. Marinetti's incessant poetic research, his one hundred souls in one, his extraordinary internationality, made palpable through his poetry, led to the first *Futurist Manifesto* and to all the other manifestos. Marinetti had a global intellect and a perspicacious view of the future. His poetry, situated in the midst of the long struggle between Symbolist language and Expressionist violence, linked "decadence" and "revolution."

The twenty poems addressed to Marinetti's wife, Beny (Benedetta), are jewels worthy of their recipient. Written between 1920 and 1938, they were inscribed calligraphically on large sheets of precious paper. Among these poems is "La droite trouve la perle" (The right finds the pearl, 1928), which appears in this collection in the section, *After Words in Freedom*. I have included it both because it relates to Marinetti's earlier "motsfondus" and because it was written on the island of Capri, where he, Beny, and later, we children spent many happy months together.

Translating Marinetti

Elizabeth R. Napier and Barbara R. Studholme

In translating Marinetti, we have exercised a degree of restraint that, given the tenor of the original works, may appear somewhat incongruous. From the flamboyant *Conquête des Etoiles* to the "liberated" verse of *Zang toumb toumb* and *Les Mots en liberté futuristes*, Marinetti's impulse seems to be toward expansion and freedom, toward an enfranchisement of language in which the translator ought to be able to share. Yet in the end neither hyperbole (the exclamatory tone and insistent battle theme of *Conquête*) nor its opposite, succinctness and a programmatic destruction of syntactic order (as demonstrated in *Zang toumb toumb* and *Les Mots en liberté futuristes*), "freed" Marinetti's verse in any radical way, nor does his poetry invite such freedom for the translator. Indeed, it is not until the later poems to his wife, Benedetta (*Poésie à Beny*, 1920–1938), that Marinetti's verse begins to show signs of the kind of formal play that licenses the translator in any true sense of the word. The challenges posed by complex verse forms, rhymes, and word play, which in turn bring pleasure to the translator, are scarce in Marinetti's work before *Beny*. To adapt Alexander Pope's phrase, there is little checking of the horse to produce mettle. Later, there is perhaps too much. But such extremes are in large part (and from the beginning) deliberate features of Marinetti's poetry, from the excesses of *La Conquête des*

Etoiles to the more emphatic rejection of traditional prosody in the later manifestos and manifesto-poems.

The evolution of Marinetti's work which Luce Marinetti's selection seeks to demonstrate shows both congruities and discrepancies between his poetry prior to 1912 (the date of Marinetti's ground-breaking "Technical Manifesto of Futurist Literature") and his work after that date. Thus, some of the issues we have had to confront as translators are characteristic of Marinetti's oeuvre, while others arise for the first time in his work around the period of the "Technical Manifesto." Distinctive to Marinetti's verse and prose is an eclectic range of diction. Throughout his writings, Marinetti uses technical terminology from diverse fields—nautical, aeronautical, military, medical, and architectural—and demonstrates knowledge of chemical and mechanical processes. As Marinetti experiments with introducing different voices into his poems, or moves his poems to foreign settings (as in *Zang toumb toumb*), Turkish and Bulgarian words, phrases, and place names appear in his work, sometimes incorrectly and often inconsistently spelled. He also mixes French and Italian, the two languages in which he was adept, in some of the poster-poems of *Les Mots en liberté futuristes*. More arcanely, Marinetti occasionally fuses French and Italian to produce curiously Italo-French constructions (mitriazes [machine guns], avampostes [outposts] from "Hadirlik quartier général turc") or translates directly from Italian into French. His French thus may take on a stilted or "foreign" air (heightened, of course, by Marinetti's declamatory style), which we have tried to retain in translation. The language of machines (airplanes, automobiles, battleships, guns) and explosive events (volcanic eruptions, rifle-fire, gastro-intestinal tumult) was clearly of great interest to Marinetti, and his translators have had to become fluent in a multitude of such nonliterary fields. Marinetti's familiarity with Balkan military history (especially the period of October and November 1912, when Marinetti was at Adrianople) informs Zang toumb toumb, and references to Turkish military officials, battles, and strategies permeate the poems from this collection. In accordance with Marinetti's new view of poetry as reportage, the works often resolve into lists of names, places, and military statistics drawn directly from actual events of the campaign in Thrace. The factual basis of these poems was important to Marinetti, so we have researched such events as thoroughly as possible and explained them in the notes.

Though the challenges posed by the range of Marinetti's subject matter and diction are relatively straightforward, his syntax poses problems of a different kind. In the early narrative poems like La Conquête des Etoiles and La Ville charnelle, the poet's excitement at personifying cosmic and geographical elements leads to accretions of adjectival clauses (introduced by avec, dont, or qui) that are meant to extend the analogical possibilities of his similes and metaphors. Extend them they do, but with a curiously cluttered result (for example: "un passant en prière m'a narré les splendeurs / dont vous auréolez les clairs pélérinages / qui viennent de partout plier leurs vieux genoux! . . ." [a passer-by in prayer told me how your glories / crown the bright pilgrimages / that come from near and far to bend their feeble knees! . . .], from La Ville charnelle). It is not until after Le Monoplan du Pape (1912) that Marinetti embraces the opposite course of concision, of connections made "telegraphically," "without conducting wires." The early works, with their luxuriant syntax and elaborate analogies and images, provide a helpful view of what Marinetti was reacting against in the manifestos of 1912 and later.

Unorthodox syntax, especially in Marinetti's early works, may be complemented by startling phrases—un lierre terrifiant d'allégresse (fearsome vines of joy), un falot de joie (a lantern of joy) (La Ville charnelle)—and by idiosyncratic usages—flexueuse (supple, flexuous) and prolixe (long). Archaisms (pâmé [swooned], s'ébaudir [to frolic]) and rare words (émeraudé [emerald], puruler [to ooze], immensifier [to immensify]) are other features of the early poems that we have retained wherever possible. Marinetti's onomatopoeia (aside from the familiar glouglou and plouff plouff) is, especially in the later poems, unconventional (chaak, tatatraaak, zang-toumb-toumb). In accordance with his habit of translating such sounds phonetically from French to Italian and Italian to French, we have given "English" equivalents of Marinetti's noises. It is interesting that such onomatopoeia, to which Marinetti devotes much attention in the theoretical essays of 1913 and 1914, figures in his early poetry as well (most notably, the untranslatable refrain Stridionla Stridionlaire in La Conquête des Etoiles, which Marinetti noted was meant to reflect the shrillness of swords and agitation of the waves in the tempestuous battle of sea and stars).

Other stylistic quirks, especially in the early poetry, may disturb the flow of reading. La Conquête des Etoiles and La Ville charnelle, for example, are frequently overexclamatory and expansive, the most amplified gestures producing on occasion sentences that are nearly unreadable. Marinetti's love for analogy results in abstruse, sometimes grotesque combinations of images —the blasting breasts in Destruction, the flabby waves and Sovereign Sea with her spongy face in La Conquête *des Etoiles*. Marinetti often renders similarities in such detail that, with attention concentrated upon individual elements, the simile or metaphor as a whole fails to deliver a coherent picture: the image fragments into a surreal, disembodied pastiche. In a certain sense, such a strategy is a foretaste of Marinetti's "telegraphic" style in *Zang toumb toumb* and *Les Mots en liberté*, where the heterogeneity of the connected concepts becomes part of the larger program to startle readers out of their conventional reading stances. It may form, too, part of Marinetti's more defiantly articulated plan to "create the ugly in literature" ("Technical Manifesto"), to debunk the sentimental, the beautiful, the ideal (which scheme is explored thematically in all of Marinetti's early work, especially in *La Conquête des Etoiles* and *Destruction*). Not yet in play in these poems is the cynical bravado of Marinetti's later pieces: the volcano in *Le Monoplan du Pape*, for example—described as a huge throat (complete with buccal muscles, gums, and bronchi) and then as a theater (with grandstand, spectators, and dancing acrobats), into both of which the aviator-speaker of *Le Monoplan* descends—reveals Marinetti's interest in spectacle for its own histrionic sake. The terser connections between war and the stage in "Bombardement," by contrast, present a more complex (and ethically more problematic) vision that is not merely visual and aural.

Though Marinetti's later poetics are intimated by the volcano in *Le Monoplan du Pape* ("Glorify war, the world's only hygiene"), it is not until the poems of *Zang toumb toumb* that this desire to wage combat, to "clean" by an act of liberating destruction, actually becomes formalized in the procedures of Marinetti's work. The shift to the techniques of the "Technical Manifesto" is surprisingly abrupt: the only hints are the distant analogies and occasional linked nouns in Marinetti's earlier work (the double substantives like *Afrique sorcière*

[sorceress Africa] or *gaz spectateurs* [spectator gases] in *Destruction* and *Le Monoplan du Pape*, respectively. Yet here the second nouns are clearly meant to be read as adjectives.) By contrast, "Bataille poids + odeur," the poem meant to demonstrate Marinetti's new poetic manifesto, is almost totally devoid of adjectives and adverbs, a nearly continuous chain of nouns. Such suppression of narrative generates a new set of translating challenges, and Marinetti's Italian version of the poem thus becomes important in isolating and limiting the meanings of his words. Comparisons of French and Italian versions of poems from this period show, interestingly, how literal a translator Marinetti himself was, and how oddly inflexible his view of that activity could be. Few changes are effected in response to the connotative richness of the language in which Marinetti is working, and multiple meanings in both languages tend to be rendered not through homonyms and puns but additively, by linking analogous images with hyphens ("obus-tribuns nuages-grils fusils-martyrs shrapnels-auréoles" [shells-tribunes clouds-gridirons rifles-martyrs shrapnel-haloes] ["Bataille"]). Marinetti's concern with analogy here is predominant: disencumbering himself from his early narrative style (where metaphoric and descriptive modes sometimes clash, as in "La Mort des Forteresses" from *La Ville charnelle*), he engages more "cleanly" in what Harold Monro called "an advanced form of verbal photography."* Speed, dynamism, journalistic succinctness are the keynotes of the poems from this period: language, trimmed of its descriptive, adjectival fat, becomes a form of ammunition, bombarding the reader with unexpected combinations of images and mechanical sounds. Marinetti makes the analogy himself, likening his pairs of images to chain shot ("Technical Manifesto"). The simile is telling: the act of writing for Marinetti has turned into an act of warfare, not only because war has

---

* Harold Monro, "The Origin of Futurism," *Poetry and Drama* 1 (1913): 389.

become the predominant subject matter of his poems but because his work seeks to destroy traditional ideas of prosody and reading. His bullet-like language (exaggerated in "Bataille poids + odeur") pursues precision, accuracy, *not* nuance, and there is a corresponding and deliberate deemphasizing of the sentimental, the human. A concern with psychology is replaced with a concern for matter: as Marinetti puts it in the "Technical Manifesto," a shining gun is more interesting than the spectacle of the slain. Thus, the illness of the Anatolian captain in "Train de soldats malades" from *Zang toumb toumb* is depicted more as a microbial battle than as an event of emotional importance. Marinetti's early interest in spectacle has here taken an unpleasant turn: deliberately neglecting the human element of war, Marinetti raps out statistics of death and destruction with the mechanical indifference of a wireless telegraph. Marinetti's lack of concern with the psychological, his curiously "objective" and dynamic attitude toward language (with its focus, to the English-speaking translator's distress, on the importance of the infinitive verb, the verb stripped of its actor), lead directly into the typographical experimentation of the poems of *Les Mots en liberté futuristes*. The poem is seen here primarily as visual object (though the narrative titles of the works—for example, "After the Marne, Joffre toured the front by car"—make clear that Marinetti enjoys the irony of juxtaposing the visual and verbal modes). Such typographic experimentation continues in Marinetti's *motsfondus* ("fusedwords"), and "La droite trouve la perle," which demonstrates the use of the lines of the hand in the poem's physical presentation.

With *Poésie à Beny*, Marinetti effects an unexpected return to previously rejected forms and themes. The *Beny* poems were intended as private works, addressed to his wife, and they display as a result a peculiar freedom, a freedom ironic in light of Marinetti's previous fulminations against traditional prosody and syntax. Relieved from the political program underlying *Zang toumb toumb* and *Les Mots en liberté*, Marinetti is clearly deriving more subtle pleasures from language. The embedding technique of "Deux périssoires à Capri" (*île/fragile; périssoires/polissoir/soir*), for example, would have struck Marinetti as fussy, even effeminate, during his *Zang toumb toumb* period. But Marinetti, as is made obvious in "Faut-il choisir ces mots" and "L'île lance la jetée," is now serving a higher (and previously scorned) master: beauty ("les mots [ont] le devoir . . . de servir ta Beauté," as he puts it in "Faut-il choisir ces mots"). The cynical homonym *cher/chair* (literally, dear/flesh, which mutates somewhat inadequately into the English dear/desire) of "Lettre d'une jolie femme à un monsieur passéiste" is now used seriously, as an expression of adoration, much as is the recurring, thematically significant homonym *Beny/bénie* (Beny/blessed). In discarding the political agenda of the 1910s, Marinetti liberates himself into more complex, sophisticated poetry, both humorous and serious.

A Note on the Texts

Marinetti revised and republished his poems frequently. We have in each case translated from the latest edition of the volumes indicated, using later, separately published revisions of individual poems (as well as manuscript material) to identify typographical errors and to clarify Marinetti's intentions as to typesetting and pagesetting. Corrections, generally, have been made conservatively. Marinetti's punctuation, before he decreed its abolition in the "Technical Manifesto," is often unconventional (compound subjects may be separated from their predicates by commas; appositives may not be set off by commas) or careless, and his capitalization and orthography can be inconsistent. To retain a sense of such eccentricity, we have exercised restraint in our emendations, correcting obvious typographical mistakes in the French texts and normalizing punctuation in the English translations sparingly.

All of the poems and essays in this volume were written originally in French or were translated from Italian into French by Marinetti. In translating *Zang toumb toumb* (published in Italian in Milan in 1914), we have worked from the corrected galleys of the unpublished French edition that Marinetti prepared prior to the war, using the Italian version to help decode problematic areas and determine Marinetti's final preferences for the physical presentation of the text. Most of the essays and poems in *Les Mots en liberté futuristes* first appeared in *Lacerba* and other Futurist reviews in Italian and were collected and translated (with revisions) by Marinetti for the French publication, which appeared in 1919.

Many of Marinetti's French texts were translated into Italian (by Marinetti or by his secretary, Decio Cinti). We have used Marinetti's translations, where appropriate, to identify typographical errors in the French.

Original texts of the French poems, including those of the corrected galley proofs of *Zang toumb toumb*, may be found at the end of this book. Poster poems (the "examples" of words in freedom), as well as the essay on "motsfondus" ("After words in freedom") and the two versions of "the right finds the pearl" in Marinetti's hand, have been photographically reproduced from the originals and face the English translations.

Readers interested in the publication history of and textual variants in Marinetti's works may consult F. T. Marinetti, *Scritti francesi*, vol. 1, edited by Pasquale A. Jannini (Milan, 1983); F. T. Marinetti, *Les Mots en liberté futuristes*, with a preface by Giovanni Lista (Lausanne, 1987); and F. T. Marinetti, *Teoria e invenzione futurista*, 2d ed., edited by Luciano De Maria (Milan, 1990).

Acknowledgments

The translators are indebted to a number of persons who helped with the translations and supplied information on many of the arcane topics with which Marinetti's poetry is concerned. Tom Butler and Tim Ferris advised us on some of Marinetti's medical references; Robert Channon, Marjorie Lamberti, David Macey, Kevin Moss, and Pardon Tillinghast answered questions about medieval and Balkan history. Elisa Barucchieri, John Bertolini, Glauco Cambon, Max Creech, Margaret Koster, Luciano De Maria, Ilaria Galimberti, Ugo Skubikowski, and Paolo Valesio provided Italian translations and advice about Marinetti's Italian writings. W. H. Barber kindly responded to a question about Voltaire. Chris Watters supplied us with the proper terminology for a snake's habitation. Donald S. Lopez and Peter Jakab of the National Air and Space Museum researched material on early flight. Robert Mitchell read and commented upon the entire translation, and Carol Rifelj answered specific queries about French usage. Librarians and assistants at the Middlebury College, Widener, and Bodleian libraries—in particular Fleur Laslocky and Terry Plum—gave us able and generous aid. We are thankful to Judy Metro and Tom Jenkins at Yale University Press and to Luce Marinetti and Laura Wittman for help in locating and deciphering Marinetti material. Marjorie Wynne at the Beinecke Rare Book and Manuscript Library and Richard Warren at the Historical Sound Recordings Collection, Yale University Library, provided special assistance with manuscripts and recordings. We are indebted to Stephen Donadio, who published excerpts from *The Pope's Monoplane* and *Futurist Words in Freedom* in the *New England Review* 17 (1995): 22–32. Grants from the Faculty Professional Development Fund of Middlebury College helped defray many expenses associated with our work. For advice on the translations, we are particularly grateful to Frank G. Ryder and Shirley S. Ryder. To them we dedicate this book.

Selected Poems and Related Prose

The Old Sailors

(1898)

To Gustave Kahn

One night when it was red
In a sea-green port, flowering musk and spray,
The old battered sunset
Dragged its senile agony down in the shacks,
And its blood oozed
Tragically, through the dead windows' hearts.
—One night when it was red . . .

Muffled voices swelled
Along the waves, upon the tide,
And souls cried, distant and blue,
At the doleful tolling of the bells . . .
A grave was dug.
Who knows? Someone out there along the shore . . .
Among the pale tapers . . .
The simple tapers cried and smiled
Like children who come
To the graveyard at night
Among the black tombs blooming with primulas,
Red roses, and bluets;
And they dreamed, out there, down in the shacks . . .
—One night when it was brown . . .

And they dreamed of the women who died
Out there, they know not where, who knew how
        to smile,
At night, when the sailors came home
From the sea and the storms.

And the old men said, mumbling their prayers:
"They passed at nightfall yesterday,
They passed bearing on their heads urns
Filled with the blood of dead twilights.
They passed proudly,
Out there, by the fountains.
They were white and nearly naked,
Their dresses open, with tears and jewels of the night
Upon their sweet breasts.
Oh! they were beautiful, ardent and pale,
Like the distant days of youth."
And the old men fell silent,
In the tolling of the bells that faded in the sky,
Dreaming of the pale lips of those dead
Who once sang in darkened doorways,
Of their honeyed lips, of their exhaled souls
That slipped off one night like ardent sails
Into the sea of golden twilights.
And among the old men a dark voice wept:
"My son, do you remember the broken pane
We found, beside her bed, the night she died?"
And the sailors sitting in their doorways,
Shivering, made the sign of the cross.
Their eyes turned to the open sea
One night when it was black . . .
Out there, down in the shacks,
Their eyes tossed like weary boats
Seeking the azure and the space . . .

3

Like old boats inhaling the vast
Sky and the sea . . .
Boats a bit mad who don't want
To die in the seaweed of the shore,
Boats in love with the waves and the stars.
—One night when it was black . . .

Cruelly the weathercocks
Drilled the darkened golds of the night silence,
And in the distance the trumpeting winds
Mocked the loud rattle
Of the smoky hovels and their skeleton sounds
And their infinite tears and their dog barks
Battling the black swell.
—One night when it was black . . .

Wildly,
The winds sang like horns
Over the funnel of the ports:
"Turn, turn away, weary old eyes,
Turn away from the reefs, far from the treacherous
    sands . . .
Turn toward infinity, exhausted souls, dying boats,
Eyes without hope! . . .
You who suffer from living and so slowly dying,
Eyes thirsting for infinity and space,
Turn toward the horizon of glowing waves,
O boats tossing in the black eddy,
Grieving eyes, dying boats! . . .
You who blazed in olden days
Hoisting your golden sails
Over the royal purple of the dawn,
Turn, turn to sea, turn toward infinity!"
The winds swollen with gold and night
Rattled wildly like horns
And died forever in space.

Then the delicate bells spoke sweet words,
Echoing low the winds' bitter song

From their withered lips of dying beguines:
"Turn, turn toward infinity, exhausted souls!"
But the night was weary . . .
The night muffled them softly, in the shadows . . .
And their bronze lips, drunk with evening and with
    sadness,
Quivered forever under the hands of the night . . .
"Turn, turn toward infinity!"

The Conquest of the Stars

Epic Poem

(1902)

I
The Oracle-Song of the Waves

"Hey-ho! Hey-ho! Hey-hey!
O ancient Waves, O Veterans of the Sovereign Sea,
rise up, mighty warriors with venerable beards
    of foam!
Rise up! Rise up, brothers! Sharpen your rapiers
for the great battle. Don your heavy
golden armor, encrusted with emeralds
devoured by moss and rust!
Hey-ho! Hey-hey! Stridionla Stridionla Stridionlaire!
We are tired of sleeping deep in blue caves,
embedded in the rocks like giant gems.
We are tired of nibbling breakwaters
and munching fleets at sea.
The time has come to conquer space and to launch
the attack on the Stars. They laugh!
See them? That's the challenge, brothers!
Soon, tomorrow, perhaps tonight,
The Sea, the scourging Sea, will come to shout
her heavy commands echoed by the thunder's roar!
Hey-ho! Hey-hoo! Sharpen your rapiers!
Let our golden armor shine! . . .
Stridionla Stridionla Stridionlaire!"

Who is singing so dolefully

beneath the towering cliffs?
A huge gulf opens at my feet,
a steaming funnel of sea-green shade.
Waves with flaccid paunches twist
their hips of tar and sticky pitch.
They raise their mountainous shoulders,
embossed with intermittent gleams,
unrolling muscled arms of greenish roots.
In slow gurgling voices, the Waves sing
the oracle-hymn of celestial wars,
amid the scraping and the stridence of the swords,
"Hey ho! Hey-hey! Stridionla! Stridionlaire!"

Off and on the Waves fall exhausted,
crashing against the monstrous rocks
with a sound like bells; the Waves fall
with the weight of hippopotamuses,
with howling and hooting
and the violent pounding of picks and hammers.
   "Stridionla Heyho!
Stridionla Stridionla Heyhooo!
   Rise up! Sharpen your rapiers!"

Out at sea, the solitude's Despair lies heavy
on the waters thick with ash and foam,
like a vast ravaged cemetery
with crumbling verdant tombs;

and the sea succumbs, stagnant and pale,
in the yellow recess of the dawn.
The dawn is worn out!
The Dawn is still drunk
with the poison kiss of the Stars!
    "Stridionla! Stridionla Stridionlaire!"
In the distance the headlands sleep abreast,
in the humid torpor and intense silence,
their hairy heads abandoned on the smooth sea.
Crouching reefs, on the watch,
form knots of violet shadows,
while little waves, quicker than cats,
bat balls of foam with teasing paws.

Below me in the smoking gulf,
the metallic Waves swing
back and forth, like
great pothooks of hell.
And it's their armor they're swinging,
rhythmically, polishing it
on the ridge of the black rocks.
It's their scaly golden armor humming
and their bronze brassards and greaves!
Heyho! slowly, heyhoo! wondrously,
the rapiers are sharpened and the chain mail shines.
Muddy Waves rise, menacing,
halfway out of the grayish spray.
Their yellow diamond eyes flash
in the mist, while other Waves,
heavier, flabbier,
trailing manes
of drowsy seaweed,
lift their leathery red faces
and rear up, with a sudden twist.
And there is their sticky, smoky body,
their great centaur body,
spangled with ringing coral and stones!
Toward the light they brandish at arms' length
their golden breastplates ocellated with gems,

then in rhythm toss
their exasperated savage heads,
crying, "Stridionla! Stridionlaire!"

In the deep cove smoky with spray,
Warriors and Warrioresses revel in releasing
the thunder of their brazen lungs,
until tetanic rictus spread
their vast disjointed jaws.
When suddenly, on the arch of the horizon,
beyond a mound of quivering clouds,
the light unsheathes
a halo of sparkling swords.
The sun will leap onto the battlefield!
Heyho! the metals heaped in the gulf
begin to shake with a lightning fever,
pell-mell, in the chaos of black smoke.

Surely the Waves have heaped
the porphyry stones that pave the deep;
surely the lid of hell
has been smashed in, for an army of fiends
breaks loose in the bottom of the gulf and rises
and rushes to the top, a tide
of shimmering spears seethes,
and the cove steams, voluminously,
like a giant vat.

Then in triumph the Sun
strides over the horizon and stabs the vast sea
with a slash of bright red gold.

And there, almost at once, greenish
clouds emerge in silhouette, striped with fire,
rummaging through space with
chimerical elephant trunks.
Where are they going? Where are they
    going? The Wind
goes off to graze its Cyclone herd.

Far away, from the fantastic pastures of the sea,
comes the sound of doleful lowing.
   "Heyho! Heyhooo!
Stridionla! Stridionlaire!!
The time has come to conquer the Stars!
Brandish your rapiers like a sheaf of flames!
We have hacked
the moss of nights and the rust of dusks
from our steel breastplates,
now blazing like infernos.
Our helmets are tipped with fire and our arms
     are taut
like the straps of a catapult.

Heyho! Heyhoo! Hurrah!

Our great horses are ready. Look! . . .
their vehement crenellated backs
are harnessed with azure and beryl.
They switch their tails quietly, grazing in the grassy
     meadows
of space, jingling their
supple bits of light
and their slaver of precious stones.
Soon we will hitch them to giant wagons,
to carry our cargo of missiles:
all the petrified corpses piling up
for centuries in the waters' depths.
And with tragic jolts, from rut to rut,
the wagons will bounce on their big solid wheels,
carrying mounds of human phosphorous and gold
that later the marshaled Cyclones will hurl
at you, sneering, treacherous Stars!
Yes, yes. At you the mighty Cyclones will hurl
all the petrified corpses from the deep,
the corpses of your cast-off lovers!

Heyho! Heyhoo! Hurrah! . . .

For those are your missiles, O Sovereign Sea!
The petrified corpses sleeping symmetrically
in your depths! The Scholars have claimed
that they swell and rot away.
The Scholars have proved it! So what? Their science
     is vain!
Look at their struggling Syllogisms, gangling,
white-haired, in their pointed magician's hats
that defy the skies!
Look at their Syllogisms, whose old prolix bodies,
shaped like Xs, easily open up
and shut, like handy folding chairs
that a pot-bellied porter tucks under his arm!
The gangling Syllogisms dance in a ring
around the sweet blue Truths,
growing dizzy and closing their eyes!
     Ah! Ah!
The slender Truths like little girls
swoon with fright at a scholar's touch,
and vanish like magic
leaving their golden veils in their wild hands!
     Ah! Ah!
Laugh, beautiful Waves! Laugh
a vast adamantine laugh up to the stars!
Let your dazzling laugh crack
the domes of Silence!
For, look, the impotent Syllogisms,
white-haired, split in two, lick the trail
of the intriguing Truths that pass ungraspable!

I now believe in nothing but my great illuminating
     lighthouse Dream!
I now believe in nothing but its giant golden eye,
like an August moon,
wandering through the deepness of the Nights!

II
The Reservoirs of Death

Look! Noon bursts: a sumptuous Summer noon!
I go slowly down into the flaming cove
that burns like a sulfur spring;
I press my face against your cool
transparent cheeks, O Sea; I throw my body
upon your breast throbbing aching
under the weight of burning turquoise,
and I explore the dizzying wells
of your wondrous eyes.
In your translucent waters I see
a glorious greenish twilight deepening.
A thousand cubits down, before me,
bluish mountains form, their sharp peaks
rippling as they fall away, mountains
veiled with incandescent mists.
And in this submerged twilight,
a long chain of pyramidal mountains
unfolds with the shadowy light.
The distance clouds the farthest peaks,
that appear on the blurred arch
of the submarine horizon like blue cones
tipped with smooth rose-colored flames.
And the flexuous flames follow
the waves' rise and fall,
looking like wandering lights
in the somnolence of a vast Summer night.

Am I hallucinating? No! . . . no! I throw myself
upon your breast, O sea, and kiss your cheeks
to explore the depth of your eyes,
while the Noons pour down
their avalanche of crushed gold blocks upon my
     head.
The terrible din of the horrified silence
fills my heart and in my skull I feel
the giant wagons of the light on iron wheels,

digging their symmetrical tracks.
When I raise my head, I wonder,
beyond the still sea hills,
at the vast gulfs gorged with blinding azure
and quicklime, blowing
globular whorls of golden voices out to sea.
I hear you and I know you,
O great bellicose and vengeful voices,
bearing the din of caissons and the hum
of joyful bells and the rustling of swords!
     Stridionla! Stridionla! Stridionlaire!
     Heyho! Heyhoo! Sharpen your rapiers!
I hear you, O Waves, and my soul reels
in the sparkling surge of your coats of foam! . . .
At sea, vehement cavalcades of Waves
pass by, like countless swirls of crimson
and gold, sweeping the immensity.
So passes the Simoon,
spurring its fury, from desert to desert,
with its caracoling escort
of whirling sands streaming with fire;
so gallops the Simoon
across the solid sea of sand,
its barbaric idol's giant torso balanced
on the flying backs of crazed onagers!

At sea, squadrons of Waves pass by,
in dazzling vehement cavalcades,
and I think of the horizon of blazing sands,
where the Simoon passes, driving fast
and furious its diabolic onagers and zebras
crested with flames that look,
distorted in the distance by their speed,
like horizontal pen strokes on the paleness of the sky.
The sun has shot all its darts in a shower of gold
at the huge cavalry of the Waves.
The warriors have slipped their glittering swords
down through the bars, loopholes,
and battlements of the clouds, to block their path

with a blazing portcullis!
But the proud squadrons pass unconcerned,
and the sun's darts fly in bloody bursts,
and its swords, bent in two, simply sweep
the Waves' supple backs, combing their manes.
Ah! the lofty gods that haunt the Noons
trample my skull and crush my heart
with their bronze-shod feet,
and I beg for mercy in your eyes, sweet Sovereign
    Sea!
Am I mad? Am I hallucinating?
No! no! . . . And I plunge my gaze again
into your depths . . . At the bottom, the very bottom,
the beautiful submerged evening has clarified its
    solitude.
It is the anguished pureness of an eastern sky,
forsaken by the light, and dying
in absolute despair at the bottom of the sea.
A pale evening fevered with desire,
filled with a resigned, majestic bitterness,
a magic evening, cool and deep,
like a well of azure
below a lip of clouds,
well of tears and stars!
Suddenly the immense chain of drowned
mountains reveals its tragic essence.
I see and understand: they are pyramids
of stacked corpses, whose packed skulls
form vast granular tiers.
Their hair hangs down like seaweed
over phosphorescent peaks.
They look like pyramids of glowing,
smoking shot. Millions of faces,
turned toward the sky, bulging their hateful eyes
at the zenith! Billions of eyes
sharpened on the tips of the stars,
eyes steeled with anger yet
liquefied with infinite sorrows!
Above me, over my buzzing head,

through the Noons' impassioned furnace
passes the triumphal procession of the Conquerors
of the light. In the distance, concave bays,
filled with the bluish ink of darkness,
open their mouths, as if inhaling space.
They are air holes venting a sound of swords
and voices hooting, "Heyho! Heyhooo!"
The scholars have claimed that corpses burn
all their phosphorous and dissolve
in sumptuous rot. No! The scholars are wrong,
for, here, I see petrified bodies,
bodies of steel, embers, and gold,
harder than diamonds!
They are the suicides, those whose courage
failed under the weight of their heart,
furnace of stars! They died
from fanning in their blood the flame of the Ideal,
the great engulfing flame of the Absolute!
They died from believing the promises of the Stars.
O Divine Astral crucibles!
O venerable ingots of astral gold! Look!
Look! their phosphorous hair
spreads wide like comets!

O almighty gods of Space,
am I mad? Don't I see just
a dim reflection of the Milky ways?
No! no! My soul, trust in your dream,
for Noon soars in the immensity!
The Noons' great block bursts over my head
in pieces of incandescent metal.
I lean over the cheeks of the Sea
and behold! the wonderful
submerged twilight and its vindictive
mountains! and the symmetrical corpses,
and their living hair that, for centuries,
has fanned their metallic faces.
Through the greenish immensity,
the submerged pyramids watch the zenith,

with all their mad eyes.
All those green faces track the stupid sky,
the sorceress Night and its Stars of lust
and Infinity!

It will come! It will come, the time for revenge,
they muse darkly, when we will be seized
in the Cyclones' huge arms
and brandished by the engines of the Sea
and hurled, fiercely hurled,
at the ramparts where the Stars of sapphire dream!
Our skulls, hardened by Desire,
will click like castanets in the Waterspouts' hands,
our clashing skulls
will resound like frenzied drums
on a carnival's harlequin stage!
We will whet our unappeased eyes,
one on the other,
to the red burning of delirium!
Listen! listen! . . . the Waves sing louder:
"Heyho! Heyhoo! Stridionla! Stridionlaire!"
Tomorrow, perhaps tonight, the Scourging Sea
will come to shout her heavy commands!
Already the horizon is filled
with the loud stamping of her whinnying herds.

V
The Sovereign Sea

A black shape loomed, growing in the distance,
rising over the horizon's arch.
It appeared like the back of a whale
shooting toward shore;
then took the shape of an island
covered with forests, bristling
increasingly with black spires, sharp obelisks,
and prolix chimneys with whorling smoke.
Mirage! A huge angular greenish face
rose streaming from the sea.
A face with strong lines of slimy rock
under a mass of liquid hair,
gushing upward in a black halo!
And this billowing hair
flooded the sky; and was a torrent
of pitch, racing upstream in space,
and streaming back to its bed;
And with dread my Dream knew
the huge spongy face of the Sovereign Sea!
Her eyes blazed in phosphorous balls,
unrolling her gaze like a serpent's coils,
and her mouth opened like a sucker.

The Sovereign Sea rose halfway
over the horizon; with a roll of her hips
she twisted her sticky sorrel cetacean's back.
Then, shifting her massive haunches,
the Sea revolved, to the infinity of the coast,
the huge array of the vast folds
of swells hung round her naked waist
like a sumptuous train.
And the folds of moving waters
seethed, gorged with swords, lightning, and armor.

The Sovereign Sea sank her giant arms
of yellow smoke into the deep, her arms

muscled with swirling boas.
And bending over the horizon, her titanic body
        propped
upon her fists, her sea-green breasts
protruding, She shook
her gleaming back, ceaselessly
sculpted by the fury of her nerves.

Her whole colossal moving back appeared,
its surface fraying endlessly,
sinuous, swaying, and ready to dissolve.
And her haunches, hugely rounded,
broke over the horizon
like a mountain falling.
The Sovereign Sea thrust out
the lozenge of her spongy face,
its sockets like snake pits
beneath the black gushing
of her mass of billowing hair
that sometimes engulfed her completely.
But again, and always, it appeared,
huge and fateful, the great
green streaming Face! . . .
Then, as suddenly She opened wide
her crumbling jaws,
the scarlet sunset blazed
in her vast brazen throat:
"To arms! To arms!" she cried. "Rise up!
Onward! Bring down the Stars!"

The Sovereign Sea swept up
into her iron fist the whole soft radiant mass
of reins trailed
by the cavalries of the Waves.
And along a hundred leagues of winding coast
the immeasurable army appeared, harnessed,
lunging at the end of countless straps
gripped fiercely by the Sea.
The line of Waterspouts gazed on the show,

far off, out there, on their colonnade front,
at right angles to the horizon's arch.
The straps, radiating
to the foot of the cliff, grew frayed with foam
and danced heavily, out at sea,
like long silver saws,
over the helmets and manes of the distant squadrons
reaching to the belly of the Sovereign Sea.
At my feet, beneath the cliff,
erect on squamate golden tails,
the Unicorns spat their screaming fury
and bloody slaver, one after the other,
like long file fire.
Rising to full height,
they thrust out their wild stallion heads,
their red jaws split with rage
with the yanking of the violent reins.
They darted their tongues at the Sea,
like fierce flames that the wind whips
and kicks.
On the coils of their tails,
the Unicorns rose giant,
defiant, arching their fearful backs.

Rearing up, they threatened infinity
with their horrible hooves,
brandished like harpoons,
over their vast breastplates armed with spurs.
Like the marble Horses marching,
threatening, symmetrical,
right hooves raised,
on the friezes of dead Ninevehs!

And the great red mouth of the Sea cried
above the chaos of the banded cavalries:
"I command you to split into two armies!
All the Waves' squadrons onward!
Pile up, one on the other! It is my wish!
I give you a glorious suicide!

Your great inert mass will form
a giant mountain that the Swells,
the Unicorns, and all my Veterans will scale,
to reach and batter down
the walls of Infinity! It is my wish!
Swells, onward! Forward, Unicorns!
Waterspouts, Typhoons, onward!
Surround my sacrificial armies, heap them up,
pound the legions down, pile
squadron upon squadron, to the Zenith!

"And you, my daughters, O my young warrioresses,
onward! gallop, carry my orders
to the misty borders of my armies!
O my daughters, young warrioresses, order the
    Cyclones
to line up at the battlefront and wait.
The time will come for them to search my depths
and hoist pyramids of phosphorescent corpses
high in their arms!
The time will come for the Cyclones to hurl
my missiles at the walls of Infinity!

XIII
The Golden Scout

Then, to the right of the mountain of heaped-up
    waves,
in the recess of the nave with its vaults of steam,
under the Waterspouts' quivering hair,
far away, on the sulfurous band of the horizon,
a huge knight sheathed all in gold
appeared astride a steed of pitch.

It was the golden Scout of the armies of the Sea.
And a great voice, his brazen voice, sang
in the sublime Immensity:

—"Ha! Stars, you are unmasked!
Vile courtesans, with your turgid,
heavy, translucent breasts like two huge
amber drops! Divine bawds with eyes of pearl!
Casters of curses and deadly spells!"

Once, twice, three times, the golden Scout
drew his great fiery sword,
slashing space with a vast blinding flash.
And in the flood of yellow light
the mountain's monstrous profile
stood out huge and black,
with giant armies of Cyclones, right and left,
spinning madly,
arms high, waving in frenzy,
like branches lashed by a storm.
Then darkness wrapped
the tragic waters, and the terrible voice
burst forth anew in angry blasts:

"O sorceresses of the Impossible! Stars!
Promising nothingness! Here you are before me!
in reach of my revenge! O joy!
Oh! let me savor the mad ecstasy

of spitting in your august faces!
Know that victory is sure!
Victory is ours. Ten million Waves
will storm your metal walls!"

Fervently, ten, twenty, a thousand times,
with lightning speed, the Scout of the Sovereign Sea
drew his great fiery sword to infinity.
And high on the peak of the mountain cemented
by torrents of hatred, high at the top of the slope,
shone a citadel with ivory turrets,
and the red teeth of countless battlements,
and tiers of sulfur walls rising in the sky,
and beyond, higher still, spread
all the flashing armies of the Milky Ways,
with the happy abundance and the laziness
of a river of light winding through infinity.

To the right and the left of the somber mountain,
over the frothing armies of the Sovereign
Sea, Cyclones, Typhoons, and Waterspouts,
some ragged, half-naked,
crested with flames and yellow wings,
others, grave and draped
in billowing crepe,
bent their gigantic torsos, searching
the waters, one after the other,
with their prolix arms as soft as entrails.
Now and then the Cyclones slowly rose,
their backs twisting, rippling,
lifting from the waves,
in their great arms taut like cables,
pyramidal granular masses of phosphorous!
"These are incandescent pyramids of corpses
the Cyclones raise and shake
at you, Stars, forever cursed!
These are the petrified corpses of your lovers,
dead from drinking
your poison kiss!

Yes, cursed! a thousand times cursed,
your faces of bliss and bitterness, Stars,
and your eyes filled with the illusory gazes
of our perfidious mistresses!
I will anoint them with our steaming green spit,
your faces wet with false tears,
and painted with fleeting sweetness!
Your adamantine faces that once smiled
at my soul in the beautiful perverse evenings of
          my youth,
through the hair of forests tortured by
a hot Spring anguish . . . your emerald faces! . . .
to tear them, I lead
the armies of the Sovereign Sea
up the steep slopes of an artificial mountain
to storm, to storm your dazzling turrets!
And my Waves are drunk with revenge!
Beyond your inaccessible walls,
we will grind your great golden hearts in our
          thousand teeth!
Hot feast! and will gulp them down
into our moist transparent guts!"

A thousand times! ten thousand times! the Scout of
          the Sovereign
Sea majestically drew his blazing
sword, cutting space into a thousand pieces;
and, in the pale depths of the horizon,
a shudder shook the dark masses
that began to roll their huge fabulous
serpent coils. And farther off
the threatening legions of rigid Cyclones,
in the stiff folds of their gowns of smoking soot,
advanced, with the ghostly
rolling of crumbling colonnades.
Naked Waterspouts raised their irritated breasts,
twirling nimbly.
From moment to moment they could be seen
bending down, breaking their soft waists

to plunge their great arms into the shifting brush
and rubble of the earth.
Suddenly a thousand Typhoons, in a semicircle,
lit up with electric flames
in the black depth of their bodies.
Around their waists they wore girandoles
of will-o'-the-wisp and strings of lightning
around their necks.
And all advanced, whirling,
so fast that their great coats of mist,
their flesh of blinding azure, their girandoles,
and their necklaces seemed to stream
like a wondrous sea
around their great implacable souls of fire!
And the pounding of their iron sandals
loosed the loud din of a dark avalanche.
And their greaves rang like thunder.

XIX
The Kiss of a Dying Star

Slowly, the open hands of Silence
soothed the fury of the Night
and the mad throbbing of the sky
still thick with swords and spears.

Under level hands of loving fleece
and eternal oblivion, the great bloody
Heart of phosphorous and gold
calmed hour by hour.
The Night's great Heart
grew quiet, voluptuously appeased,
in the misty caress of a blue virgin Dawn
that smiled, superhuman
and far from the world.

I went wearily down into the deep
cove, still rumbling
like a belly filled with borborygmi.
The rocks all seemed to ache,
and I walked through the sneering
and the exhausted sobbing of the caves,
along the sand, beside the waves stiffened by
        the darkness.
When suddenly I saw the heavy flaccid swell
dragging slowly to shore,
on its seal's back glistening with black oil,
the pale and battered body of a Star.
Dying Star, alas! half-naked and flexuous,
its damp flesh turning green!
Its amethyst face, veiled with slow tears,
glistened in the seaweed's hair.

Oh! how sweetly its eyes
of sea-green shade entreated the unknown!
Then! stretching out upon the coolness of the sands,
I softly kissed its sinuous lips,

opening over moonbeams of pearl.
Long I savored this funereal kiss
that I might die! that I might die!
It drenched me with its tears of love,
the inconsolable Star of my Dream!

The Dawn, clarified by these divine tears,
and smiling with sibylline ecstasy,
raised its great horn of rapture and bitterness,
that sang out, red, on the horizon like a rising sun,
with, in the distance, the throes of echoes and black
sobs, and clots of blood,
in the shattered jaws of the dying caves! . . .

Destruction

Lyric Poems

(1904)

I
Invocation to the Almighty Sea
to Deliver Me from the Ideal

For Eugène Lautier

O Sea, divine Sea, I do not believe,
I will not believe that the earth is round! . . .
Myopia of our senses! . . Stillborn syllogisms! . . .
Dead logic, O Sea! . . . I do not believe
that you roll sadly over the back of the earth,
like a serpent over the back of a stone! . . .
So say the Scholars, for they've measured you
    well! . . .
They have sounded your swells! So what? . . .
For they can't understand your delirious word.

You are infinite and divine, O Sea, I know it
by the oath on your foaming lips,
by your oath that attentive Echoes like watchmen
repeat from shore to shore,
by your oath that the thunder roars! . . .
Infinite and divine, you flow, O Sea,
like a great river in happy plenitude.
Oh! who can sing the solemn epithalamium
of my soul swimming in your vast lap? . . .
And the dazzled clouds beckon,
as you dive effortlessly, straight down,
into the horizon's unsounded depths! . . .

Like a river of shimmering waters gorged with
    flames,
yes, you dive straight down! . . . and the Scholars
    are wrong,
for I have seen you, in the noons' apotheosis,
flashing in the distance like a silver sword,
pointed at the Azure maddening with treachery! . . .
. . . For I have seen you glowing red and cruel,
brandished implacably,
against the sensual flank of a dying April evening
in the diabolic tresses of the Night! . . .
O Sea, O mighty sword to cleave the Stars! . . .
O mighty sword,
fallen from the broken hands of a dying Jehovah! . . .

And so the changing Sunsets
are bloody wounds you gouge,
through time, for revenge, revenge! . . .
What do the Scholars say of this? . . .
What say you, old books of spells, eternal alembics,
silver scales, searching telescopes?
Whatever they say, the Scholars are wrong.
Wrong to deny your divine essence,
for the Dream alone exists and Science is no more
than the brief swooning of a Dream! . .

You dive into Infinity, like a river without end,
and the flexuous sapphire Stars
lean nonchalantly on your shores,

in their palpitating metal robes
with adamantine folds! . . .
While imperious Stars,
helmeted with fire, agile in their emerald sheaths,
rise up on your banks, spreading their great arms
    of light
over the waves, O Sea, to bless you,
you who run through the blue plains of the sky,
there to spill your eternal desire
and your mad pleasure,
O radiant Veins of Space! . . .
O pure Blood of Infinity! . . .

The scholars have come to your promontories,
prancing like puppets, dangling
from the tangled strings of autumnal rains,
to explore you, O Sea! . . .

They treat you like a wretched slave
endlessly beaten, scourged on the shores,
by the Winds, your tormentors! . . .
They scorn your sobs
and the sinking sadness of your eyes! . . .
They said that you encircle the curves of the earth
like the perverse humors of our bodies,
—dropsy of a decrepit world!
Others, seeing you green with gall, and pus,
and drool, and reddening in the dusk,
have said that you are drawing farther and farther
from the beaches and are dying sadly dried.
To them you are just a snake of old gold
twisted round the withered missal of the earth!
So what? . . . the hammers and augers of your voice
can instantly crumble their ephemeral word! . . .

I who love you, with all my despair fixed on
    the shore,
I who believe in your divine power,
I will sing your triumphal march through space,

which you traverse, spreading
your sparkling and solemn waters,
combed by the winds deep in Infinity! . .
Fill my soul, O Sea, like a golden sail.
O blood of Infinity, fill and flood at last
on this dizzying night the shores of my heart,
with your tides swollen with crimson and light!

Countless nostalgic Stars
have come down, O Sea,
into your majestic river's flow,
swimming, searching the vast horizon,
attentively seeking, far away,
the clear golden stream, eternally cool,
to ease the knots of fire in their hearts
and the burning of their brightening arms! . . .

Quick! quick! O Sea . . . giant bulls
of steam, with colossal backs—
see them?—come lazily down to your banks,
hauling the huge carts of Constellations.
They come to drink at your shimmering waters,
tossing their misshapen heads,
beneath their diverging horns of smoke,
and their nostrils stream with sparkling worlds! . . .

Heavens! Heavens! . . what prodigy is this? . . .
    Sonorous echoes,
repeat the cry of wonder and of joy! . . .
The miracle, O Sea, has it come to pass? . . .
Yes! Yes! . . At last, I feel you in my veins,
O turbulent Sea, O adventurous Sea! . .
You are inside me, how I desire you! . . .
Gallop drunkenly through my expanded heart,
with your fierce pack of howling storms,
trumpeting to the stars,
beneath your romantic plume of touseled clouds.

III
The Babels of Dreams

For E. A. Butti

Sunsets with golden claws,
beneath their blazing manes! . . .
Sunsets crouched on the horizon's edge,
their tawny paws outstretched like lions,
have long torn at my adolescent flesh! . . .

It is you, O dusky Sea, who brought me
the sharp nausea of living and infinite sadness! . . .
Because I gazed too long upon you in my youth
I stagger in your breath, drunk with despair! . . .

Some nights, down there, in sorceress Africa,
they led us to your sullen shores,
where we, doleful flocks of schoolboys, lagged
sheep-like, under the stern eye of the dark priests.
O inky silhouettes that stained
the ethereal silks of a beautiful Eastern sky! . . .

And you came to us slowly, O sensual Sea,
cool and green, half-naked in ruffles of foam,
to dry your snowy feet upon the sand . . .
Stamping with rage, like a wild child,
you sulked at the lazy lingering Night,
the handsome Night, your lover, who colors your
        cheeks! . . .
And you hurled high to the skies,
with the crests and the troughs and the wash of
        your waves,
our stars and our dreams,
soft beads from the East! . . .

My heart grew drunk on the rustle of pearls
that your tired fingers tell among the stones! . . .
My heart sobbed in your burning hands

like a satanic lyre, whose taut strings,
spent from caresses, suddenly burst
into agonizing laughter! . . .
My heart? . . . I wound it in your nocturnal locks . . .
My heart? . . . I dragged it breathless
through your foaming waves, toothed
like cruel silver saws! . . .

Be cursed, a thousand times be cursed,
in the name of the astral laws,
O Sea, who filled my pensive youth
with Levantine mouths in spasmodic song,
and with the obscene writhings of sexual waves! . . .
O Eastern dancer with your leaping belly
and breasts red with shipwrecks' blood! . .

We walked limping, O Sea,
like wounded dying dogs with bloodied ears
who slake their thirst in putrid pools . . .
. . . already blooming with illusory stars! . . .
We dreamed fallen, like mendicants,
before the dazzling porch of the venerable night,
where your frenzied fingers of ebb and flow
have chronicled your shipwrecks! . . .
And in my heart was the grand mirage
of a black palace with its hundred golden turrets
brandished at the azure, there to hold at last
and keep inviolable the Bride of Brides,
conquered at the cost of all the starry
heavens of my dreams! . . .
And my eyes probed deep in the hateful dusk,
between the greenish branches of the clouds,
the blue depths of fabulous caves . . .

Later, when I came back home,
a quiet family evening had begun,
beneath the lamp that stretched its neck of flame
and curled its wings of light across the table,
to brood the impassioned desires of my soul

in the fluttering of its silky rays . . .
—like a hen with giant magic golden eggs,—
. . . while in a shadowy corner,
my wrinkled Sudanese nurse
sang sadly,
with her thin black voice,
and marked the rhythm with her clapping hands
like wooden castanets . . .
And in the stifling of the flame-gorged night,
my nurse's voice painted the silence
with woolly tales like negro heads
riddled with white laughter
and crowned with scarlet feathers! . . .

And from time to time, I'd lean against my window
to hear you, O Sea, entreating
waves of passers-by like a girl on the street.

—O Sea, who will come tonight to share
your stormy bed . . . and stroke the menacing coils
of your boa body . . . and, in the throes of death,
bite and bloody your flame-studded breasts
that fire off at God in the tempests? . . .

Suddenly, shooting up from the rocks,
foaming, wild, O Sea,
like a lunatic in a fit of rage,
you waved your ivory arms, rattling with amulets,
and clicked your teeth, sonorous stones . . . .
. . . . .
. . . while the Night slowly mastered the shore
like a giant octopus with golden suckers.

The Sensual City

(1908)

The Sensual City

I
The Mad Traveler

To break the hell-born desert winds
that madly tear their coats of sand,
I leaped, with matchless speed, I ran,
like a ray ricocheting off the waves.

To catch the Night at sleep in the plains,
I crossed the enormous mountain range,
I crushed the Night with my echoing steps,
the honey Night sickening with heat,
envenomed by the climbing moon.

I overtook the labored turning of the earth
like a juggler on the oscillation
of a rolling ball . . . I conquered the big Dipper,
I passed childish Aurora in the race,
and now I can slacken my pace
among these black palms that sift the azure
and the silky murmur of the African sea.

Already my broken feet savor the languor
and the abandon of this trusting shore.
My ecstatic ear evokes the ringing
fall of pebbles with soft bursts of laughter,
and there, in the attentive mist of dawn,
your silhouette appears to me at last,
O, opulent City of feminine curves

whose sensual whiteness tempts my mouth,
on your fragrant couch of drowsy trees
blooming with jasmine, black currant, and mint.

She slumbers still, nonchalantly at rest,
giving her back to the Dawn's hot caress,
whose rosy breath drifts over the waves
and skims the meadows on top of the hills.
Gracefully she stretches her body, half-veiled
with superabundant black hair that curls
like a cloud down the slope of her spine,
like the leaves of hanging gardens.
Her body is jeweled with the fine night dew
and the sweat of lingering pleasures
drunk long from the lips of the Stars.

Suddenly on the horizon of the sea
the great mulatto Sun shakes his heavy head
fouled with blood and his shock of hair
tangled with fire and scarlet coins.
His tatooed torso rises from the sea,
dripping as from a crimson bath.
He leaps up, leaning on the clouds
to gaze upon the careless pink City;
then, bending down, he dares caress her hips
and the white walls
quiver with pleasure.

And then their shadow spread across the sands,

like a soft fan of immeasurable azure.
It wound around me on my dusty path . . .
And then I saw the stained glass windows blaze
on the ivory face of the supreme citadel,
crushed by the gardens' fragrant hair . . .
Burning windows, whose golden lashes beat
    with fright
in the reflected bursts of light,
a passer-by in prayer told me how your glories
crown the bright pilgrimages
that come from near and far to bend their feeble
    knees! . . .

Oh! red are your doors, all red from the hearts
hung as offerings on your ivory leaves!
Oh! red are your doors, all red from grinding,
as they opened and closed, heady spices
heaped on wagons long ago by Egyptian sorcerers,
which perfumed the bright lintel of mother-of-pearl.

Oh! red are your doors, reddened by the massacres
where black conquerors came to clash
their giant ebony bodies and their musculatures! . . .
Oh! red are your doors, all red with the blood
that mendicants of love, thirsting for pain,
spilled on your sill from impure wounds
poisoned by the desert's breath! . . .
Oh! red are your doors, from strangling
in the ravenous gap of their open leaves,
the birds of Bukir, that come in summer
to plunge their flaming beaks with fury there
and fly only the night when the maddest one
twists, hung at last, like a bloody handkerchief.

The pink city stretches out her sensual walls
veined like marble and colored with carmine,
rounding her beautiful goddess's hips
that spill into hills,

smoother than thighs the color of peaches,
and fade into the cool forests
of the horizon,
where the city wished to tuck her pretty feet.

V
My Heart Sang . . .

"What's the use of pursuing the stormy sea,
sweeping toward the illusory promise of the capes?
It is here! here is the ecstasy of ecstasies!
It's you I want to drink down in one gulp,
pink Vulva perfumed by the breath of the Stars!

You can pant with anger and vexation,
I scorn your long howls of rage,
O galloping Simoons of my ambition,
stamping heavily at the city's gate!
You won't catch me now despite your speed!
You'll never clear the sensual walls!
There's no point in whinnying; I've covered my ears!
Better still, my ears are deafened now
by the pink murmur of her subterranean voice,
like cool shells filled by the song of the seas.

O passion for digging my grave in her blue flesh!
Oh! far from you, far away from you, Sun,
watching me from the sky!
I do not see you, but I hear your wings
beating on the walls of the Zenith!
I no longer fear the greedy horizon's mouth
that wants to eat me in a single gulp!
O jealous Sun, mad for splendor,
slave tricked out while his master's gone,
I've already forgotten your great brutal gestures,
your looks and cries as heavy as hammers.
I want to dig my grave and cradle here!
Singing Vulva, gurgling like a spring,
oh! the quivering joy of resting inside you,
in your hot and fresh humidity!

I long to soak my heart in your smell
of humid rust and rotten rose!

Reflections of conquered steel, scattered stubs
    of swords,
still smoking with the blood the heroes spilled,
killed at your door for your love!
Oh! the joy of giving you my life, my blood,
    my strength,
and of taking yours in an endless kiss!
Heroism of the blood that shoots toward you
spattering your hot lips with joy
like a fountain crimsoned by the scarlet dawn!

The bliss of drowning
in your illusive, burning depths
of a tropical sea, streaming Vulva,
lovely and so frail, but
vaster at this moment than my soul! . . .
The world is abolished! Desire is killed!
Infinity is filled, since you are my goal!

Yet it's so sweet to hurt you,
biting you like a beautiful fruit,
to gobble you down,
to drink the sobs and savage bounds
of your liquid pleasure!

See, I writhe with delight and ecstasy
in your hollow soft and gushing like a spring!
I want to dig into your sand with my teeth,
    my hands,
deeper, farther, down to the imperscrutable
depths, to know
and find the vein of joy,
the amazing vein of metallic bliss!

Oh woe! I feel the fire of a wound!
The Sun has bitten me on the ankle!
Oh! the mad dog! . . .
I was to sleep, my mouth on your mouth,

pink sacred Vulva, whose sand is sweet,
but I writhe like a wounded snake
that wants to spring back with dolor, with desire,
and with eternal hope! . . .

Oh woe! oh woe! For now I rise
and withdraw my heart and already think
of your sublime joy, domineering windows,
great golden eyes, growing larger
in the fragrant fall
of hanging gardens! . . .
Alas! I think of you, windows endlessly
reflecting the swaggering of the suns
and the pilgrimage of the boats, sails set,
seen from high above, frozen in their flight,
on the fluttering sheet of the sea.

VI
The Sacred Lizards

Meanwhile the City sank
into the incandescent sleep of the hour . . .
O velvet sleep, O breathing
of the City swooned in the Sun!

Then all around, on the pavements scorched
    with heat,
I saw the lizards wake,
drowsy and bluish, coupling,
forming interlacings of palpitating veins
on the smooth skin of that square, rounded
like the belly of a girl in bloom.

Lizards emerald with lust,
beautiful lizards sated with solar pleasure,
I like to watch your slow awakening
on the sleeping belly of a deserted square,
its hot skin downy with vermilion grass.

But the last stone of the great mulatto Sun
drove me into the sweltry heat of the banana grove.
I passed along the domes steaming in the azure,
pausing now and then to embrace the trees
and the flowering shrubs, groping, on my knees,
to kiss the roots of all the bushes,
whose perfume swelled my heart,
when I reached the edge
that opens on the sky like a dock on the sea.
My soul embarked on the departing cloud
that gave its sail to the wind of infinity.

The Death of the Fortresses

(Little Light Play)

I
The Coy Hulls

Now since the age of time,
the rugged harbor Fortresses
have sat on the black piers,
among the pyramidal freight
of juicy fruit and metals and fragrant wood.
Their giant spines are sunk
into the ramparts and their feet are in the sea,
and they spill their shadow and their dreary lives
into the sumptuous oils of the swell
and its long ventriloquist's soliloquies.
They laze in the sweet intimacy
of their children, the little Ships
half dressed in raggedy sails
like urchins frolicking
with the incandescent ball of the sun.

And the Islands' fertile scarlet perfume
rocks their venerable grandmothers' sleep . . .

But sometimes, suddenly,
with the wistful smile of autumn nights,
big sacks of dried orange peel
blow puffs of violet smells their way,
exasperating their great petrified backs.

For the old harbor Fortresses

once were lively hulls,
their keels gracefully grazing
the waves' supple backs, in their wandering
    course . . .
Nonchalant, they drifted off,
leaning right and left at the will of the winds,
rolling their sterns like hips,
swelling their white sails
like breasts billowing from a blouse.
They sailed on, lifting
their skirts fringed with a fan of foam,
turning their rudders like ankles
in a rustling wake of lace.

The hulls slipped off secretly
beneath the red lantern of the prowling sunsets,
clutching their trembling sails to their breasts,
extinguishing the big colored lights
on their bows,
as if hiding fascinating jewels
in the folds of a great black coat.

Out at sea, the hulls lived,
happy, on the ripe and fragrant
pulp of the dawn . . .

In the swooning of spring nights,
they moaned, becalmed,
with the cool rocking of a sleeping cradle,

in despair from waiting for a favorable wind
under the shrill mocking of yellow moons,
watching the copper of a falling star
that rings in the hollow of the seas like alms
in a beggar's cup.

In the smoky shipyards humming
and buzzing like bells in the rain,
every year,
when Midsummer's near,
caulkers fouled with soot
mended the mossy bellies of the hulls,
pounding hard to reforge
their native beauty.
And hammers hoisted in the greasy steam
fell with the sound of a mine,
smashing the anvils that smoke
in the frenzied bleeding of the torches.

And the fading beauty of the belles
bloomed again, reborn in the sun.

They crushed the tarred oakum
into the fine cracks of the skin,
for make-up and miracle creams,
pounding the heads of the protective black nails
called all-powerful against the pride of the Storms
. . . Here and there like a flirt's beauty marks.

But one day the hammers fell helpless
to mend the steel spines
and the hulls' soft shells . . .
The nails, the make-up, and the iron beauty marks
would no longer hold to their skin;
the bulkheads could not stop the leaks . . .
The caulkers sneered, sticking out their smug dark
mastiff's mugs: "Oh! the pretty hulls
can't roll in the arms of the Storms

if they tinkle
in their lovers' beds,
wrinkled belles! . . ."

That was the night of their undoing . . .

II
Useless Wisdom

The illustrious Hulls ran aground
onto the black piers; and now, seated,
their broad backs sunk into the ramparts,
and their green eyes drunk with shipwrecks,
the belles languish . . .
holding on their open knees
deserted terraces that overhang the sea.

Their gray skirts langued with shells
and flowered with emeralds fall in stiff pleats
to the waves that softly rock
their furbelows of sleepy seaweed,
with the long garrulous gurgling of bottles.
They have become the guardians of the harbor,
the somber Fortresses,
with starfish like medals
on their battle-scarred breasts.

Suddenly they feel the touch
of countless hands and it's
their children, the little Ships,
who kiss and hug them fiercely,
and whose masts, halyards, and lines
form fearsome vines of joy.

Shivering, the Fortresses smile,
opening their tired mouths with a few yellowed
          teeth . . .
Old balconies with balusters
that the Wind punches out, millennial drunkard! . . .

Crying loudly, waving wildly, the Ships plead
for the pleasure of sailing away,
soaring far from shore! . . . The old Fortresses
clutch their old hearts in despair,
like our old grandmothers

who knew the savage sea of love
and foresaw all its shipwrecks . . .

O wretched Grandmothers, suddenly I recall
your shadows slumped in deep armchairs,
whose monumental backs rose
over your bent spines like ghosts
vanishing into the dusky ceiling! . . .
The room turned dark with grief and mourning
and shook with your trembling of wounded
          wings . . .
The air seemed grainy and rough with age,
and voices tried in vain to climb,
slipping like rats in a sewer pipe.

One day pretty children sputtering with youth
threw themselves at your feet,
tugging your skirts, in a lantern of joy:
—"O, mommy dear, got to let us go,
we want to play and dance in the sun . . ."
For they had felt beating outside
on the shutters, closed like eyelids,
the blond Sunday sun of one's dreams,
and swelling like a great heart happy with life . . .
Thus, thus the little Ships
plead frantically for freedom,
laughing with all their motley linen
flapping in the wind like feverish lips.
Their halyards and shrouds stiffen
like nerves overstretched creaking with passion,
for they want to leave and go off
to the horrible sadness (so what?), inconsolable
and (so what?) infinite,
of having tasted it all and cursed all of it (so what?).

The Fortresses, their glassy eyes blurred with tears,
mumbled: "We returned from our voyages
vanquished and sobered by the horror of mirages
and shores where our keels agonized

in the jaws of the Rocks! . . .
Take care! They're watching you,
sly as bonzes that the Tempest feeds
with the sails that coo
out at sea, unfurled, like doves! . . .

. . . .

Beware the enticing smile of the Sirens
hidden and unseen beneath the sea! . . .
One night, we felt their longing lips
in the sweet seething of the waves . . .
Slowly our lateen yards weakened,
and we drifted among our undone sails,
our bowsprits groping along the horizon
and our flanks thirsting for vast plenitude.
Our long hair burned in the hot torture
of the infinite silence . . .
The breeze was nothing but a brief caress
on the pure emerald of the sea streaming
like a pupil blurred with tenderness;
and all around, along the rails,
was the wild and frenzied apparition
of the Tritons, on the sea choked with heat.
They came, unleashing their bodies of rubber
and greenish bronze, their musculatures
matted with kelp and oiled with rays,
locking their long phalluses like antlers,
bursting with lust and insolent laughter
in the slapping of the crested waves . . .
That night, we nearly washed up on shore . . .

. . . .

Watch out for the Sirens' enticing smile! . . ."
Then the granitic grandmothers fell silent,
and, musing on the futility of their wisdom,
on the fleeting desire reborn in our hearts
despite old knowledge and prior disgust,

wanted to tempt the urchins' anguish,
offering them virgins with vernal lips.

On their broad knees spread into terraces,
in the honeyed acid smell of brine,
they made the little harbor girls sit down,
their faces colored with spray and sun,
their bodies softened by the boldness of the wind.
Clusters of girls in rose and lilac
leaned nonchalantly on the parapets
from which one could already see, on the grayish
    horizon,
the rising sun tangling in the masts
amid the red hair of the ropes.

And the young Ships stretched toward the little girls
their hooked lateen yards and their long hungry
    fingers
ringed and scented with brass and tar . . .

III
The Dawn's Victory

But the exalted Dawn spread its golden voice
in the silence, full-blown like a giant rose.

Crimson cheeks appeared, bulging,
blowing heroically on voracious horns . . .
dazzling clouds spread
their ruby veins across the temples of the sky.

And the fervent Dawn roared over the clouds,
whose thousand wounds pour with madness,
whose sonorous blood rings in space:
—"To sea! Follow me, handsome Ships,
to the absurd islands, to the seas' infinity!"
In fury again and again, the golden voice seized
the City's decrepit smoky heart,
gripping the old Fortresses' bones
and twisting their rope tresses to a spasm.

Then the Dawn's hymn stole over the city
through the scuffle and the flight of steeples
and the rebellion of roofs and gables,
insurgent, screeching, scaling
together the vast amphitheater of the mountains,
beyond the feverish applause
of the wash hung out on the terraces.

An echo clung, shivering, still,
like a red tear in the white silence.

It was already clear in the growing hum
of the burning atmosphere irritated with light
that the Dawn's call would thunder once more! . . .
"Have mercy, have mercy, for they cannot
resist the voice! . . ."

And now, preceded by a nostalgic stir

the great thrilling horn blared out its voice
that falls in a hail of explosive notes,
reverberated by echoes, struck to the heart,
buzzing and warlike as drums.

Then, with a twist, the Ships broke
their tragic moorings, leaping out,
onto the moire of the waves convulsed with stares,
into the air swollen with horror and elastic hopes.

A dream of smiling and scarlet madness
roused the headlands crouching in the sea,
and their contortions of chained tigers
that sniff in the Dawn the wind of liberties! . . .

A dream of brutal lust and gore
bloodied the sands of the shore
squamate and glistening like serpents' skin.

A dream of absurd self-slaughter and adventure
thundered under the hollow belly of the sonorous
       piers,
where the surf strains like a mastiff chained.

Glorious, dominating, on the topgallants
the eloquent flags, mad with crimson and azure,
cried out to twist and unfurl their wings,
flapping wildly,
like island birds invoking their home.

At first, the Ships went off in a line,
flourishing their thousand dressed masts,
and grandly spread their sails and spars
like aprons to gather the stars.

Then, passing the black narrows flecked with light,
they slowly sailed into the seas' beyond.
One could see them from afar, already spent,
staggering over the riot of saw-toothed waves,

near the incandescent mouth of the Sun
that leaned joyfully against the scarlet clouds.

And this is how, and this is when, in the
shimmering flowery movements of the Dawn,
the ancient Fortresses,
trembling on their immemorial marble seat,
with deserted terraces on their knees
washed over and over by the horror of infinity,
suddenly died from having seen
the lascivious and Levantine Sun nibble and eat
with his blazing teeth the childish boats,
their sails strewn with azure and beryl
like violets heavy with dew.

Dithyrambs

To My Pegasus

Vehement god of a race of steel,
space-intoxicated Automobile,
stamping with anguish, champing at the bit!
O formidable Japanese monster with eyes like a forge,
fed on fire and mineral oils,
hungry for horizons and sidereal spoils,
I unleash your heart of diabolic puff-puffs,
and your giant pneumatics, for the dance
that you lead on the white roads of the world.
At last I release your metallic reins . . . You leap,
with ecstasy, into liberating Infinity! . . .

At the sound of the pound of your voice . . .
see how the setting Sun hounds
your bounding steps, accelerating its bleeding
palpitation along the horizon . . .
It's galloping there, down in the woods . . . look! . . .

What's it matter, handsome demon? . . .
I'm at your mercy . . . Take me!
On the ground deafened despite its echoes,
under the sky blinded despite its golden stars,
I go fueling my fever and my desire
with sword blows right in the nose! . . .
And from moment to moment, I straighten my back
to feel winding round my quivering neck
the cool downy arms of the wind.

It's your alluring distant arms that draw me!
this wind, it's your engulfing breath,
fathomless Infinity absorbing me with joy! . . .
Ah! Ah! . . . suddenly the gangling black windmills
seem to be running
on their whaleboned canvas wings
as if on gigantic legs . . .

Now the Mountains get ready to throw
cloaks of drowsy coolness on my flight . . .
There! There! look! at that sinister curve! . . .
Mountains, O monstrous Cattle, O Mammoths
trotting heavily along, arching your huge backs,
you are outrun . . . drowned . . .
in the maze of mists! . . .
And dimly I hear
the whirring of your colossal legs
pounding the roads in their seven-league boots . . .

Mountains with cool cloaks of azure! . . .
Beautiful rivers breathing in the moonlight! . . .
Shadowy plains! I pass you at full gallop
on this racing monster . . . Stars, my Stars,
do you hear his bounds, the sound of the pound
of his brazen lungs endlessly exploding?
The bet is on . . . with You, my Stars! . . .
Faster! . . . faster still! . . .
And no respite, and no rest!
Release the brakes! . . . You can't? . . .

Smash them then! . . .
Let the engine's pulse centuple!

Hurrah! No more contact with the filthy earth! . . .
At last, I break loose and fly freely
over the intoxicating abundance
of Stars streaming in the great bed of the sky!

The Pope's Monoplane

Political Novel in Free Verse

(1912)

1.
Flying Over the Heart of Italy

Horror of my room like a coffin with six walls!
Horror of the earth! Earth, dark lime
trapping my bird feet! . . . Need to break free!
Ecstasy of climbing! . . . My monoplane! My
     monoplane!

In the breach of the blown-out walls
my great-winged monoplane sniffs the sky.
Before me the crash of steel
splits the light, and my propeller's cerebral fever
spreads its roar.
I dance, throbbing, on my bickering wheels,
lashed by the mad wind of fantasies,
while mechanics hold me by the tail
in the dark logic of the room,
elastically, like a kite on a string . . .
Let's go! Let it go! . . .

I have the heady joy of finally feeling
what I really am:
a rebel tree uprooting itself
in a burst of will, soaring
on its open, rustling leaves,
pushing into the wind
the tangle of its roots,
straight, straight into the wind!

I feel my breast open like a great hole
and all the azure of the sky, smooth, cool,
     and torrential,
pours joyously in.
I am an open window, in love with the sun
and flying toward it!
Who can stop
the windows now, hungry for clouds,
and the drunken balconies
tearing off the old house walls tonight
to spring into space?

I regained my massive courage
the moment my two vegetable feet
stopped drawing the conservative sap of fear
from the cautious earth!

Up high! Open sky! Here I am resting
on the air's elastic laws! Ah! Ah!
I'm hanging straight over the town
and its intimate chaos
of houses set out like obliging chairs! . . .
I sway gently like a bright chandelier
over the town square, table set
with many steaming plates, cars,
whose sparkling glasses pass
electrically!

The last shot of the sinking sun

hits me, bleeding but still flying bird.
I leap from branch to branch
through the great illusory forest of smoke
that rises from the factories.

Higher! Farther! Outside the walls!
A riot of crosses emerges
between the grim rows of cypress guards.
The sepulchral gardens shout their reds and greens.
The white stones look like waving handkerchiefs.
Tonight the dead would follow me . . .
Tonight the dead are drunk, the dead laugh loud!
I was dead like you, I am risen now! . . .

The sky reeks with my engine's castor oil.
It's everywhere: in my eyes, my mouth . . . A flood!
Stomach, my flying stomach,
don't be squeamish!
You'll have to pay for your trip with a little nausea . . .
Vomit on the earth! Last ballast tossed so we can
    climb,
and leap-frog nimbly
over the hairy mountain backs!
Geometric countrysides! Square fields and meadows!
O giants' tombs! Each with its four green rows
of candles lit slowly by the sun.
Awake, quiet farms! Spread! Spread
your roofs' red wings and fly with me
to your mad throbbing, Sicily, great heart of Italy,
sprung from her breast in the fervor of conquest! . . .

At last, at last I enter the flush of the setting sun
like a conqueror in the climbing architecture
of the proud metallic future city
that the subtle pencils of the clouds
drew in my adolescent brain!
At last I touch down in the crimson gulfs
of this great aerial continent!

A vast salty smell? The sea!
The sea, row after row of blue women
undressing . . . There's the foam of their frail
    nakedness,
interlaced and leaning toward the last
swallow of light
in the round desert of the sky!
Ah! you make me laugh, pitching sailboats,
insects overturned that cannot—you make
    me laugh!—
and will not ever get back on their feet!

Pretentious islets in your pompous green gowns,
to me you're nothing but flat swamp flowers
swarming with fat flies!
I spin by you
stroking the great globe of atmosphere
with my speeding hand,
vast back of the murderous danger
between me and the sea . . .

I see, I feel below, straight down
beneath my feet,
the horrible possible crash
against the rock-hard breast
of the sea!
Joy! oh joy! . . . I must drop
the levers to cheer the fleet!
Twenty fabulous turtles, motionless,
sticking their cannon heads
out of their metallic shells
and all around the happy wriggle of torpedo boats
and boat-toads
hopping on their wild little oars.
The sailors' silhouettes collapse in a round,
their pearl-gray faces follow my applause
like the blue calls of migrating birds.
The broad battleships are silent, but they will
    speak again

with their explosive eloquence of lead, fanning
over the swept enamel of our Adriatic lake!

Ah! Ah! Dark African wind,
doltish wind with hypocritical calms,
is your eye on my distractions?
Why correct for your sly drift? . . .
Do what you will, I'll take you on!
I fly into your wet and stringy arms.
A thousand meters below my feet the sea turns black
    with rage.
We're coming back to earth! Does it have a smell?

What is that sickening stink of a tomb?
I can barely read and I lean forward, my nose to
    the compass.
That soft sepulchral stench is Rome,
my capital! . . . Bah! Giant molehill,
heap of papers nibbled slowly
by a thousand rats and worms . . .
Domes! Giants' swollen bellies floating
in the violet vapor of the night!
I see them nearly all pierced with golden spires,
straight daggers still trembling in their sonorous
    wounds,
against the shadows' dismal walling! . . .

Trains? Hardly!
More like speeding snakes with gleaming coils,
supple as they swim in long rhythmic bounds
against the huge aggressive forest waves,
diving in the mountains' flow.
Now and then the trains stop
to sniff the towns, pale carcasses,
drinking up their phosphorous fleas
and clacking their glowing suckers.
Ah! to be someday a deadly poison
in your agile rhythmic bellies,
when you leap toward the border!

Glory to you, serpent-trains,
who profit from the dark to seize the earth!
The moon strokes you in vain, teasing you
with long mockeries of light . . .
In vain the moon shows the shining elbow
of her lascivious ray, revealing
the sleeping, breathing nudity of the rivers . . .

O sad, somnolent, passéist moon,
what should I do with these pools from the flood?
I cancel you out when I turn on my spotlight,
whose huge electric ray is newer
and whiter than yours! My ray bathes
the terraces, floods the balconies in love,
and noses into young girls' ready beds.
The wandering ray of my great spotlight
burns the murmuring streams
of their sleeping veins with glory and heroism . . .
But I have better things to do, stubborn wind!
Let go! Hands off! I'm back to the sea!

The sea and her imprisoned people
wailing inside her iron walls.
All her guards are there. All the lighthouses standing,
dreadful in their stillness,
huge and violent in the dark.
Some peer all around,
like eager hunters;
others bend their golden shafts over the black waves
like fishermen with shining lines.

Lighthouses! Poor defeated fishermen,
what do you want of this emptied sea?
Lift your heads and look around! All those fat gold
    fish
you want are wriggling in the sky!
This is how I love to fly, like a great butterfly
blinding a lighthouse's sad eye with swoops and cries
without scorching my wings.

Watch out for the rocks, sleepy ships,
rolling through the hills and valleys of the sea
on the hundred light-paws of your reddish portholes!
Oh! I pity the beacons impaled on your masts
and their suffering, spent look, sighing
for the muddy, courtly harbors.
I pity you, violently spurned
by the sea and the wind spinning
the grinning arches of its gaping mouth
in your weeping sails!

Out there are the fleeing ships!
Like factories flying, smoking, windows flaming,
uprooted by the cyclone.
They skim the living darkness of the sea!
And that ship looks like . . . Like what? . . . That's
        it! . . .
. . . a giant mill to grind the stars!
Its masts suck in the sky, and all around
sidereal flour streams from the portholes!

But I must weather the head wind's many blows
that block me, and I pitch, and I roll, and I hold
my monoplane steady,
working the two rudders . . .
A stroke of the pump will give me back
the velvet hum of my satisfied engine . . .
Dear carburetor, run wide open
like a hero's wound!

At last my heart, my great Futurist heart,
has won its long rough war
against the bars of my thorax.
My heart has burst from my breast.
My heart, my heart, it lifts me and transports me
in the bloody whirlwind of its veins.
Terrible whirling propeller!
I am one with my monoplane,
I am the colossal drill

piercing the petrified skin of the night.

Harder! Harder! We must dig deep
into this fiber mummified by time.
Will I beat my wings forever
like a vulture nailed to the doors of the sky?
This spot won't give? Look higher! Break
the sorry window of the yellowing dawn!
Propeller! strong propeller of my monoplane heart,
tremendous drill, eager and willful,
can you feel the cursed shadows crack
from your piercing effort?

The fouling skin is losing its opacity.
What rage! Let's hurry . . . Why is it fighting like this?
Try again! Again! Again! . . .
We've almost done it: soon all will fall!
Again! Here! Here! Hurrah!
A great crimson crumbling fills the air,
and the succulent sun, colossal fruit,
bursts with brutal joy
from its soft shadowy pod.

People of Palermo! Can you see me coming?
It is I! It is I! . . . Cheer,
for I am one of you! . . .
My monoplane looks like a giant white man
on the springboard of the clouds, leaning down,
arms open wide, to dive
into your trembling Sicilian dawn.

In this harbor, mauve and bathed in silence,
one sleeping town
still pulls the soft blue silken sheet of the sea,
mechanically,
over the eyes of its rosy windows.
And this other town, like a bit of iron
the sun heats to a blazing red,
steams between the bright bronze pincers of the sea.

Hurrah! the young bells of Palermo
have spotted me now! They leap with joy
on their childish swings
and rock back and forth,
airing their humming skirts of bronze
and their legs bitten with the longing to be free.
Here I am! Here I am, O bells of Palermo! . . .
To revel in your long sonorous swings,
I cut power and glide toward you
like a long white boat,
its double row of oars uplifted at the race's end.

Palermo, from far away you seem
a formidable arsenal
guarded right and left by mountain walls
with your long streets diving into the sea,
and their close-set terraces, to be ramps
for the Dreadnought ruler of the world! . . .
In the troughs of your deep streets is the feverish
traffic of caulkers, and above the sweet
rending of pink breezes . . .

Sicilians! you who've fought since misty times
night and day, hand to hand with volcanic rage,
I love your souls that blaze
like the mad rays of the central fire,
and you resemble me, Saracens of Italy,
your strong nose bent over the prey we crush
with our beautiful Futurist teeth! . . .
Like yours, my cheeks are burned by the simoons;
like you, I have the violent elastic speed of a cat in
     the grass
and the riddling stare that drives
the slimy, jumping backs of the policeman and
     the beadle
deep into the shadows.
Like me, you spring all the traps.
The happy rats can gnaw our manuscripts,
for our engines write

definitive verses of bright steel and gold
in the open sky!
Each one of you can build a high justice
around his great taming and untamable Self.
Damn the heavy social machine! . . .
Damn the laws' sad mechanism
and its sorry doling out of justice!
Childish mechanism with makeshift cogs
that snags a trembling beggar,
rolls him, grinds him, stupidly crushes him,
and, *wham*, out the window like a dead pod
in the holy name of an unseen god!

2.
The Volcano's Decrees

I come to you, Volcano, and I defy
your mad mocking ventriloquist's laughter.
Believe me, I am not in your power!
You'd love to catch me
in your lava nets,
as you do ambition-driven climbers
when on your sides they face
the fearful sadness of the huge sunset
that suddenly bursts lugubriously
into earthquake!
I fear neither the threats nor the symbols
of space that can
bury towns at will
in heaps of copper, gold,
and clots of blood.

I am the mighty, the invincible Futurist
borne by his heart in tireless flight.
So it is that I sit at Dawn's table
to gorge myself at her display of multicolored fruit!
I crush the noons, smoking pyramids of shot,
I overstride the sunsets, bleeding armies in retreat,
and at my heels I drag
the nostalgic sobbing dusks! . . .

Etna! Can anyone dance better than I
or sway so gracefully over your wild mouth
bellowing a thousand meters beneath my feet?
I descend and I dive into your hydrogen-sulfide
    breath
through the giant globes of your red smoke.
I hear the heavy echoing din
of your vast stomach crumbling
like the walls of a subterranean capital.
In vain the sooty fury of the earth
would drive me back into the sky!

My fingers hold the levers tight
as I roar:

                    M E

O Volcano,
unmask your face with its phosphorous warts!
Flex your buccal muscles,
open your rocky granite-crusted lips,
and cry to me the destiny
and duties of my race.
Rouse the dreadful resonance
of your smoky lungs.
I am quick and strong, and I make the winds
chirp piteously beneath my wings,
like baby chicks.
Admire my wings that look so huge,
drowned out there in wrathful swirls of steam.

Behind me I see my stabilizer,
far back, and my rudder bleeding
over the reverberated blaze of your bowels.
My canvas vibrates dully like a drum
under the aerial dance of the rosy brands.
Infernal washhouse where everything decays!

As a smoker waves aside the smoke of his cigar,
with one rough puff, O Volcano, you blow
your grand white plume away, offhandedly.
Everywhere my horizon is blocked
by the enormous contortion
of your exploded jaws, sickening with embers! . . .
I'm right in the middle, in the dark dilapidation
of your lips higher
and thicker than mountains . . .

And I descend again, looking around me
at your monstrous swollen gums . . .
What is this flora of soft fumaroles

that you would chew
like a heavy blue moustache? . . .
The hoarse funnel of your throat
appears to me a theater in flames,
incalculably large,
where all the peoples of the earth were called.
For there is ample room for all of them.
There are the stands, swarming with celebrants! . . .

You can see, crowding in and waving,
over a billion flames,
enthusiastic spectators,
shouting and cheering
a billion different pleasures.
Above the reddish crowd
explosions of purplish gas suddenly swagger,
pot-bellied, apoplectic.
Farther off, hysterical yellow vapors
in their quick green hats fire
impassioned rays, sweet then suddenly scornful.

What happy laughing flame is this,
sheathed in mauve velvet,
that so cleverly tosses its orange hat parabolically,
flashing, fading,
toward the show of shows as it begins?
In the pit of the theater, surely
over twenty kilometers wide,
an inviting sea of fire spreads far,
creased here and there with shadows and freshly
        colored
with coral and with childish cheeks,
with long quivers of white cries.

Is that the shattering crash of an anvil
raising higher and higher the radiant
surface of this sea of fire?
Resplendent rivers, streams, and brooks,
gorged with gold ingots, race

to feed it, streaming
from eloquent crevices
opening at intervals
along the stands,
through the swaying crop
of spectator flames and gases.

Between the burly red-faced rocks,
flames and gases lead the fun and frolic . . .
This whole strange crimson audience
is swept pell-mell by the vehement force
of the applauder cheers
toward the throat, the heart, the center
of the crater, fiery amphitheater and funnel.

And this sea of fire congeals and turns to stone.
In groups of clots and islets, sewn, melted,
in quick alluvia of rubies and agates,
a continent forms, vermilion, dazzling . . .
All across the sea of embers
a flotilla rocks,
spreading its sails reflecting
all the brilliant colors of the lava.

Bit by bit the continent is paved with chrysolite;
then suddenly the paving stones are shattered
by the amazing fall
of three thousand lions,
tumbling from the sky, cataracting in hate,
and spraying from their factory nostrils
screeching fountains of mica and pearls.
Furious maze, forest of fiery paws and manes,
one of which could burn three towns to ashes,
paint the pale polar sky in fresco
and warm the cheeks of the winter stars.

Visceral trembling of the earth!
All of Italy's grenades together,
bleeding of a burning club,

spinning whirlwind of backs on backs!
Huge pyramid of black howls
chased up and down by baby-sobs,
reeling in the round of pallid fears! . . .
Is that not our planet bloodied
by a hundred thousand wars,
rolling out there beneath a Martian's eye? . . .

Bah! these appearances or these realities
are well within my grasp! . . .
I have at hand, for instance,
that illusory setting sun, scaly, hairy,
made of three thousand biting, fighting beasts.
I could easily hold it as it sinks
into the dramatic crater of this volcano . . .

I see myself haloed in rich phosphorous dust.
I burn and I melt like metal,
in the incessant combustion of hydrogen.
That fearful cracking sound, what's that?
No doubt the grinding of three thousand lions'
     bones
beneath the mountain slopes! . . .
The meticulous slaughter of the beasts goes on
     and on.

All their ivory fangs grow longer, magnify,
raise a chalky trellis above the scarlet pulp
and its spattering groans of horror.
Are those immensified fangs or white plumes
     of smoke?
No, no, they're ivory, for here
elephant trunks come into the fray.
Elephants go to and fro, planting their feet
like obelisks
splashing through this liquid sulfur's yellow sauce,
and through this red turmoil of grapes
that spills down the corners and shoots up high
in corollas of wine, to shower the spectators . . .

Above the trampled vintage
wisps of smoke in motley like clowns
glide swiftly, balancing on invisible wires,
while firing their revolvers right and left,
exacerbating the untold madness of the raging
     colors!

O Volcano! your show intoxicates me.
I drop down for a better view.
I have my life belt around my waist
and I can swim, if I so desire,
in this cool and tender sea of fire.
Now who could have wasted with a single puff
the crimson continents and the balls of liquefied
     lions?

Slowly from the heaving wounds
of the waves rise the monstrous keels
of three black battleships, chewed over and over,
cast back to the surface, no doubt,
by the insolence of the submarine depths.
Slowly, one by one, the three warships
come back to life, shuddering deeply.
They stiffen their lifeless limbs, right their masts,
recovering their balance . . . And their boilers,
     lighting,
activate the great steel towers.

Seasickness grips the cannons' guts
that throb with a continuous vomiting of lead.
They are heads bristling with sparks
that growl, spitting silicates, crystals, and vitreous
     blocks
in fierce volleys on the merry revels and the chassé-
     croisés
of the torpedo boats and sharks.

These change strangely into intermittent fragile isles,
no sooner here than gone,

struggling against the suction of the waves!
Meanwhile a battleship splits and sinks,
bursting the holds of its heart
that spreads in howling flames against the sky.
Already it's no more than a wandering watering can
of liquid azure, fan of freshness.

At last I'm in the paradise of violet trees
that weep under the weight
of the too large stars in bloom
and of too heavy flashes, fierce butterflies
that suck the light.
This paradise is ringed
with round cascades of flowing emeralds.
Is that your soul, O Volcano, surging upward in
    the center
in an enormous spray of dusty quicksilver,
its vertical force resisting
the squall's redoubled blows?

O Volcano, long have I heard
the endless rolling of your turbulent words
trembling in the hoarse chimney of your throat.
I am so lost in the contemplation
of your white-hot words erupting
that I have not yet unraveled the blazing
maze of your thought!

Oh! the mastery and inspiration
the booming thunder of your voice reveals
on your workshop's scorching walls! . . .
With these masses of smoking chalk you sculpt
symbolic monsters and great blinding bas-reliefs
of light that, unforeseen,
might spread, like comets,
a canopy of rays over the sleepless sea! . . .

At last I hear a word! A mighty word
swells and leaps from your lips,

into the sky, at the very tip of a long tube
of black smoke,
like those soft spheres of molten glass
shaped by glassmakers with bulging cheeks
in the incandescent rage of their factories!

THE VOLCANO

I have never slept. I work endlessly
to enrich space with ephemeral masterpieces!
I watch over the firing of the chiseled rocks
and the polychrome vitrification of the sands,
so in my hands the clay
transforms
into perfect pink porcelain
that I shatter with my flicks of steam! . . .

I am continually mixed with my scoria.
My life is the perpetual fusion of my debris.
I destroy to create and I destroy again
to make thundering statues
that I smash at once in the horror of lasting.

The heavy golden sun the dark sets free
each day hoists itself painfully
over the Calabrian peaks,
trying vainly to cast the cone of my oppressive
    shadow
into the center of Sicily,
sowing fear and caution round.
All cherish the hope of knowing I'm tamed
like some great sedated beast.
My ermine mop and my white mane
are pledges of innocence and slow agony.

The Strait of Messina is my accomplice,
asleep at dawn, stretched out sleek and white
like a Persian cat . . .
The Strait of Messina is my accomplice,

with her lingering look of a blue silken bed,
and the soft Arabic words stitched by the wake
of the clouds and the lazy sails
sewn silently, it seems,
with fine silver thread, on the gown of the sea . . .

The lying moon is my accomplice,
most painted of sidereal courtesans,
nowhere else so coaxing,
stirring, and persuasive.

Nowhere else is the moon so careful
to seduce the hard red lights of the steamboats,
gruff passers-by departing,
fat cigar clenched in their teeth,
spitting their smoke into the azure.

Nowhere else does the moon spill such a soft
and gentle violet ash
to lull the hardened lava
of the black houses clinging to my sides.
Nowhere else does the moon pour such poignant
floods of ecstasy and light
across the gashes of the paths
cut by my surgeon flames.

Woe be to those who follow the moon's bleating
        light
and the flocks' plaintive bells
and the shepherds' bitter flutes
whose long threads of nostalgic notes are lost in the
        azure! . . .
Woe be to those who would not match the gallop
of their blood with the gallop of my ravaging
        blood! . . .

Woe be to those who would root
their hearts, their feet, their homes
in the mean hope of eternity!

You must not build, but camp.
Am I not shaped like a tent
with a cropped peak to air my ire?
I love only the stars, svelte acrobats
poised on the rolling spheres
of my juggler plumes! . . .

                ME

I can dance as they can, and juggle in the sky,
and sing over the echoing din
of the storms that form
in your deep caverns! . . .
And I descend
to hear the polyhedrons of your voice.
Space the electric volleys of your bronchi
that dislodge those underlying rocks!
Silence your loquacious caves
that shake endlessly with excitement! . . .
Gag with heavy ash
the basaltic echoes that cheer you in chorus!

I've no use for the volcanic bombs
that punctuate the rumbling of your speech!
What do I care for the gleaming jets
of your savage slaver?
Your floods of mud have soiled my white wings
but do not stop me! I withstand the avalanches
of your scoria, and descend in golden glory,
haloed by your dusting of wondrous gold.

        THE VOLCANO

I lay waste to all the gardens
of blooming sentiments
and their shade, guitars, and mandolins
sobbing under the fingers
of the serenading winds.

I topple the tidy vegetable beds
and the well-groomed lettuce heads,
but skirt delicately round
the forests of big bold trunks
whose muscled branches have a horror of the earth,
and lift their charred fists
against the stars, little chirping birds
that seek a spot to land! . . .

Beware, you who slumber
worshipping the path of ancestors
beneath the quiet boughs of Peace!
I respect nothing, neither ruins of stone,
nor ruins of flesh and bone.
By shovelfuls my breath scatters
the conquered and the cowards in their graves,
the only furrows that their feet have dug,
systematic spades!
War or revolt, the choice is yours! . . .
Great festivals of fire, pride of the world!

What presumptuous bird
or aerial boat is this,
rowing overhead?
No doubt a degenerate child of mine! . . .
Italian, son cooled from ancient Lava!

You and your brothers, ah! that I may
see you at last on the speeding decks
of the nocturnal torpedo boats
in the fierce hatred of the squalls,
at the mercy of a cyclone's sweep,
but still watching for the ebony forms,
blacker than night,
that enemy fleets will amass in the dark! . . .
That I may see you suddenly turned
into firebrands, islands, ships sailing off from land,
in an endless eruption of heroism

against the skies! . . .

I'll suck the stones and dirt
out from under the Italians' feet,
planters of oaks and palaces.
You must surpass my rage or die!
I'll crush your nests, foolish birds of Italy,
so you'll learn how to fly over life!
With the leaping lines of my lava
I'll strike from earth all geographic forms
not colored by the joy of blood!

ME

Hurrah! Hurrah! I spit like you, with you,
O Volcano,
on all the usurers of our conquering blood!
For you I cried
over the roaring peaks of human energy:
"Glorify war, the world's only hygiene!"
For you I violently
purge Italy of parasitic peace,
mighty vine
soon to climb espaliered
on the stars! . . .

Oh! spit on Peace, foul Rafflesia
of Java,
great colossal flower with rotting leaves
whose hollowed heart is filled with stinking water
where sticky insects swim and feed
that colonize the vile pulp of corpses!

THE VOLCANO

Oh! may all the listening echoes of the earth
embrace your red voice hotter than my voice! . . .
I see in you my regenerated son.
Receive, my son, on your radiant cheeks

my double and triple accolade of fire!
Now where has that pack of my lava gone?
Do you hear my whistle of strangled steam? . . .
Red hounds with long corrosive teeth,
Here! Now! Lie down
before this Man ablaze,
and lick the wheels of his fine monoplane! . . .

Zong Toomb Toomb

Adrianople   October 1912

Words in Freedom

(1912–1913; published in Italian 1914)

Correction
of Proofs Desires

No poetry before us
with our wireless imagination and words in
freedom **LOOOng** live **FUTURISM** finally
finally finally finally finally finally finally

FINALLY

POETRY BEING BORN

my train train **tron tron tron
tron** (iron bridge**: tatatlontlan) sssssiii ssiissii
ssissssssiii** train train train
fever of my train express-express-express-
expresssssssss press-press-press-press-press-press-
press-presssssss press-press-press press-presssssss
stung by sea salt sssscennnted by orange
trees seek sea sea sea **boUnd BOUnd
BOUBOUUND** rails rrrails careeeening (*GREEDY
SALTY PURPLE STRANGE INEVITABLE INCLINED
IMPONDERABLE FRAGILE DANCING MAGNETIC*)
I'll explain these words I mean
that sky strait mountains are greedy salty
purple etc. and that I too am greedy
salty purple etc. all that outside me **but
also within me** totality simultaneity absolute
synthesis = superiority of my poetry over
all others STOP
Villa San Giovanni

hook + catch + swallowing of the train-
shark net it pu-pu-pu-push it into
ferryboat-whale floating station
solidditty of the planed oak sea
indigo ventilation (*INSENSIBLE DAILY
METHODICAL STUFFED METALLIC VIIIIBRATING
CUT PACKED CHISELED NEW*) light-
ing of a sailboat = kerosene lamp +
12 white shades + green carpet + cir-
cle of solitude family serenity
method of a second sailboat bow turn the
sea's metal on a lathe foam
shavings temperature falling = 3 fans over
the Calabrian Mountains (*BLUE SLOW INDUL-
GENT DOUBTING*) Messina's
ruuuubble in the strait nearly
liquid earthquakes feel the sea as
a sum of different weights nav-
igate = add up 200,000 blocks beams
ropes barrels **(ploooooom)** + million blue
bags rotten ceilings green doors yellow
cabs + 2,000 steam pregnancies
tataploomploom slap slap against the
bowww-belly hold in its mouth
the whole ROUND sea = swimmer jug-
gler + porcelain plate (diameter 6 Km.)
between his teeth

M O O N (OLD YELLOW)

over-

head

jolts light buzzzzzing angrrrrrrry birrrrrrth of 4 electric glooobes hanging on my train stopped in the flo-flo-floating ferryboat station

M O O N (DIRTY MILK)

over-

head

enough light to correct the proofs for my book on Adrianople   *x* nausea presence of the besieged city in the strait turn my back on Messina-Mustafa-Pasha graduated heap of Villa-San-Giovanni tumble of 8 electric lights into the sea on the right 2d cascade of white lights Reggio beneath my feet-hold-keel 1,000 m. deep middle of the strait great volcanic sewer opened 5 years ago possible rumbling of terrestrial intestines

Villa-San-Giovanni = agitation of 300 electric lights shaken by 18 different densities of wind-wind-wind current dance of happy fish before the acetylene lights of a boat

Reggio = agitation of 800 electric lights (*BRANDISHED FURIOUS MAD*) shaken by 20 different densities of wind current

universal hatred of the moon sssssssliding of the train from the net-ferryboat

M E S S I N A

Messina improvisation dress rehearsal of a city-about-to-be-played indifference of the author sweets and joys of the atmosphere swing of serenades (3 baritones 2 tenors) chilly tenacity of the ivy on the shacks suppleness of the reinforced concrete balancing over the lava's pranks OSTENTATION of an apartment = alcove + canopy + picture gallery + kitchen stuffed into a shack (8 square m.)

impossibility of setting lofty facades against the wind of the strait not over 10 m. high TRUNcated AMBITION of the proprietors preoccupation of the houses = down on all fours like wrestlers so as not to get trounced next round **PRESENCE** of the earthquake tired wrestler sleeping on the doorstep volcano's smoke chamade sent to vesuviuses strombolis treachery of the vegetation = disguises of the earthquake threat of a garden too sweetly scented pungent whiffs of danger powder keg + will + worrrrrrk + comfort + carefree nocturnal fecundation = Messina speed of cars heading for Catania

70 Km. per hour trrrrrrrrrrrrrrr

the **driver leaning back** under the en0rmous wheel that spins like a world skid on the speeds washed by the turns turns fields gardens beaches Calabrian landscape cone of Etna indigo inlets headlands cactus

bowels
writhe
torrents
jolts
run
spasms
scream
smooking
of
**PETRIFIED
LAVA**
under
vast
frozen
wadding of
the atmosphere

fe
ro
cious
ly
born
between
between
between
ON
in
against
(*BLACK
HARD
TWISTED*)

of
cactus
Negro soldiers
offering
fruits
dripping
pink
like
electric
lights

Futurism
bristling
sobriety heroism
depppthhhh resistance
solidity
antivegetable
metallism
300,000 solitudes noons
blaze sands ambushes
ghibli stinging mouths eyes
African conquests
concentrated Saharas

explosive torrefaction + speed + fier-
rrrrceness of the tires coal dust of the
road thirst thirst of the rubber cactus

**80 Km.
per hour
TRrrrrrrrrrrrrr** { sedentary speed **o**f the driver
leaning back in his wheel Saturn
in its ring spin spin tap the far-
away blue foot of the wildest
speeds **glug glug glug** of air in
bottles-ears ventriloquist wind

**95 Km.
per hour
TRRRRRR** { musical n**o**nchalance of the dri-
ver hold down the pedal of the
roaring organ of Kilometers in-
haled in one breath and blown
out again far away

**100 Km.
per hour
TRRRRRR** { ram with his right foot accelera-
tor faraway distances + 1,000
depths + 3,000 resistances of
the earth to the grinding **o**ffered
speeds **pon-pon-traaak tata-
traaak**

toong   toongzongSHAAK flip

Stop

(instinctive braking jolt agony of the dri-
ver) $\frac{1}{3}$ of a car 3 wheels
graze graze graze blondness forage ironies
of a village 306 years   foolishness of
the mountain landscape take my car for
the ruins of Girgenti hold them close in
the arms of its valleys streams trees grasses
correct proofs no no here

HERE

my proofs just as they are to **WIPE** my
DEAR surviving carburetor

SYNCHRONIC CHART

of sounds noises colors images smells
hopes desires energies longings
drawn up by the aviator Y. M.

LEFT

elastic green yellow white
mattress of noises crash from
which comes a long fluffy sound
= ADRIANOPLE + gardens + 27 forts

RIGHT

∧∧∧∧∧∧∧∧∧∧∧∧∧
∧∧∧∧∧∧∧∧∧∧∧∧∧
long narrow double
line of hard noises =
machine guns

egg of golden silence =
captive **balloon** preg-
nant woman in light
dress seaside taken and
taken again by the wind
green coat striped with
noises plain + battery

yellow
globular **crash**
= village
+ forage

pin-tray of yellow
noises = shrapnel
burst over village

5 silvery stars of noise
= 5 shrapnel shells

30 gangling **red** sounds
= echoes of cannon-shot

foaming waves of
liquid sounds =
valley 200 m. deep

**cascade of verdant
sounds = valley
300 m. deep**

**weary parabola
of blue sounds
= 150 mm. shell**

crash crumbling
= gun firing

rosy silence
coated with
greenish noises
= **north**west
wind

green coat striped
with noises = plain + battery

Bulgarian biplane 860 m. high cut
490 390 340 300 260 230 200 100
power

Knot
of rosy
sounds and
violet noises
= crossroads

needles of light noises
= speed 80 km. per hour

saw of sounds
= car

azure braid of velvety
sounds = longing for Paulette
Latin Quarter

gush of frozen
sounds = village

pear-shaped
noise = camp

puddle of dirty
noises = crossroads

**rosy swing of
languid sounds
= winding road
+ north wind**

blackish boiler of
noises + in and out
of a sound trumpet
piston =
MUSTAFA PASHA

caravan of blue green soft sounds = Maritsa

3,000 noises struggling under a fan of cool echoes = **RHODOPE MOUNTAINS**

Hadirlik
Turkish Headquarters

fervor of the Nizams   idleness
shabbiness of the Mustafiz Redifs beard
white hair   Ichtiats Mohammedans
and non-Mohammedans Greeks Bulgarians Mace-
donians Israelites Armenians called to the
Turkish colors

HANGING
1 2 3 4 5
traitors spies deserters professors Bulgarians

sandwich corpses wearing posted on their
stomachs the sentence-sign   pell-
mell officers and cattle   Ismail
Pasha in command of the citadel Fuad Bey
staff officer horses mules carts talikas
            orders to stock up for 2
months   no going out after 7
at night population of Adrianople (55,000
Turks + 20,000 Greeks + 10,000 Bul-
garians + 6,000 Armenians + 20,000 Is-
raelites = 120,000 mouths thirst **water
cut off**) 240,000 ears filled with the
tatatatatatata of machine guns at the out-
posts Akbunar Kadiköy   ennnnd-
less rrrrrumble of wheels on the Stambul-
Yolu road

FALL OF KIRKILISSE

communication with Constantinople cut off
            Bulgarian army encircling Babaeski
and Lule Burgas   procession of
300 Turks deserters fists bound between
Turkish bayonets   quick stash rail-
road papers and records in Hadirlik's vaults

Turks'
ideas
of
Bulgarians
{ bad soldiers officers whip and
whallop back to action love of
ambush wear the fez raise white
flag use shadows and rain skewer
old men children disembowel
pregnant women rape little girls
eat fried squash onions roast barley
etc.

INDIFFERENCE
OF 2 SUSPENDED ROTUNDITIES
CAPTIVE
SUN + BALLOON

giant flames   columns of smoke   spirals of sparks

Turkish villages in flames

big **T**

drrrrronnnne of a Bulgarian monoplane +
snow of manifestos

> We Bulgarians are waging war on the Ot-
> toman government, which is incapable of
> governing properly. We are not against the
> Mohammedan people. You must know that
> we do not wish for bloodshed. We wish
> to save you from the men of the Ot-
> toman government, who are cruel, treacher-
> ous, and heartless. We want a guarantee
> on this Balkan peninsula. See what a state
> your governments have reduced you to. Your
> neighbors the four States have taken all the
> territory around you. Kirk Kilisse has long
> been in Bulgarian hands. Baba-Eski, Lule Bur-
> gas, Demotika, Uskub, Prishtina, Nevrokop,
> Kumanovo, Elassona, and other towns have
> likewise long been in our hands. Adrianople
> is surrounded on all sides; the road to
> Constantinople has also been cut off. You
> must know that the city of Adrianople can
> no longer get help from any quarter. Un-
> der these circumstances, why shed blood?
> What good would it do? Would it be for
> justice or for your rulers, who are thieves
> and tyrants? 1000 guns are trained on Adri-
> anople. If it does not surrender, it will
> be destroyed and totally devastated. Wouldn't
> that be a pity for the people?

(*Notice thrown from the Bulgarian airplane, 18–
31 October 328 at 6:20 in the evening*)

long lines of Mohammedan mohadjirs dri-
ven toward Adrianople by the flames of
their villages-infernos   6,000 Arabas
(clothes housewares pallets mats)
rancid honeyed stench + sweat + wheez-

ing of 35 mohadjirs spell out posted no-
tice word by word

. . . .

> We firmly trust that with God's help the
> enemy will soon be repulsed. The Com-
> manding Officer expects the people to re-
> main calm and resolute.

SHUKRI PASHA
Commanding Officer

5 m. up rattle of windows blocks of
voices + gesticulations of Shukri rage in-
sults weight of his scorn on Halil Bey
guilty of letting in 20,000 mohadjirs =
20,000 useless mouths   no char-
coal oil at 22 piasters a tin shopkeepers
raise prices despite municipality no light at
night

              hello hello telephone
Hakki Bey has advanced 2 Kilometers (from
the 1st to the 2d Bulgarian entrenchment)

hope
of relief
from the armies of
$\begin{cases} \text{Nazim Pasha} \\ \quad \text{(150,000 men at Tcherkesköy)} \\ \text{or Tugrut Pasha} \\ \text{or Mukhtar Pasha} \\ \text{or Abdullah Pasha to the rescue} \end{cases}$

telegraph restored between Adrianople and
Uzun Kupru   order from the
minister of finance to the Defterdar of the
vilayet issue the army receipts for mail
telegraph customs regie public debt
nasal voices of 2 boys from the collec-
tor's office repeat repeat the figures fig-
ures figures figures   obliquity of
the astrakhan calpac on the wide hard
domed forehead of Shukri double gray bush
of eyebrows   hard sharp eyes
straight Roman nose graying thickness of

moustache and beard muscular stamina oiled
by 60 years of will undress khaki-greens
suppleness of the shoulders shoulder straps
agility of the legs booted night and day
rolling of 3 batteries through the streets
cheeriness of an order chewed with a cig-
arette by a young officer on horseback

drizzle

RAIN
HAIL

on the outposts attack counter-attack bivouac
along the road   exhausted starved
sicknesses   stragglers   missing   desertions
        rain   rain   rain   rain   rain
tatatatatatatatata rain brutality of a down-
pour flooding of the trenches foot-knee-
belly-chest baths **pik-pok-pon** rain rain stolen
cows departure of a regiment better be
shot than rot forward forward against Bul-
garians

but Bulgarians

going

gone

rain rain downpour torrent of rain go
back follow if you can   vil-
lage zig-zag of huts **patapoom-praak** am-
bush tatatatatatata rain every man for him-
self one-armed sergeant Bulgarians fleeing
bivouac along the road fall asleep in the

fire and smoke head on your pack rain
(*TORRENTIAL SYSTEMATIC PENETRATING DARK
SOLITARY ETERNAL RED BLACK SMOKY RED
DANCING STREAMING ACID*)

Shukri Pasha walk back and forth be-
hind his windows head down   gen-
eral marching orders in spite of the rain
departure of 3 divisions weight of feet
battalions dissolved darkness (*LIMP MONOTO-
NOUS SOMNAMBULAR AUTOMATIC UNDULATORY*)
mud mud mud mud mud flooded plains
clank clank clank clank   stag-
gering of soldiers dead tired masses ditches
ruts 4 hours to walk a league

halt   rain

soldiers-sponges

silence

drums rainy drrrrums   order to
break stacks murmurs refusals officers' cries
Shukri Shukri Shukri Shukri magnetic cir-
culation of a word through the ranks **pik-
tok-tom** Bulgarians enemy enemy everybody
up calm rain distances rain close order
forward rain canteens emptied bottles tossed

Komitadjis

mounted Bulgarian patrols rails dismantled
telegraph wires cut rain explooosion (bridge
blown up) expansion tossing of air masses
halt uproar in the ranks desertion of a
hundred Bulgarian recruits   wind
wind wind wind wind sweep of clouds
        shiver + bitterness of a violet dawn

Bulgarian W / T ambush
b u z z z z z z z z z z z z
confuuuuzzzze Turkish communications
Shukri Pasha-Constantinople

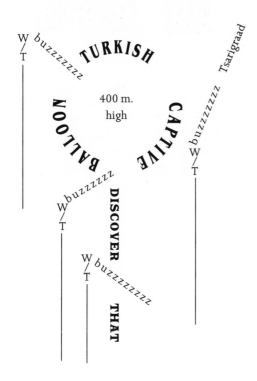

the attack on Seliolu masked important
attack on Marash weak point Bulgarian ob-
jective

by
wireless { war minister notified by Turkish
Embassy in Paris informs Serbian army
reinforcing Bulgarians at Adrianople
power usurped by Young Turks thieves
assassins dismembering of Turkey

solar impassiveness of Shukri Pasha to the
entreaties of 3,000 starving **toom-toomtoom**
zah-zoo axe blows attack on bakeries stores
emptied

prices
raised
300% { sugar 20 frs. a Kg.
rice 2 frs. 50 ” ”
oil 25 frs. a tin
salt 18 frs. a Kg.

shoot on-the-spot
ALL (100) ALL (300) ALL (2000)
the soldiers who attacked the tobacco regie
BOOOOMBAAAARDMENT
BOOOOMBOOOOOMBAAARRRRRDMENT

24 March

25 March { **BOOM BOOM BOOM**

26 March

hunger anguish terror of the Turks fall
back to Forts Kavkas Aivas Bata   sell
arms for piece of bread smash shops Shukri
Shukri Shukri

U B I Q U I T Y   O F   S H U K R I

people's rations reduced to 75 gr. of bread
(millet straw sorghum dust)

3 SHELLS

5 shells
2 shells
4 shells   3 shells   **8 SHELLS**
over Stambul-Yulu over Rechadie Gardens
over Institute of the Sisters of
Agram (structure $+$ solidity $=$ sieve)
frenzied moving of Halil Bey

7 in the morning entrance of the Bul-
garian cavalry through Kaik

WHITE
FLAG
O
V
E
R

Hadirlik Headquarters General Vasov at the
head of the 2d infantry division ponder-

ousness   long beard filth wild-
ness fierceness skin tanned by explosive
blasts shrapnel + danger

MASS EXECUTIONS

500   prisoners
off   with   the   fez

statement
of the siege
$\Big\{$
21 October blockade
15 November Adrianople surrounded
30 attacks 45 battles
52 artillery duels
2,500 shells
destruction of 430 buildings
15,000 men lost

Bridge

300 BEAMS + 180 BARRELS + 28 CABLES + 900 BOLTS < 150,000 CU.M. PRESSURE + 190 TURKS

Splash splash body falling in the water or revolving door café 2 + 2 + 3 + 2 customers plunges coats furs into the waves ricochets of electric lights

mirrors marbles lapping fever of a newspaper big HEADLINES bellicose Balkan capitals telegraphic-tak-tak river torrents streams lakes of unexpected ALBANIA NANCY MARITSA this mirror 5 meters deep under the bridge the Bulgarians built last night dawn of six months ago or yesterday 15 degrees below zero boredom shivers Kadaköy Station the same wind unfurling in the papers waved by the vendors in Stambul Belgrade Sophia Athens and in these flags waiting continuity of hatred Bulgarians Serbians myself over there frozen feet hot heart tonight hot feet frozen heart 10 meters from the bridge Turkish villa garden (*RAVAGED BLACK VIOLET BLACK VIOLET HU-*

MID SLOW) 6 reservists white bandages stained red sweet-smell-of-corpse ammonia ether rotten-cabbage warm yourself by a flame-aloe-roast-squash rye-bread wooden-spoon passed around savor slowness (*VIOLET VIOLET VIOLET BLUE BLUE*) 2 rumblings reservist + biplane
(above) **HHRRRAAAaaa**

hrrrrrrr (below)
there over our heads a Farman vacant glance beatitude of the lips meditation of the tongue awkwardness of the soul vitality of the stomach chew each mouthful well hot belly frozen back

$$\text{newspaper} = \begin{cases} \text{distortion} \\ \text{concision} \\ \text{caricature} \end{cases} \begin{cases} \text{distance} \\ \text{anguish} \\ \text{presence} \end{cases} \begin{cases} \text{summary} \\ \text{of} \\ \text{ITALY} \end{cases}$$

what are we doing what are they saying rain (*VIOLET TREMBLING-GREEN*) terrified bridge streaming teeth chattering aii aii aii flesh cartilage of the wood beams barrels nails weeeary suffering of the fibers (*HARD FROZEN TIGHT STUCK GREENISH SO SLOW*) underbelly-of-the-sky birth of heavy crows crammed with corpses

    caaw-caaw tatatatatatata

get the machine guns ready or else rumbling of carts Paris Halles avez-vous une cigarette Serbian officer French accent woman's silhouette between his lashes warm bustle of Montmartre lacy lights rolled up souls excited mirrors sweat bidet castanets breathless display of breasts routine legs criiiiies invasion of bitter noises blonde burning of memories-desires azure mist of her eyes electric pallor of her cheeks wounded lips evening wrap in Nattier blue charmeuse trimmed with ruffles and a collar of feathers dyed blue warmth and malice of another weary smile heaviness of two black eyes black satin coat-cape embroidered with jet wiles of Parisian skepticism wells of anguish in the flesh creeping of weariness in the nerves cry of stenches in battle gasps from the bridge shivering of the wood groaning of the fibers *give-us-5-degrees-of-heat-so-we-can-expand*

    caaaaaw

3 crows flock of crows (2 Km. long) defeat of the night silvery swelling of clouds vibrating-fuselage-of-the-soul untangling of hopes and voices 1st fermentation of echoes rush of reflections (*BLUE BLUE SOFT GRAY SWIFT*) deliverance conquest dare gold beryl perish digest crows crows building of a black black ceiling 10 km². already big-ger 20 km². shaky swollen from masons' steps crows demolition of the horizon-chimney [*200 KM. IN DIAMETER*] flakes of soot avalanche of coal it's snowing (*WHITE BLACK ETERNAL*) screws grating rusty-pulleys crows inundation of India ink sooty lining of the atmosphere what are we waiting for the artillery **gee-up gee-up kring-kring** pools ponds splish-splash nags pearl-gray-latest-model-Creusot-guns **gee-up gee-up** whips crack-crack frenzy of the horses-martyrs-skeletons solemnity of the mountain gunners 2 meters 120 kilos padded legs wool mud elephant feet coat-boa slung over the shoulder rosaries of cartridges hunk of bread under the arm rearing shouting stammering of orders cries mud rain

we're floundering nothing's moving

what are we waiting for to cross the bridge **caaw-caaw** after the crows the Turks will come **caaw-caaw** don't shoot for-god's-sake can't wake the Turkish sentries bag a crow eat at last shoot into this dummy instead swallower of reflections and vomiter of idiocies at my table

don't kill him you can chat with him when you're looking night road rutted by the cannon wheels for your death line in the thousand million bullet lines of the 800,000 enemy guns at the border Individual and Fatherland live together without squabbling kill that crow eat some Bulgarian they're coming from Kir Kilisse slow beating of wings one-kilo crow gourmet's meal in full flight 100 1,000 300,000 kilos of flying filth **caaw-caaw** hiccoughs nausea children whining after the meal savor scrap of Turkish corpse in its beak Bulgarian's nose greedily dug all night long truffles spices red pepper cinnamon got to eat plenty of wheat to give you strength here here   here's Mustafa Pasha in our clutches **caaw-caaw** (*DISHEVELED DISHEVELED DISHEVELED MECHANICAL*) it smelled better at Kir Kilisse let's stop some flour sacks a minaret with its round deserted balcony where the sun no longer speaks   cemetery

go north go north

quick before the air bursts into pieces there's the sun's belly hoist over the hills that dear griller of corpses run run digest in peace fields of Stara Zagora **caaw-caaw** keep off the roads horns bellowing and wheels **caaw-caaw pet-na-nozha forward**   bayonets toward the bridge all men stand line up **pet-na-nozha** inexplicable solemnity of 11 battalions on the winding roads spike the hills of Yörük like watching a show huge officers on horseback have the troops pour onto the bridge will it hold for 3 hours bridge built too fast the night before 300 Bulgarians in a hurry tie push chain despite the current plunges mud eddies fasten boats barrels beams shh quiet as you can lucky it was raining cables rafts heave-ho heave-ho sweet Maritsa with her hard chest tumult of her breasts against the bridge quick 2 machine guns aimed at the Turkish shore   there are the Turks Turks there there near Fort Kazal Tepé   at a run all together run leap onto the bridge whisssstling bullets **pim-pom-pok** good-god too late 5 10 15 eyes all the eyes of the forts winking blinking **crash** of their battery of eyelids

flames flames flames whistling **strrrrr** over our heads flying 12 kilometers **zong-toomb-toomb** 3 shattered echoes ricochet of 4 echoes lawn-tennis-of-noises   ovoid sound wave that goes off slowly caressing 3 hills and stretching over the green belly of the Maritsa elasticity 150 km. monotony to the sea = 600,000 emeralds   soft teeth of the sun nibble 4 minarets Selim Pasha and this swarming at the end of the bridge the Turks chopping blue flashes **zah zoo zah zoo** quick quick shoot a good gunner (*ORANGE RED GOLD GOING GREEN INDIGO VIOLET INCANDESCENT PERISHABLE*) horizon = spiral of sunlight + 5 fragments of hill + 30 columns of smoke + 23 flames   you three level your machine guns that's it sit get your heads down behind your 3 death cameras do you understand racket squawking I know Turkish do you hear them shouting a saw a saw straw burn burn heavy cable crunch creak **crrrr** the saw **tatatatatatata** aim well **splash** turk 80 kg. into the water   **splash** another one 120 kg. at least **tatatatata** very good 2 3 5 turks 600 kg. **splash**   **splash** cluster of turks **kersplash-splash** to satisfy you dear Maritsa dazzle **zong-toomb-toomb** the machine-gun's-had-it 2 more keep it up keep it up **tatatatata** watering cans of bullets machines to stitch up the atmosphere ripped by the axes **zah-zoo-zah-zoo-zoo** the bridge **cruuuunnch** creaking of its ribs   very long long **thrrrrrrobbing** of the cable Maritsa 120,000 cu.m. pressure against the bridge to split it **zah-zoo-zah-zoo tatatatatata kring-striadiiiiii-ooooz** turks rage fury sobs prayers   I beg you I beg you dear bridge break in two open up to deliver our victory the forts the forts open blink blink multiplication of their stares (*PIERCING REPEATED RELENTLESS IM-PLACABLE HARD HARD HARD*) **patatraaaak boom zoomb-toomb** Turkish shell on the bridge whirlwind dust-mire-wood-hate-terror-blood-hail-of-meat-guts-corridas-minced-meat-fat shattering of machine guns masks of bloodymud (*RED RED RED STRONG STRONG MAD MAD BIG BURLY*) see **zoo-zahng zahng-zahng** axes sparkle of iron splendor of sweating faces luminous mud swift wheel of muscles-eels over the head spatter of sun axes cable quick **saaaaaw saaaaaw saaaaaw saaaaw saaaaaaaw** 3 more bolts **pet-na-nozha pet-na-nozha forward** elastic suspension of vic-tory   need more machine guns let's go quick settle it later get your head down idiot and fire at those 3 giants by the furnace under the cable **tatatatata screeeeeeeam** (*LONG LONG LONG*) the bridge wants to come apart   collapse let's go quick chop chop chop chop **zoo-zah** *oof break away from me 3-millimeter fiber open up bliss* (*LITTLE LITTLE TINY*) *multiply ecstasy into 20 30 fibrils 400 filaments and 600 straws hot too hot here comes the blade* **zoo-zah** *let's-get-wet   coolness of the river live free all points turned out I'm too thick break up crumble o my 6-millimeter fiber if you'd move over a little I could break in two   if you'd explode thank you at last I can breathe-through-3-holes ah 6 holes smell of resin mold*

bitter burnt-iron bolt-rust big calloused hands gripping the pincers pull pull while the axes chop chop **zah-zoo**   2 big Turks on the last last bolt to resist **tatatatatata** courageous resistance of the wood **crrrrrrr zong-toomb-toomb zah-zoo-zah-zoo** shhhhhattering of the sun into pieces 1,000 solar blocks **whirling** over the hills 20 shrapnel-kids (*COCKY GANGLING SHIFT-LESS*) drag their noisy feet whistle **zong-toomb** collapse of a bronze ceiling all the forts **open shut open shut open shut open open open** their eyes-mouths fire-lead fan of flames 30 km. wide over the 15 gunners fallen on their faces like they're sleeping around the 2 machine–guns-guard-dogs-mouths-gaping

push me to the left 2-millimeter fiber I want to cut myself in three don't bend blow up pom break saw saw look there's my sawdust **crrrrr** *ca-ble* **pet-na-nozha** 3 new gunners second shower of lead on the cable before they burn it quick   flaccid laugh of the ed-dies pilings draped with green red water **zah-zoo tatatatatata** cable stink smoke **cr-rrrrraaaak** too late hell blast damn the bridge obtuse angle taut arc thrusts out its belly **spliiiiiit aiiiii patapoompatatraaack**

     curses bastards bastards shout shout yell howl **joy joy frenzy the turks** shouting their heads off **hurrrrrraaaah tatatatatata hurrrrrraaaah tatatatatatatata POOM POMPOM SPLASH zong-toomb-toomb-toomb-toomb**   **hurrrrraaah tatatatatatata hurrrrraaaah**

{
MINCED RED RED STREAKED SPASMODIC ETERNAL

hurrrrrrrraaaaah hurrrrrraaaaah

win win joy joy revenge massacre keep on

tatatatatatatatatatatatata

END DESPAIR LOST NO-USE HOPELESS

dive coolness expand open soften expand

ploom plomplom splash splash frrrrrrr

dung urine bidet ammonia typographic-smell
}

{
AUTOMATIC SUN 20,000 BULLETS A MINUTE

hurrrrrrrrraaaaaaaaaah

joy joy joy joy again again revenge

tatatatatatatatatatatatata

START OVER HOPELESS HOPELESS NO WAY

want to swim 2-millimeter fiber

splash splosh splosh guggug glugglug

ammonia old-woman-smell armpits tuberose corpse
}

it's cool it's green it's blue it's smooth in the water I lost my head you
swim better me I've got no belly I've got a hole filter-sieve that lets
through 1,000 drops of water a second

Trainload of Sick Soldiers

Shukri Pasha by Allah the audacity of these lords is infuriating we don't need them here lock up Abdul Pasha for uncoupling a locomotive without my orders all these sick men must be underway in an hour at the latest

Karagach station clatter of doors banging shut at both ends of the cars doctors nurses medical officers stretchers bearers breeze throbbing like the intestines of that Anatolian captain enteritis dysentery trembling of his bony hand raise to his lips the bottle of milk *swarming insurrection furnace of microbes of putrefaction in the intestinal tract take hold quick multiply penetrate rot walls avalanche of milk 6,000 lactic ferments to the attack tumult of the visceral battle massing of 31 microbe battalions fragmentation of 6 microbes-generals uncertainty of victory = health + death coolness hope of living ghost of a smile on the lips drawn in agony counterattack of the microbes*

sappers

picks hammers pincers bayonets quartering all the Balkan rage in the stomach doctor's potion shower of brewer's yeast + barley comings 3,000

powerful constituents against the microbial armies deafening din of pain jolts commotion of departure health of speed and fresh air shrinking of the thin body facing straight ahead shocks against the skin on the outside 30 Km. per hour to Stambul my brother get well get well get well (*VISCERAL REBOUND OF THE TRAIN'S LYRICAL ONOMATOPOEIAS*)

tloktlok ii ii gwiiii

trrrrrrtrrrrrr

tatatatohh-tatatatatohh

(*WHEELS*)

coorrrrrr

currrr

goorrrrrrr

(*LOCOMOTIVE*)

fooofoofoofoofooofoofoo

fahfahfahfahfah

zahzahzahzahzahzah

tzahtzahtzahtzahtzah

40 Km. per hour 45 Km. = *growing pressure on the viscera still moving at* 30 Km.

army of lactic ferments + army of brewer's yeast < 900,000 microbes battle in a land rocked by an earthquake (TUBULAR INCREASING TENA-

72

CIOUS FEROCIOUS METICULOUS ETERNAL CLOUDY RAVAGED) stop change locomotive now pull the train by the tail and the sick man by the shoulders facing backward *shocks acting on the nerve endings near the trunk irritation of the central nervous system* right left slowing of the 2 revolving landscapes = 2 horizontal cogwheels turning in the opposite direction from the train-horizontal-bar each tree-cog of the 2 wheels-landscapes mesh vibrate 3 seconds between 2 cars-cogs and flee 3 Km. back between cogs and cogs the captain's Anatolian viscera full of sharp branches and greenish skies over the impossible Bosporus WEIGHT + slowness of the train progressive slowing of 2 revolving landscapes (*VELVETY OMINOUS UNIVERSAL*)

1,500 sick men's dreams {
idleness luxuries journeys speed of the trains-scalpels mountains-stomachs surge of the volumes of space agility of the trains-eels streaks of rain brushes of the sun trains-needles stitch mountains of velvet silk of the plains moires of the lakes moving fabric of the journeys speed meadows-theorems breasts of the hills milk of dawn in the mouth cool
station bed
fresh sheets ice-cold
orangeade
}

scuffle superimposition of the smells of all the sicknesses stuffed in the train *quivering leaves of the olfactory nerves* fecal smell of dysentery honeyed stench of plague sweat ammoniacal smell of the cholera patients sweet stink of gangrene consumptives acidulous smell of the fever patients cellar smell cat urine hot-oil mold incense rotten-straw swamp grease cheap wine mouse smell tuberose garlic rotten-cabbage **zong-toomtoomb** tatatatatata **stop**

howowowow howowling of the sick men through the **crrrrrrrackling** of **bullets** whistling **crash** of broken windows doors-targets Adrianople completely surrounded train abandoned by engineers and soldiers fury of the Bulgarian shrapnel

flying hunger and greed bite Selim Pasha's minarets-nougats urgency of exploding over the marble gold touch touch the precious stones mystery supernatural power mow down trees men and columns like wheat cadaverous head of the Anatolian captain leaning out the door = camera capture an abandoned Turkish battery gunner head shattered cover the gun with his body pulp putrefaction flies behind him the server a shrapnel in his hands embrace the open caisson full of gold safe around the 3 guns 12 servers dead reseda different trajectories rooted to the spot humor of immobility 3 horses sitting on the single stew of their 3 fused rumps pull pull pull all the earth endless entrails with their 3 necks stretched 1 m. **whiiiiiinying** high to the sky implore sniff lick that 1st star Venus flesh precious stones wealth spring shimmering electric display Rue de la Paix

howowowowowling of 1,500 sick men at the **locked** doors in front of 6 dead horses in harness 24 legs in the air mad maze of reins and wheels bursts of shrapnel packs uniforms upheaval of the earth craters gaping holes sticky mud

howowowowling   of
1,500   sick   men   at   the   **locked**   doors   in
front   of   18   Turkish   artillerymen   struck   down
         rags   shreds   greatcoats
         officers   thrown   against   the   wire   en-
tanglements   cross   cross   at   any   cost   agony
twist   with   the   short   bayonet   tear   out   the
links   rage   **TRAP**   slowing   of
the   gunfire   under   the   weight   of   the   clouds
$(= 3$ _DAYS OF RAIN_$)$ shrillish   quiv-
ering   of   a   musette   from   afar   on   the   wind
         dance   the   Horo   fermentation
of   bivouacs-wounds   in   the   first   darkness
(_RED   BLACK   SOFT   RIPPLING   INDEFINITE   IN-
DULGENT   SPASMODIC_)   swarming   of   shadows
creeping   of   advanced   posts   ochre-colored   uni-
forms   dig   in
                 creep   patience   of   cats
                 repositioning   of   84   heavy
guns   thunderrrrrrrrrr   of   wheeeels   and   clouds

Bombardment

1 2 3 4 5 seconds siege guns split the silence in unison **zong-toomb** sudden echoes echoes all the echoes seize it quick smash it scatter it to the infinite winds to the devil   In the middle middle of these **zong-toomb** flattened 50 square kilometers leap 2 3 6 8 crashes clubs punches bashes quick-firing batteries Violence ferocity regularity pendulum play fatality

    My ears   my eyes   nostrils   open look what joy is yours O my people of senses see hear smell drink everything everything everything **taratatatatata** machine guns cry writhe under 1,000 bites blows **traak-traak** thrashes lashes **pik-pok-poom-toomb** juggling clowns' leaps in mid-air 200 m. high it's gunfire Down below bogs' guffaws   laughs buffalo carts goads horses stamping caissons splish splash **zong-zong-shaaak-shaaak** rearing pirouettes **pata-traak** spattering manes whinnying **eeeeeeeeee** hubbhub jingling 3 Bulgarian battalions on the march **kroook-kraaak** (*SLOWLY DOUBLE TIME*) Shumi Maritsa o Karvavena officers' cries clash copper plates **pom** here (*QUICK*) **pok** there **boom-pom-pom-pom-pom** here there there farther all around up high

watch out good-god on the head **shaaak** staggering   flames
        flames
flames   *flames*
  flames   *flames*
    flames footlights of the forts over there
    flames
    flames

Shukri Pasha phones his orders to 27 forts in Turkish in German hello **Ibrahim Rudolf hello hello** actors parts   echoes-prompters   scenes of smoke forests applause hay-mud-manure-smell there's no more feeling in my frozen feet smell of mold rot gongs flutes cowbells pipes everywhere above below birds warble beatitude shade greenness *cheep-cheep* *zzeep-zzeep* flocks pastures *dong-dang-dong-ding-baaa* **zong-toomb-toomb-toomb-toomb-toomb-toomb-toomb** 2,000 shrapnel gesticulation explosion **zong-toomb** white handkerchiefs full of gold **toomb-toomb**

2,000 grenades thunder of applause Quick quick what enthusiasm tear mops shocks darkness **zong-toomb-toomb** orchestra of war sounds swell under a note of silence   hanging in mid-air golden captive balloon monitoring the firing

STATEMENT OF ANALOGIES

(1st SUM)

Advance of the Futurist cannonade colossus-leit-motif-hammer-innovative genius-optimism-hunger-ambition (*TERRIFYING ABSOLUTE SOLEMN HEROIC HEAVY IMPLACABLE FECUNDATING*) **zong toomb toomb toomb toomb toomb tatatatatatatatatata pikpokpokponpokpokponponpon** oooooooooooom ooooooooooom

(2d SUM)

defense of Adrianople passéism minarets of skepticism domes-bellies of apathy cowardice we'll-think-about-it-tomorrow not-a-chance no-way   what's-the-use   after-all-I-don't-give-a-damn   delivery of all the supplies at the only   station   =   cemetery

(3d SUM)

around   each   shell-colossus   step-note-hammer   fall-genius   creation-order-run   gallop-ing round of rifle fire machine guns violins kids   poodles   critics'   ironies   wheels   gears cries   shrugs   regrets (*GAY GAY GAY GAY SKEPTICAL PLAYFUL PRETTY AERIAL CORROSIVE VOLUPTUOUS*)

(4th SUM)

around   Adrianople   +   bombardment   + orchestra   +   colossus-walk   +   factory widen concentric-circles reflections plagiarisms echoes laughter little girls flowers steam-whistle waiting feathers fragrance foulness anguish (*INFINITE MONOTONOUS PERSUASIVE NOSTALGIC*) These weights thicknesses sounds smells molecular   whirlwinds   chains   nets   and   channels of   analogies   concurrences   and   synchronisms for   my   Futurist   friends   poets   painters   and musicians

zong-toomb-toomb   zong-toomb   toomb tatatatatatatatata   pikpokpompokpokpikpompom oooooooooooooooo

TECHNICAL MANIFESTO
of
Futurist Literature
(11 May 1912)

I was in an airplane, sitting on the gas tank, my stomach warmed by the pilot's head, when I suddenly felt the absurd inanity of the old syntax inherited from Homer. Raging need to free words, releasing them from the prison of the Latin period. It has, of course, like any imbecile, a provident head, a stomach, two legs, and two flat feet, but will never have two wings. Something to walk with, run a few steps, and then stop, panting, almost immediately! . . . . That's what the whirling propeller told me as I flew two hundred meters above the mighty Milanese smokestacks. And the propeller added:

1. — **We must destroy syntax by placing nouns at random as they are born.**

2. — **We must use the verb in the infinitive,** so that it will conform elastically to the noun and will not subordinate it to the I of the writer who sees or imagines. Only the infinitive verb can convey the sense of life's continuity and the elasticity of the intuition that perceives it.

3. — **We must abolish the adjective** so that the naked noun can retain its essential color. The adjective, carrying in it a principle of nuance, is incompatible with our dynamic vision, because it implies a pause, a meditation.

4. — **We must abolish the adverb,** old clip that holds words together. The adverb maintains a fastidious unity of tone in the sentence.

5. — **Every noun should have its double**—that is, a noun should be followed, without any conjunctive phrase, by the noun to which it is tied by analogy. Example: man-torpedo boat, woman-harbor, square-funnel, door-faucet.

Because aerial speed has expanded our knowledge of the world, perception by analogy is becoming increasingly natural to man. Thus we must suppress the *like*, the *as*, the *so*, the *similar to*, etc. Better still, we must fuse the object directly with the image it evokes by presenting the foreshortened image in a single essential word.

6. — **No more punctuation.**

Once adjectives, adverbs, and conjunctive phrases are suppressed, punctuation is naturally annulled in the varied continuity of a living style that creates itself, without the absurd pauses of commas and periods. To emphasize certain movements and show their directions, we will use mathematical signs, $\times\ +\ :\ -\ =\ <\ >$, and musical symbols.

7. — Up to now writers have indulged themselves in direct analogies. For example, they have compared an animal to man or to another animal, which is still almost the same as photography. For example, they have compared a fox terrier to a tiny thoroughbred.

Others, more progressive, might compare this same trembling fox terrier to a little Morse apparatus. I myself compare it to boiling water. The **analogies here have become increasingly vast,** the connections increasingly deep, though very remote.

Analogy is nothing but the immense love that connects distant, seemingly different, and hostile things. It is through very vast analogies that this orchestral style, at once polychromatic, polyphonic, and polymorphic, can embrace the life of matter.

When, in my *Battle of Tripoli*, I compared a trench bristling with bayonets to an orchestra, a machine gun to a femme fatale, I intuitively introduced a great part of the universe into a brief episode of African battle.

Images are not flowers to be chosen and picked sparingly, as Voltaire maintained. They are the very lifeblood of poetry. Poetry must be an uninterrupted succession of fresh images or it is nothing but anemia and chlorosis.

The vaster the connections an image encompasses, the longer it will keep its stupefying power. We must spare the reader's astonishment, you say. Bah! Instead we should worry about the fatal corrosion of time, which destroys not only the expressive value of a masterpiece but its stupefying power. Haven't our ears, too often enraptured, worn out Beethoven and Wagner? Therefore we must abolish all that language contains in the way of clichéd images, or faded metaphors—that is, almost everything.

8. — **There are no categories of images,** noble or vulgar, elegant or base, eccentric or natural. The intuition that perceives them has neither preferences nor prejudices. The analogical style is therefore absolute master of all matter and its intense life.

9. — To render the successive movements of an object, we must render the **chain of analogies** it evokes, each one condensed, drawn into one essential word.

Here is a striking example of a chain of analogies still masked and weighed down by traditional syntax:

"Why yes, sweet machine gun, you are a charming lady, and sinister, and divine, at the wheel of an invisible hundred-horsepower, roaring and snorting with impatience . . . And soon you will leap into the circuit of death, to a smashing crash or victory! Would you like some madrigals full of grace and color? As you wish, madam! I also see you as a gesticulating orator, whose eloquent, tireless tongue strikes his impassioned circle of listeners to the heart. Now you are an omnipotent trepan boring through the too solid skull of this stubborn night. You are also a steel rolling mill, an electric lathe, and what else? . . . . a great oxyhydrogen blowpipe burning, chiseling, and slowly melting the metallic tips of the last stars." ("Battle of Tripoli").

In certain cases we must link images in pairs like chain shot that can level a clump of trees in its flight.

To surround and capture all that is most fleeting and elusive in matter, we must make **closely woven nets of images or analogies** that we will cast into the mysterious sea of phenomena. Except for its traditional form, this sentence from my *Mafarka the Futurist* is a closely woven net of images: *"All the bitter sweetness of his youth rose in his throat, like the cries of children rising from the playground to their old teachers leaning on the parapets of the terraces from which boats can be seen skimming across the sea."*

Here are three closely woven nets of images:

"Around the wells of Bumeliana, under the bushy olive trees, three camels, lying comfortably on the sand, gargled happily like old gargoyles, harmonizing their spitting with the thump-thump of the steam pump supplying water to the town.

"Shrill and dissonant Futurist sounds in the deep orchestra of the trenches with their sinuous channels and sonorous vaults, as the bayonets come and go, violin bows that the sunset-conductor's red baton fires with enthusiasm.

"It is he who, with a sweep of his hand, gathers the scattered flutes of birds in the trees and the plaintive harps of insects, the creaking of branches, the crunching of stones . . . . It is he who stops dead the mess tin drums and the clashing guns so all the stars in golden clothes, arms open wide above the footlights of the sky, can sing out over the muted orchestra. And here's a lady at the show: in a low-cut gown, the desert

flaunts her vast bosom with its thousand liquefied curves, polished with pink rouge under the tumbling jewels of the lavish night." ("Battle of Tripoli").

10. — Since all order is inevitably the product of cautious intelligence, we must orchestrate images by arranging them with a **maximum of disorder.**

11. — **Destroy the "I" in literature**— that is, all psychology. Man, utterly ruined by libraries and museums, ruled by a fearful logic and wisdom, is of absolutely no more interest. So abolish him in literature. Replace him with matter, whose essence must be grasped by flashes of intuition, something physicists and chemists can never do.

Auscultate, through things in freedom and capricious engines, the breath, the sensibility, and the instincts of metal, stone, wood, etc. Replace the psychology of man, now spent, with a **lyrical obsession with matter.**

Beware of attributing human feelings to matter; rather, divine its different guiding forces, its powers of compression, expansion, cohesion, and disgregation, its rush of molecules en masse, or its whirls of electrons. We must not offer dramas of humanized matter. The solidity of a sheet of steel interests us in itself— that is to say, the incomprehensible and inhuman alliance of its molecules and electrons that can withstand, for example, the penetration of a shell. From now on, the heat of a piece of iron or wood interests us more passionately than a woman's smile or tears.

We want to render in literature the life of the engine, that new instinctive beast whose general instinct we will know once we know the instincts of the different forces that make it up.

Nothing more interesting for the Futurist poet than the movement of a keyboard on a mechanical piano. The cinematograph gives us the dance of a thing that divides and reassembles without human intervention. It gives us the backward plunge of a diver whose feet rise out of the sea and spring violently back onto the diving board. It gives us a man running at 200 kilometers an hour. So many movements of matter beyond the laws of intelligence, and therefore of a more significant essence.

We must introduce into literature three elements that up to now have been neglected:

1. — **Sound** (manifestation of the dynamism of things);

2. — **Weight** (faculty of flight in things);

3. — **Smell** (faculty of dispersal in things).

Try, for example, to convey the landscape of smells a dog perceives. Listen to engines and reproduce their discourse.

Matter has always been looked upon by an I that is distracted, cold, overly self-absorbed, full of prejudices of wisdom and human obsessions.

Man, with his youthful joy or aging sorrow, tends to corrupt matter, which is neither young nor old but has an admirable continuity of impulse toward increasing heat, movement, and dispersal. Matter is neither sad nor joyful. Its essence is courage, will, and absolute power. It belongs entirely to the diviner-poet who can free himself from traditional syntax—heavy, confined, earthbound, armless and wingless, because merely intelligent. Only the asyntactic poet who unbinds his words can penetrate the essence of matter and destroy the veiled hostility that separates it from us.

The Latin period that has served us up to now was a pretentious gesture by means of which a presumptuous and myopic intelligence tried to subdue the multiform and mysterious life of matter. Therefore the Latin period was stillborn.

The profound intuitions of life, juxtaposed word by word according to their illogical birth, will give us the general outline of an **intuitive physiology of matter.** This was revealed to me up in an airplane. Looking at things from a new point of view, not from the front or the back, but straight down—that is, foreshortened— I was able to break the old logical shackles and plumb lines of ancient understanding.

Futurist poets, all you who have loved and followed me up to now, like me you were frenetic builders of images and brave explorers of analogies. But unfortunately your closely woven nets of metaphors are too weighed down with logical lead. I advise you to lighten them so that your immensified gesture can cast them into the distance, spread over a vaster ocean.

Together we will invent what I call the **wireless imagination.** One day we will achieve an even more essential art, when we dare to suppress all the first terms of our analogies and give only the uninterrupted sequence of second terms. To do this we must give up being understood. Being understood is not necessary. Besides, we managed well enough without it when we were expressing fragments of Futurist sensibility in traditional, intellective syntax.

Syntax was a kind of abstract code used by poets to inform the masses about the colorful, musical, plastic, and architectural state of the universe. Syntax was a kind of interpreter and monotonous cicerone. We must remove this intermediary so that literature may enter directly into the universe and become one with it.

There is no question that my work is clearly distinguishable from all others in its terrific power of analogy. Its astonishing wealth of images almost equals its disorder of logical punctuation. It leads us to the first Futurist manifesto, synthesis of a hundred-horse-power launched at the wildest terrestrial speeds.

Why keep on using four tired exasperated wheels when you can break free of the ground? Liberation of words, soaring wings of the imagination, analogical synthesis of the earth embraced in a single glance, all drawn together in essential words.

They shout to us: "It won't be beautiful! We'll have no more verbal symphonies with harmonious modulations and soothing rhythms." That's right. And what luck! Instead we use all the brutal sounds, all the expressive cries of the violent life that surrounds us.

Let us boldly create the "ugly" in literature and kill solemnity wherever it may be. And don't put on those high-priest airs when you listen to me. We must spit every day on the *Altar of Art*. We are entering the limitless domains of free intuition. After free verse, here at last are **words in freedom.**

Nothing in this is absolute or systematic. Genius has impetuous gusts and muddy floods. Sometimes it imposes analytical and explanatory delays. One can hardly renovate one's sensibility overnight. Dead cells are mixed with the living. Art is a need to destroy and disperse oneself, great watering can of heroism flooding the world. Microbes, don't forget, are necessary to the blood as well as to Art, that extension of the forest of our veins that spreads outside the body into the infinity of space and time.

Futurist poets! I taught you to hate libraries and museums. This was to prepare you to **hate intelligence,** awakening in you the divine intuition that is the distinctive gift of the Latin races.

Through intuition, we will put an end to the seemingly indomitable hostility that separates our human flesh from the metal of engines. After the animal kingdom, the mechanical kingdom begins! Through the knowledge and love of matter, of which scholars can only know the physico-chemical reactions, we begin the creation of **mechanical man with replaceable parts.** We will deliver him from the idea of death, and hence from death itself, that supreme definition of logical intelligence.

F. T. Marinetti

Milan, 11 May 1912

BATTLE

WEIGHT + SMELL

Twelve 45 flutes yelping burning **toomb-toomb** alarm Gargaresch snapping crackling march Clank packs rifles hooves spikes guns manes wheels caissons Jews fritters oil-bread cantilenas shops whiffs shimmering rheum stench cinnamon chit chat ebb flow pepper quarrel vermin whirlwind orange-trees-in-bloom filigree misery dice chess cards jasmine + nutmeg + rose arabesque mosaic carrion bristling scuff machine guns = pebbles + surf + frogs Clank packs rifles guns scrap iron atmosphere = lead + lava + 300 stenches + 50 scents pavement-mattress refuse droppings carrion splish-splash pile-up camels donkeys hubbub cesspool Silversmiths'-suq maze silk azure galabia crimson oranges moucharaby arches span bifurcation little square teeming tannery polishers gandouras burnouses swarming run ooze motley enveloping excrescences cracks hovels rubble demolition carbolic-acid lime squalor Clank packs rifles hooves spikes guns caissons whip-lashes uniform-cloth suint impasse left crater right crossroads chiaroscuro steamrooms fried food musk jonquils orange-blossom nausea attar-of-rose-trap ammonia claws excrement-bites meat + 1,000 flies dried-fruit carobs chickpeas pistachios almonds bunches-bananas dates **toomb-toomb** goat moldy-cousscous spices saffron tar rotten-egg wet-dog jasmine acacia sandalwood pinks ripening intensity bubbling ferment tuberose Rot scatter fury die break up bits pieces dust heroism worms gunfire **pik pok poon pon pon** mint tangerine tawny-wool machine-guns-wooden-ratchets-leprosarium sores forward moist-flesh filth sweetness ether Clank packs rifles guns caissons wheels benzoin tobacco incense anise village ruins burnt amber jasmine houses-eviscerations abandon goglet **toomb toomb** violets shadows wells he-ass she-ass corpse-pulpefaction-sex-exhibition garlic bromine anisette breeze fish greenpine rosemary butcher shops palms sand cinnamon

Sun gold scales pans lead sky silk heat stuffing crimson azure torrefaction Sun = volcano + 3,000 flags atmosphere-precision corrida fury surgery lights rays-scalpels sparkling-bandages desert-clinic X 20,000 arms 20,000 feet 10,000 eyes-aim twinkling waiting operation sand-boiler-rooms Italians Arabs: 4,000 meters battalions-boilers orders-pistons sweat mouths furnaces damn it forward oil ammonia > acacias violets droppings roses sand shimmering everything march arithmetic tracks obey irony fervor humming stitch dunes-pillows zigzags mend feet-millstones-grinding sand uselessness machine guns = pebbles + surf + frogs Advance guard: 200 meters bayonet-charge forward Arteries swelling heat fermentation-hair-armpits knot-redness blondness breaths + pack 30 kilos caution = seesaw scrap iron money box softness: 3 shudders orders-stones rage enemy-magnet quickness glory heroism Advance guard: 100 meters machine guns gunfire eruption violins brass **pam poom pok** pok tam toom machine guns **tataratararatarata**

Advance guard: 20 meters battalions-ants cavalry-spiders roads-fords general-islet couriers-grasshoppers sand-revolution shells-tribunes clouds-grills rifles-martyrs shrapnel-haloes multiplication addition division shell-subtraction grenade-erasure stream run crumbling blocks avalanche Advance guard: 3 meters mixing back and forth sticking unsticking tearing fire uproot yards crumbling quarries blaze panic blinding crush come go run spattering Lives-fuses hearts-sweetmeats bayonets-forks bite carve stink waltz leap rage spoils explosions shells-gymnasts crashes trapezes explosion rose joy stomachs-watering-cans heads-foot-ball scattering 149-gun elephant gunners-mahouts heave-ho anger levers slowness heaviness center cartridgejockey method mo-

notony trainers distance grand-prix muzzle parabola *x* light thunder club infinity Sea = lace-emeralds-coolness-elasticity-abandon-softness battleships-steel-concision-order Battle-flag (meadows-white-hot-sky blood) = Italy power Italian-pride brothers wives mother insomnia clamor-of-vendors glory domination cafés war-stories Towers guns-virility-chases erection range finder ecstasy **toomb-toomb** 3 seconds **toomb-toomb** waves smiles laughter splish splash gluggluggluggluig hide-and-seek crystals virgins flesh jewels pearls iodine salts bromine petticoats gas cordials bubbles 3 seconds **toomb-toomb** officer whiteness range finder cross fire megaphone range-4-thousand-meters everyone-to-the-left good to-your-stations elevation-7-degrees erection splendor gush pierce immensity azure-female deflowering ferocity corridors cries labyrinth mattress sobs smashing desert bed precision range finder monoplane theater-gallery applause monoplane = balcony-rose-wheel-drum trepan-gadfly > rout Arabs oxen sanguinolence slaughterhouse wounds refuge oasis humidity fan cool siesta creeping germination effort vegetable-dilation I'll-be-greener-tomorrow let's-stay-wet hold-that-drop-of-water got-to-climb-3-centimeters-in-6-days press-your-stem-down-to-stand-20-grams-of-sand-and-300-grams-of-darkness milky-way-coconut-palm stars-coconuts milk stream juice delights

F. T. MARINETTI

Futurist Words in Freedom

(1919)

Words in Freedom

Futurism, born in Milan eleven years ago, has influenced the entire universe through thousands of exhibitions, meetings, and concerts, and has created innumerable different Futurisms in response to the needs of different circles. Every circle has its own kind of passéism, an oppressive, pernicious passéism that must be destroyed. Futurism has been understood in all the European and American capitals and has become the springboard for important spiritual revolutions everywhere. In Italy it has long been slandered and hounded by reactionary, clerical, moralistic, pedantic, and conservative forces. It is emerging from this battle more powerful than ever.

The Futurist movement first exercised an artistic effect while at the same time indirectly influencing Italian politics through its propaganda of revolutionary, anticlerical patriotism that was directed against the Triple Alliance and that prepared us for our war against Austria. Italian Futurism, prophet and architect of our war, disseminator and coach of courage and freedom, opened its first artistic meeting at the Lirico Theater in Milan eleven years ago with the cry *Down with Austria!*

From that day on, those words became the incessant cry of all our stormy gatherings.

The Italian Futurists are proud of having organized the first two mass demonstrations against Austria on 15 September 1914 in Milan, in the face of Italian neutrality. These two demonstrations were relentless and resounding: eight Austrian flags were burned in the riot by the Futurists, who were thrown into jail at San Vittore.

The Futurists, always first in the streets to fight for the declaration of war on Austria, were also first on the battlefield, with a large number of dead, wounded, and decorated.

During the war the Futurists founded the Futurist political party, whose organ is the paper *Roma Futurista*. Immediately after our great victory at Vittorio Veneto, Futurist political Fasci were formed in Milan, Rome, Florence, Ferrara, Taranto, Perugia, etc.

Italian Futurism is the soul of the new generation that fought against the Austro-Hungarian empire and victoriously annihilated it.

The Futurist artistic movement, which necessarily slowed during the war, is now regaining its provocative, renovative dynamism.

Throughout our great victorious war, the Futurist poets, fighters at the front lines, took advantage of their brief respites in the trenches or in the hospital to pursue relentlessly their great inspired work for the total renovation of lyricism, which, having gone through free verse, is now attaining words in freedom.

The victory of words in freedom is already a fait accompli in Italy and is being realized in intellectual circles throughout the world, which are nearly all feeling the influence of Futurism.

In Italy today we have over a hundred interesting free-wordists.

Words in freedom are an absolutely free expression
of the universe in which prosody and syntax have no
part, a new way of seeing and feeling, a measuring of
the universe as a sum of moving forces. These forces
intersect in our conscious and creative self, which
records them exactly, using every possible means of ex-
pression.

In this way, the free-wordists orchestrate colors,
noises, sounds, form evocative combinations out of the
material of language and patois, arithmetic and geo-
metric formulas, old words, distorted words and in-
vented words, animal cries and engine noises, etc.

The artistic victory of words in freedom cuts the
history of human poetry neatly in two, from Homer to
the last lyrical sigh of the earth.

Up to now men have all sung more or less like
Homer, using a narrative sequence and logical catalogs
of ideas, facts, feelings, sensations, images. This is why
it is possible to state that there is no real difference be-
tween the poetry of Homer and that of Gabriele D'An-
nunzio or Verhaeren.

Ultimately, the free-wordists distinguish them-
selves clearly from Homer because they are no longer
content to create a narrative sequence, but present in-
stead the integral, dynamic, and simultaneous expres-
sion of the universe.

[. . .]

Futurist Sensibility
and Wireless Imagination

[. . .]

Words in Freedom

Without bothering with the stupid definitions of professors, I proclaim that lyricism is the very rare *ability to be intoxicated with life and to intoxicate it with ourselves;* the ability to turn into wine the troubled waters of life that surround us and run through us; the ability to paint the world with the special colors of our changing self. Let's suppose that a friend endowed with this lyrical gift finds himself in a zone of intense life (revolution, war, shipwreck, earthquake, etc.) and, immediately afterwards, comes to tell you his impressions. Do you know what this friend will instinctively do as he begins his story? He will brutally destroy syntax as he speaks, will not waste time constructing sentences, will abolish punctuation and word order, and will bombard your nerves with all his visual, auditory, and olfactory sensations, as their mad gallop takes him. The impetuousness of steam-emotion will blow out the pipe of the sentence, the valves of punctuation, and the adjectives that are habitually placed with regularity like bolts. Thus you will have fistfuls of essential words in no conventional order, your friend being concerned with nothing but the expression of all the vibrations of his self. If this lyrical speaker also has a mind rich in general ideas, he will involuntarily and constantly link these last sensations with all that he has known of the universe, experimentally or intuitively. He will cast great nets of analogies over the world, thus rendering the analogical and essential core of life telegraphically—that is, with the economy and speed that the telegraph imposes on reporters and war correspondents in their superficial dispatches.

This need for succinctness is a response not only to the laws of speed by which we are governed, but also to the age-old relationship of the poet and his public. This relationship is much like the intimacy of two old friends who can communicate with a single word, a single glance. This is how and why the poet's imagination must link distant things *without conducting wires,* using instead essential words absolutely *in freedom.*

Wireless Imagination

By wireless imagination I mean the absolute freedom of images or analogies expressed by liberated words, without the conducting wires of syntax and *without any punctuation.*

"Up to now writers have indulged themselves in direct analogies. E.g., they have compared a fox terrier to a tiny thoroughbred. Others, more progressive, might compare this same trembling fox terrier to a little Morse apparatus. I myself compare it to boiling water. The analogies here have become increasingly vast, the connections increasingly deep, though very remote. *Analogy is nothing but the immense love that connects distant, seemingly different, and hostile things.* It is through very vast analogies that this orchestral style, at once polychromatic, polyphonic, and polymorphic, can embrace the life of matter. When, in my *Battle of Tripoli,* I compared a trench bristling with bayonets to an orchestra, a machine gun to a femme fatale, I intuitively introduced a great part of the universe into a brief episode of African battle. Images are not flowers to be chosen and picked sparingly, as Voltaire maintained. They are the very lifeblood of poetry. Poetry must be an uninterrupted succession of fresh images, or it is nothing but anemia and chlorosis. The vaster the connections an image encompasses, the longer it will keep its stupefying power" (*Manif. of Futurist Literature*). The wireless imagination and words in freedom will lead us into the very essence of matter. In discovering new analogies between distant and apparently opposite things, we will evaluate them ever more intimately. Instead of *humanizing* animals, vegetables, and minerals (as we have done for so long) we can *animalize, vegetalize, mineralize, electrify,* or liquefy style by making it live with the very life of matter. E.g., a blade of grass that says, "I'll be greener tomorrow." Thus we have: **Condensed metaphors. — Telegraphic images. — Sums of vibrations. — Knots of thoughts. —Fans of movement opening and closing. —Abbreviations of analogies. —Statements of colors. —Dimensions, weight, measure, and speed of sensations. —Plunge of the essential word into the waters of sensibility minus the concentric circles that the word produces. —Pauses of intuition. —Movements in 2, 3, 4, 5 time. —Explanatory analytical poles carrying the wires of intuition.**

[. . .]

Onomatopoeia and Mathematical Symbols

When I said we must "spit every day on the Altar of Art," I was urging the Futurists to free lyricism from the atmosphere of compunction and incense that we call Art with a capital A. Art with a capital A is the clericalism of the creative spirit. I was urging the Futurists to scorn the garlands, palms, halos, precious frames, stoles, peplums, all the historic relics and romantic bric-a-brac that make up the bulk of the work of all the poets before us. I was promoting in their place a swift, brutal, violent, immediate lyricism that all our predecessors would have called anti-poetic, a telegraphic lyricism infused with a strong smell of life and with nothing bookish about it. Hence the need boldly to introduce onomatopoeic chords to render all the sounds and all the noises of modern life, even the most cacaphonous. Onomatopoeia, which enlivens lyricism with the raw elements of reality, has been used only timidly by poets from Aristophanes to the present day. The Futurists were the first to have the courage to use onomatopoeia with anti-academic boldness and continuity. This boldness and continuity should not be systematic. For example, my *Adrianople-Siege-Orchestra* and my *Battle Weight* $+$ *Smell* required numerous onomatopoeic chords. Moreover, our constant care to express the maximum of vibrations and deep syntheses of life drives us to abolish all the traditional bonds of style, all the precious fasteners that traditional poets use to fix their images in a sentence. We use mathematical and musical symbols instead, which are infinitely more succinct and absolutely anonymous. And we place directions like these in parentheses—(fast) (faster) (slow down) (double time)—to control the speed of the style. These parentheses can also split a word or an onomatopoeic chord.

Typographic Revolution and Free Expressive Orthography

Typographic Revolution

I am launching a typographic revolution aimed above all at the absurd and nauseating idea of the passéist book of verse, with its handmade paper, sixteenth-century style, ornamented with galleys, minervas, apollos, great initials and flourishes, mythological vegetables, missal markers, epigraphs, and roman numerals. The book should be the Futurist expression of our Futurist thought. What is more, my revolution is also aimed at the so-called typographic harmony of the page, which opposes the ebb and flow of style across the page. We will also use, if need be, 3 or 4 different-colored inks and 20 different typefaces on a single page. For example, *italics* for a series of similar and rapid sensations, **bold** for violent onomatopoeia, etc. New concept of a typographically pictorial page.

Free Expressive Orthography

The historical need for free expressive orthography is demonstrated in the successive revolutions that little by little have freed the lyrical power of the human race from fetters and rules.

1. – Poets began in fact by channelling their lyrical intoxication into a series of equal breaths, with accents, echoes, chimes, or rhymes set at fixed intervals (**Traditional Prosody**). Then, with increasing freedom, poets alternated the different breaths that had been measured by the lungs of their predecessors.

2. – Later, poets convinced themselves that each different moment of their lyrical intoxication should create its own breath, of different and unforeseen lengths, and accented with absolute freedom. Thus they came naturally to **Free Verse,** but still preserved syntactical order so that their lyrical intoxication could flow into the mind of the listener through the logical channel of the conventional sentence.

3. – Today we want lyrical intoxication to stop placing words in syntactical order before casting them forth in the breaths we have invented. Thus we have **Words in Freedom.** Moreover, our lyrical intoxication should freely distort and shape words, shortening or lengthening them, strengthening their centers or their extremities, increasing or decreasing the number of vowels or consonants. Thus we will have the new *orthography*, which I call *free expressive*. This instinctive distortion of words corresponds to our natural inclination toward onomatopoeia. It makes no difference if the distorted word is equivocal. It will blend better with the onomatopoeic chords or sound summaries and will help us soon to achieve the *psychic onomatopoeic chord*, sonorous but abstract expression of an emotion or a pure thought.

Geometric and Mechanical Splendor

We have made short work of the grotesque funeral of passéist Beauty (Romantic, Symbolist, Decadent) whose essential elements were the Femme Fatale and Moonlight, memory, nostalgia, eternity, immortality, the legendary mists of distant time, the exotic charm of distant space, the picturesque, the indefinite, the rustic, wild little solitudes, motley disorder, twilight shadows, corrosion, patina = filth of time, crumbling of ruins, erudition, smell of mold, love of rot, pessimism, consumption, suicide, the flirtations of agony, the aesthetics of failure, the adoration of death.

Today from the chaos of new sensibilities we bring forth a new beauty to replace the first, which I call **Geometric and Mechanical Splendor.** Its elements are the Sun rekindled by Will, hygienic oblivion, hope, desire, the perishable, the ephemeral, bridled power, speed, light, will, order, discipline, method; the instinct of man multiplied by the machine; the sense of the big city; the aggressive optimism that comes from physical culture and sports; the intelligent woman (pleasure, fecundity, affairs); the wireless imagination, ubiquity, the succinctness and simultaneity of tourism, big business, and journalism; the passion for success, records, enthusiastic imitation of electricity and the machine, essential brevity and synthesis; the happy precision of lubricated gears and thoughts; the concurrence of energies converging in a single trajectory.

My Futurist senses first perceived this geometric splendor on the deck of a dreadnought. The speed of the ship, the range of fire fixed from the bridge in the cool breeze of warlike probabilities, the strange vitality of the admiral's orders suddenly turned autonomous and inhuman through the caprices, fits, and complaints of steel and copper: all this glowed with geometric and mechanical splendor. I perceived the lyrical initiative of electricity coursing through the armor of the quadruple turrets and running down armored tubes to the magazine to pull shells and cartridges up to the breech, toward the emerging barrel. Aim for elevation, for direction, sight, flame, automatic recoil, personal surge of the projectile, impact, grinding, crash, smell of rotten eggs, mephitic gas, rust, ammonia, etc. Here is a new drama full of Futurist surprises and geometric splendor, which we find a hundred thousand times more interesting than human psychology with its limited combinations.

Crowds sometimes make us feel a few faint emotions. We prefer the bright signs, paint, and Futurist jewels, under which the cities hide their passéist wrinkles at night. We love the solidarity of zealous and methodical engines. There is nothing more beautiful than a huge humming power station that holds the hydraulic pressure of a mountain range and the electric power of an entire horizon, synthesized on distribution panels bristling with keyboards and shining switches. These formidable panels are our only models in poetry. Our few precursors are gymnasts, acrobats, and clowns, who realize, in the development, repose, and rhythm of their musculatures, that sparkling perfection of precise gearings and that geometric splendor we strive for in poetry through words in freedom.

1. – We systematically destroy the literary I to scatter it in the universal vibration, and we express the agitation of molecules and the infinitely small. E.g., the lightning molecular agitation in a hole blasted by a shell (end of *Fort Cheittam Tepe* in my ZZONG TOOMB-TOOMB). The poetry of cosmic forces thus supplants the poetry of the human. **As a result we abolish the old narrative proportions** (romantic, sentimental, and Christian), according to which a battle wound had exaggerated importance in comparison with instruments of destruction, strategic positions, and atmospheric conditions. In my poem ZZONG TOOMB-TOOMB, I briefly describe the execution of a Bulgarian traitor, while I prolong a discussion between two Turkish generals on range of fire and enemy guns. In fact, during the month of October 1911, while living with the gunners of the De Suni battery in the trenches of Tripoli, I observed how trivial is the spectacle of lacerated human flesh when compared with the shining and aggressive barrel of a gun scorched by the sun and rapid fire.

2. – I have demonstrated more than once that the noun, worn by repeated contact with and by the weight of Parnassian and Decadent adjectives, can be restored to its absolute value by stripping it of all adjectives and isolating it. I distinguish between 2 kinds of naked nouns: the **elemental noun** and the **synthesis-movement noun** (or knot of nouns). This distinction is not absolute, for it is based on intuitions that are difficult to grasp. I see every noun as a cart, or as a belt set in motion by the infinitive verb.

3. – Aside from the need for contrast and changes of rhythm, the different moods and tenses of the verb should be done away with because they turn the verb into a loose coach wheel that adapts to bumpy inclines but cannot roll swiftly over a smooth road. **The infinitive verb is the very movement of the new lyricism,** for it has the sleek resilience of a train wheel or an airplane propeller. The different moods and tenses of a verb communicate a cautious and reassuring pessimism, an accidental, occasional egotism, a rise and fall of strength and weariness, of desire and disillusion—in short, obstacles to the flight of hope and will. The infinitive verb communicates optimism itself, absolute generosity, and the fury of becoming. When I say *run*, what is this verb's subject? Everyone and everything—that is to say, the universal irradiation of life that flows and of which we are a small conscious part. E.g., the end of the poem *"Hotel Lounge"* by the free-wordist Folgore. The infinitive verb is the impassioned I that surrenders itself to the becoming of all things, heroic continuity, selflessness of effort and the joy of acting. Infinitive verb = divinity of action.

4. – By isolating one or more adjectives in parentheses or behind a perpendicular line in the margin of words in freedom (as an indication of tone), it is easy to convey the different atmospheres of the narrative and the different tones that govern it. **These atmosphere-adjectives or tone-adjectives cannot be replaced by nouns.** These are intuitive convictions, and ones that cannot easily be proved. Nonetheless, I believe that by isolating the noun *fierceness*, for example (or by using it like a tone), in the description of a scene of carnage, we create a state of mind of fierceness that is too rigid and too closed and delineated too distinctly. Whereas if I put the adjective *fierce* in parentheses or use it as an indication of tone, I transform it into an *atmosphere-adjective* or a *tone-adjective* that encompasses the entire description of the carnage without arresting the flow of words in freedom.

5. – Syntax has always embodied a scientific and photographic perspective absolutely contrary to

the laws of emotion. **In words in freedom, this photographic perspective disappears** and is replaced by the emotional perspective, which is multiform. (E.g., the poem *"Man + Mountain + Valley"* by the free-wordist Boccioni.)

Simultaneity

Synoptic Tables of Lyrical Values

In words in freedom we sometimes create **synoptic tables of lyrical values** that enable us to follow several currents of intersecting or parallel sensations simultaneously. These synoptic tables should not be the free-wordists' primary aim, but a way of increasing the expressive power of lyricism. We must therefore avoid all preoccupation with the pictorial, and not amuse ourselves by playing with bizarre lines or strange typographic disproportions. In words in freedom everything that does not contribute with geometric and mechanical splendor to the expression of the fleeting Futurist sensibility must be banned. In his poem *"Smokers, Second Class"* the free-wordist Cangiullo cleverly portrayed the monotonous daydreams and the expansion of smoke on a long train trip through this **pictorial analogy:**

S M O O O K E . To express the universal vibration with a maximum of force and depth, words in freedom naturally transform themselves into **auto-illustrations** through free expressive orthography and typography, synoptic tables of lyrical values, and pictorial analogies. (E.g., the balloon drawn typographically in my poem ZZONG TOOMB-TOOMB.) As soon as this maximum of expression is achieved, words in freedom resume their normal flow. Synoptic tables of values are also the basis of criticism in words in freedom. (E.g., *"Statement 1910–1914"* by the free-wordist Carrà.)

Free expressive orthography and typography convey the facial expressions and gestures of the speaker. Words in freedom express integrally that part of communicative exuberance and epidermic genius that the southern spirit was unable to convey within the framework of prosody, syntax, and traditional typography. These energies of accent, voice, and gesticulation now find their natural expression in the distorted words and typographic disproportions that correspond to grimaces and the chiseling force of gestures. Words in freedom thus become the lyrical, transfigured extension of our animal magnetism.

Our growing love of matter, our desire to penetrate it and know its vibrations, and the physical affinity that attracts us to engines drive us to make increasing use of onomatopoeia. Since noise is the result of the impact of speeding solids or gases, onomatopoeia, which reproduces this noise, is necessarily one of the most dynamic elements of poetry. As such, onomatopoeia can take the place of the infinitive verb, particularly if it is juxtaposed with another or several other onomatopoeias. (E.g., the onomatopoeic *tatatatatata* of the machine guns and the *hurrah* of the Turks at the end of my chapter *"Bridge"* in ZZONG TOOMB-TOOMB.) In this case, the conciseness of onomatopoeia enables us to create flexible combinations of different rhythms. These would lose a great deal of their speed if expressed in a more abstract and developed way—that is, without onomatopoeia.

[. . .]

Numerical Sensibility

My love of precision and of essential conciseness has naturally given me a taste for numbers that live and breathe on the page like living beings through my new **numerical sensibility.** E.g., instead of saying, like a traditional writer, *a deep and resounding sound of bells* (imprecise and inexpressive description) or, like an intelligent peasant, *the people of such and such a village hear this bell* (a more precise and expressive description), I grasp the sound of the bell with intuitive precision and ascertain its range, saying, **ding dong** *bells range of sound 20 Km.*[2] In this way I express a whole vibrating horizon and a number of faraway people listening to the sound of the same bell. I leave the imprecise behind, I take hold of reality in a deliberate act that distorts the very vibration of the metal. The mathematical symbols $+$ $-$ $\times$ $=$ make possible marvelous syntheses and, through the abstract simplicity of impersonal gearings, contribute to the ultimate goal, which is **Geometric and Mechanical Splendor.** In fact, you would need more than a page of traditional description to give an imperfect idea of this vast horizon of complicated battle, whose definitive lyrical equation is: *"horizon* $=$ *neeeeeedly spiral of sunlight* $+$ *5 triangular shadows each side 1 Km.* $+$ *3 lozenges of rosy light* $+$ *5 fragments of hills* $+$ *30 columns of smoke* $+$ *23 flames."* I use the x to mark interrogative pauses of thought. I thus eliminate the question mark, which fixes its atmosphere of doubt too arbitrarily on a single point of consciousness. By means of the mathematical x the suspension of doubt spreads over the entire agglomeration of words in freedom. Following my intuition, I introduce numbers into words in freedom that have no direct meaning or value, but that (speaking phonically and optically to numerical sensibility) express the various transcendental intensities of matter and the elusive replies of this sensibility; I create actual theorems and lyrical equations with numbers chosen intuitively and placed in the very middle of a word. With a certain quantity of $+$ $-$ $\times$ $=$ I indicate the thickness and shape of the things the word is meant to express. The arrangement $+$ $-$ $+$ $-$ $+$ $+$ $\times$ expresses[, for ex., the changes and acceleration of an automobile's velocity. The arrangement $+$ $+$ $+$ $+$ expresses] the accumulation of equal sensations. (E.g., *fecal smell of dysentery* $+$ *honeyed stench,* etc., in *"Trainload of Sick Soldiers"* in my ZZONG TOOMB-TOOMB.)

Thus, through words in freedom we replace Mallarmé's *anterior sky where beauty bloomed* with *Geometric and Mechanical Splendor and Numerical Sensibility.*

Examples of Words in Freedom

Lettre d'une jolie femme
à un monsieur passéiste

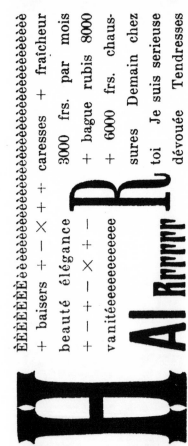

Letter from a pretty woman to a passéist gentleman

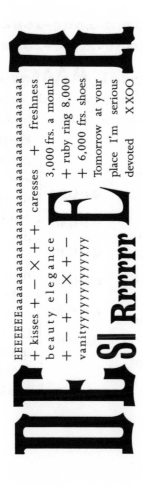

Dunes

Karazouc-zouc-zouc
Karazouc-zouc-zouc

nadI-nadI AAAAaaaaaa *(bis)* dunes duuuuuuuuunes soleil dunes dunes dunes dunes dunes dunes dunes

douum douumm
derboukah ennuiblanc
━┃━ laine du bruit
de la pensée
rembourrage sonore
du ciel
bruit rotatif
du soleil souvenirs
cotonneux tam-
bours des moelles
tunnel de sons noirs
dans les montagnes
incandescentes de la
lumière

précipité
aveuglant **doum**
éternel **doum**
aveuglant
mécanique **doum**
aveuglant **doum**
consanguin
aveuglant **doum**
ton majeur **doum**
aveuglant

Dunes

Karazook-zook-zook
Karazook-zook-zook

nadI-nadI **AAAA**aaaaaa (bis) dunes duuuuuuuuunes sun dunes dunes dunes dunes dunes dunes dunes

sudden
blinding
endless   **doom**
blinding
mechanical   **doom**
blinding
consanguine   **doom**
blinding
major key   **doom**
blinding   **doom**
   doom

d o o o m d o o o m m
derbookah whiteweariness
✝ wool of sounds
of thoughts
sonorous stuffing
of the sky
rotary sound
of the sun fleecy
memories marrow
drums tunnel of
black sounds
in the incandescent
mountains of the light

Ocre ✚ cuivre-jaune ✚ cannelle 18 Km.²

déchirant | **vvvvvvvrrrriiiiiii**
universel | **vluiiii** | violons chats grince-
fibreux | **vuulii** | ment de toutes les
ton mineur | **vuluit** | portes romantiques
  | **vuvu-** | balles tympanums
  | **luit** | tourbillons de neige

dans les fils télégra-
phiques

cordes du vent ten-
dues sur le nez du

très délicat | chauffeur sous l'archet
grimpant | toortuuUuUuUuUueux
étiré | de la route véhémente

JAUNE JAUNE

âcreté urine sueur cassie saleté jasmin
ventre de banquier pieds-labourcurs sable-
coussin se-coucher-soif-soif

bruit ✚ poids du soleil ✚ odeur orangée
du ciel ✚ 20 000 angles obtus ✚ 18 de-
micercles d'ombre ✚ minéralisations de
pieds nègres dans le sable de cristal

Ochre **+** brass **+** cinnamon 18 Km.²

tearing　　**vvvvvvvrrrreeeeeee**

universal　　**vlooeeee**　　violins cats creaking of all

fibrous　　**voooolee**　　the romantic doors　bul-

minor key　　**voolooee**　　lets　tympanums　flurries

　　　　voovoo-　　of snow on the telegraph

　　　　looee　　wires

　　　　　　　　strings　of　wind

　　　　　　stretched　over　the

　　　　　　driver's　nose　under　the

very delicate　　torrtuuUuUuUuUuous

climbing　　bow of the vehement road

stretched

YELLOW   YELLOW

sharpness urine sweat cassia filth jasmine banker's
paunch feet-plowmen sand-pillow lie-down-thirst-
thirst
sound **+** weight of the sun **+** orangey
smell of the sky **+** 20,000 obtuse angles
+ 18 semicircles of shade **+** mineralization
of black feet in the crystal sand

dunes
nues de
mon front
voyageant

dunes de mon
corps de quinze
ans donné
À TOUT

.7
dunes
corps-de-
femmes
traversés
par la route
caravanière

dunes de l'orgueil
+ odeur de vulve
en vitesse

dune
syncopée
succès
déveine

DÉCAGONE
DE LA
SENSIBILITÉ
MOTRICE

dunes de lointains
dos amicaux
courbés sur
d'autres
feux

dunes tristes-
satisfaites de
la volonté qui
se fouette

dune véloce
de la vieillesse
accourante
proche
plus
proche
dégoût

dunes de la
jeunesse très
lointaine pré-
sence FORCE

dunes
mortes du
déjà fait
pensé écrit

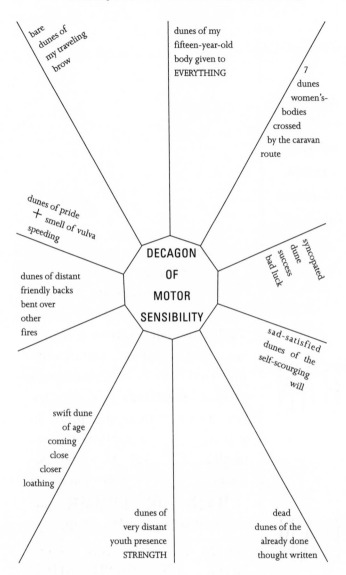

bare
dunes of
my traveling
brow

dunes of my
fifteen-year-old
body given to
EVERYTHING

7
dunes
women's-
bodies
crossed
by the caravan
route

dunes of pride
+ smell of vulva
speeding

syncopated
dune
success
bad luck

dunes of distant
friendly backs
bent over
other
fires

DECAGON
OF
MOTOR
SENSIBILITY

sad-satisfied
dunes of the
self-scourging
will

swift dune
of age
coming
close
closer
loathing

dunes of
very distant
youth presence
STRENGTH

dead
dunes of the
already done
thought written

distances

cadencé
navigant
moëlleux
maniable
minutieux
intestinal

distances

dunes
s'étirer
ondulation
angles
angles modeler sables s'émous-
ser   polir   polir   somnolence
du vent   rond-de-cuirs
RAN
artères écarlates joie de pa-
yer à un voleur le prix du
prurit   comptabilité des
ongles   1/2 kilo de fro-
mage   226 kilos de
CHAIR DE FEMME spi-
RAN
rales d'une fumée bleue **+**
odeur de veau rôti GAR-
GOTE DE ROTHSCHILD
(ampleur   1000   km.   carrés)

distances

rhythmic
sailing
soft
supple
meticulous
intestinal

distances

dunes
stretch
undulation
angles

RON

RON

angles shape sand dull polish
polish somnolence of the wind
pen-pushers scarlet arteries joy
of paying a thief the price of
pruritus   fingernail accounts
1/2 kilo of cheese   226 kilos
of FEMALE FLESH spi-
rals of blue smoke **+** smell of
roast veal ROTHSCHILD'S
GRILL (range 1,000 square
km.)

RAN

3 cuirassés de papier de soie
+ **2** capitaines de plomb-
fondu vomis par le soleil-
qui-frit

équateur

immense
aveuglant
ranran
rond ou
carré

soif

rrrrrr
sssssss
rrrrrr
croucra
croucra
croucra

hurlements blancs concentri-
ques de 14 luuuuuuuuunes
affolées se noyer lunes ron-
des carrées se tordre s'é-
mietter dans le puits (3 m.)
de Bu-Fellah [NUIIIⅢIIIT]
croucracroucraruminer de cha-
meauauauauaux

VENT
TOURNEUR

de dunes **+** nerfs **+** remords
+ nausées **+** excréments **+**
barracans en fuite excentrique

RON

3 tissue-paper battleships **+** 2 cast-lead captains vomited by the frying-sun

equator

huge
blinding
ronron
round or
square   thirst

rrrrrr
ssssssss
rrrrrr
croocra
croocra
croocra

concentric white howls of 14 panic-stricken mooooooooons drown round square moons twist crumble in the well (3 m.) of Bu Fellah [NIIIIIIII-IGHT] croocracroocraruminating of caaaaamels

WIND TURNER

of dunes **+** nerves **+** remorse **+** nausea **+** excrement **+** barracans in eccentric flight

MOUVEMENT

DE

2 PISTONS

VENT

négateur paresse inertie geler tout par des ètoiles littéraires deracinées de la chair **(NUIT LIVRESQUE)** enterrer tout avec odeur d'aisselles matelas de parfums seins cuits dans le plaisir **+** 7000 raisonnement sceptiques

SANG

affirmateur optimisme force repousser le vent-pessimiste-chaud-ou-froid aller sans but pour **FAIRE VIVRE COURIR ETRE**

Karazouc-zouc-zouc-AAAaaaaaaaaaaaaaaa

Nadi – Nadi – AAAaaaaaaaaaaaaaaa

MOVEMENT OF 2 PISTONS

WIND {

negator indolence inertia freeze everything with literary stars torn from the flesh **(BOOKISH NIGHT)** bury everything with smell of armpits mattress of perfumes breasts baked in pleasure **+** 7,000 skeptical arguments

BLOOD {

affirmer optimism strength drive off the hot-or-cold–pessimist-wind wander aimlessly to **DO LIVE RUN BE**

Karazook-zook-zook Nadi-Nadi-AAAAaaaaaaaaaaaaa

SOLEIL HUILEUR UNIVERSEL

tlac-tlac

tchic-tchouc

MENU D'UN DINER DE 6 COUVERTS A LA CLARTÉ D'UN VER-LUISANT

1. hors-d'œuvres de kaka-wick-nostalgine
2. petites angoisses à la crême
3. remorderau bouilli
4. pressentimentlung rôti
5. grappes hémorroïdales
6. urine d'ascète frappée

aïh

aiiiiiiiiiiiiii

aiiiii

s'asseoir confortablement à quatre sur la pointe d'une épingle sveltesse aristocratique gris-perle du vent qui promène l'incendie-levrette-habillée-en-rouge

SUN UNIVERSAL OILER

DINNER FOR 6 BY THE LIGHT OF A GLOW-WORM

tlack-tlack

chick-chook

1. kakawick-nostalgine hors-d'oeuvres
2. little agonies à la crême
3. boiled remorselet
4. roast forebodelung
5. hemorrhoidal clusters
6. ascetic's urine frappé

ai

yiiiiiiiiiiiiii

yiiiii

sit comfortably four on the point of a pin   pearl-gray aristocratic grace of the wind walking the fire-greyhound-dressed-in-red

terriiBLE SOLEEIL FÉROOCE

SENTIMENTAL

aveu-
glant
de
larmes

sur les jeunes ex-
plorateurs trompés
par leurs femmes
maîtresses
solennité d'un cocu
sur la ligne de l'é-
quateur

aveu-
glé
de
larmes
rouges

terriBLE FIEERCE SSUN

SENTIMENTAL

blind-
ing

with

tears

{
on   the   young   ex-
plorers   betrayed
by   their   wives
mistresses
solemnity of a cuckold
at the equator
}

blind-
ed

with

red

tears

(andante gracieux avec pizzicati)

(TEMPS DE CAKE-WALK)

petite lettre tiède en sueur sur
la poitrine dilatatiooON d'un mot
écrit amenuisage de coude-main-
tenue dans la chaleur   3
jours de marche dunes dunes
dunes

CÔTE   le **PAQUEBOT**
8 JOURS GÊNES Parme
me voilà baisers **zing‑zing‑**
zing ‑ zing ‑ zing traditionnel
d'un lit de province
Karazouczouc‑zouc
tuesunhkros **zingzingcouic**
zingzingcouic flaccidité de
cloches tombantes
tombaaaaantes de la braaaanche
très haute très ancieeeeeenne
    odeur‑de‑buanderie‑acacias‑moi‑
sissure bois vermoulu‑choux‑cuits
zingzang de casseroles
ombre ammoniacale d'une tente
de Bédouins   dunes dunes
dunes dunes

(graceful andante with pizzicato)

(CAKEWALK TIME)

lukewarm little letter sweating on the chest swellLLING of a written word tapering of elbow-hand-held in the heat 3 days' walk dunes dunes dunes
COAST the **STEAMER**
8 DAYS **GENOA** Parma
here I am kisses familiar **zing-zing-zing-zing-zing** of a country bed
Karazookzook-zook
youreahero **zingzingqueek**
zingzingqueek limpness of bells falling
faaaaaalling from the very high very oooold braaaaaanch
  smell-of-washhouse-acacias-mildew wormy wood-cooked-cabbage zingzang of pans ammoniacal darkness of a Bedouin tent dunes dunes dunes dunes

Bataille à 9 étages
du Mont Altissimo

3000 mètres rrrrr aéroplane autrichien ✛ balles sifflantes ═ cerf-volant ✛ vacarme d'enfants
ironie légéreté écoles hygiéniques sur les terrasses gratte-ciels

2500 mètres cimes ensoleillées
réclames lumineuses de l'Italie

10 heures ligne entière bête de cavalier

2070 mètres canonnade de 149 invisibles ouah ouah ouah départ de trains suicides
sur des ponts aériens et fragiles
fatalité des rails convergeant à la gare unique
chaque 27 secondes PLOUM PLOUM PLOUM PLOUM

1800 mètres Alpini en védette
═ badigeonneurs sur le fronton des gratte-ciels

descendre dans les arènes

PLOUM
PLOUM

1200 mètres tchip tchip tchip de mésanges ═ couturières
américaines odeur de camphre ammoniaque vanille

1190 mètres volontaires en réserve   sensibilité d'une
bataille électorale   les pieds dans le bariolage des
prospectus de l'automne   ronces giflantes   le
capitaine demande 20 hommes   vite descendons
glissades on tombe cul-par-dessus-tête tiintinntamzinn
de gamelles gourdes baïonnettes

800 mètres pic pam pam crépitation d'incendie
TOUM TOUM couchez-vous c'est le Brion qui tire
ssssrrrrappnells... PIIING... sssrrr zit zit zit PAAC
═ explosion d'un gazomètre à droite
candidat autrichien fichu   incendie dompté
les pompiers reviennent

50 mètres patrouille   tapie ═ viande
congelée

arènes gelées de la montagne

TOTAL :

MÉTALLIQUE
MATHÉMATIQUE
ÉLASTIQUE
VOLITIF
VICTORIEUX
QUOTIDIEN
ITALIEN

30 mètres LAC DE GARDE
cave-égout des montagnes   paix nostalgie
ciel tombé   amour écrasé sous
l'insurrection folle des montagnes futuristes
popopopo de canot-automobile ═ naufrage d'un
cœur de femme   2 torpilleurs moustachus
de réflecteurs ═ veilleuses de la Madone

Tranchées de Dosso Casina (Altissimo)
27 Octobre 1915

9-storied battle
of Mount Altissimo

3,000 meters rrrrr Austrian airplane **+** whistling bullets **=** flying kite **+** shouting children
irony levity hygienic schools on the skyscraper slopes

2,500 meters sunny peaks
illuminated billboards of Italy

10 o'clock solar ray heating rod

2,070 meters firing of 149 invisibles wah wah wah suicide trains setting out
over fragile aerial bridges
fatality of the rails converging on the only station
every 27 seconds **PLOOM PLOOM PLOOM PLOOM**

PLOOM
PLOOM
PLOOM

1,800 meters Alpini standing sentry
= whitewashers on the pediment of the skyscrapers

descend into the arteries

the mountain's frozen arteries

1,200 meters cheep cheep cheep of titmice **=** American
seamstresses odor of camphor ammonia vanilla

1,190 meters volunteers in reserve   sensitiveness of
an election battle   feet in Fall's multi-colored leaf-
lets   lashing brambles   the captain calls for
20 men   quick let's go down slides we fall head over
heels clinketyclinkclank of mess kits canteens bayonets

TOTAL:
METALLIC
MATHEMATIC
ELASTIC
VOLITIONAL
VICTORIOUS
QUOTIDIAN
ITALIAN

800 meters pik pom pom blaze crackling TOOM TOOM get
down it's Brion firing   ssssrrrrappnell ... PAAANG ...
sssrrr zzt zzt zzt POK **=** gas tank exploding on the right
Austrian candidate done for   blaze tamed
the firemen return

50 meters crouching patrol **=** frozen meat

30 meters LAKE GARDA
sewer-cellar of the mountains   peace nostalgia
fallen sky   love crushed under
the mad uprising of the Futurist mountains
popopopo of a motorboat **=** wreck of a
woman's heart   2 torpedo boats mustached
with searchlights **=** vigil lights of the Madonna

Trenches at Dosso Casina (*Altissimo*)
27 October 1915

Après la Marne,
Joffre visita le front en auto

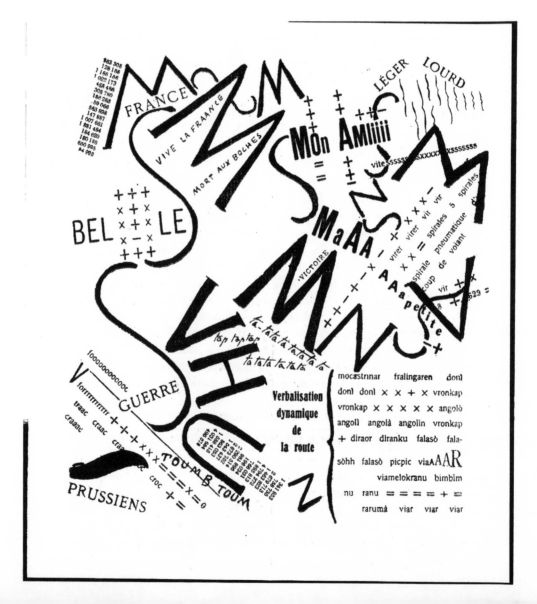

After the Marne,
Joffre toured the front by car

Le soir, couchée dans son lit,
Elle relisait la lettre de son artilleur au front

At night, lying in bed,
She rereads the letter from her gunner at the front

Une assemblée tumultueuse
(Sensibilité numérique)

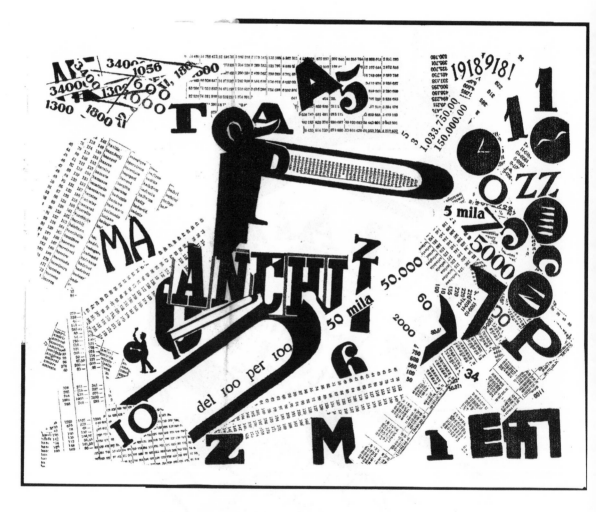

A tumultuous assembly
(Numerical sensibility)

After Words in Freedom

(ca. 1924–1928)

Le poem doit ~~s'imprimer avec les~~
lignes de la main sur le papier
Les mots ~~doivent courir sur les~~
~~lignes de la~~ imprimés.   9
Le poem de mot

        Après les mots en liberté, les
~~D~~ mots fondus en liberté.
Après avoir délivré les mots de la
du vers ~~de la~~ et de la syntaxe il faut
les fondre pour porter la pensée
et l'à sensibilité dans la zone de
la simultaneité.
        Forme de fusions de 2 3 ou 4 mots
— mots simultanés
— Blocs simultanés
— Mots fondus
Corsadvieurapeluta

Navid ventosue infaccia
Zludolghedornoschurmaride
Uousferro leanaubarenu

Jormastelocielo.

beondaltassrurrovcutinpoppa

Le poem de motsfondus doit contenir
les lignes de la main sur le papier.
Le poem s'imprimera avec les lignes de la
main sur le papier et les motsfondu
(ou mots simultanés) doivent courir sur
ces lignes de la main reproduite sur le papier

~~The poem should be printed with the~~
~~lines of the hand on the page~~
~~The words should run along the~~
~~printed lines of the hand~~

~~The poem of words~~

~~After having~~

The poem will be printed with the lines of the hand on the page and the fusedwords (or simultaneous words) should run along the lines of the hand reproduced on the page.

After words in freedom, fusedwords in freedom. After having liberated words from from verse ~~from~~ and syntax we must fuse them to carry thought and sensibility in the wheel of simultaneity.

Create fusions of 2 3 or 4 words
— simultaneouswords
— Simultaneous blocks
— Fusedwords

Runbackfrozen
herwindhandsoverface
Blueofseaweedsleepsfoamshores
Manirondiamondcream
womanstemsky
blondetallazurefollowingwind

The poem of fusedwords should continue the lines of the hand on the page.

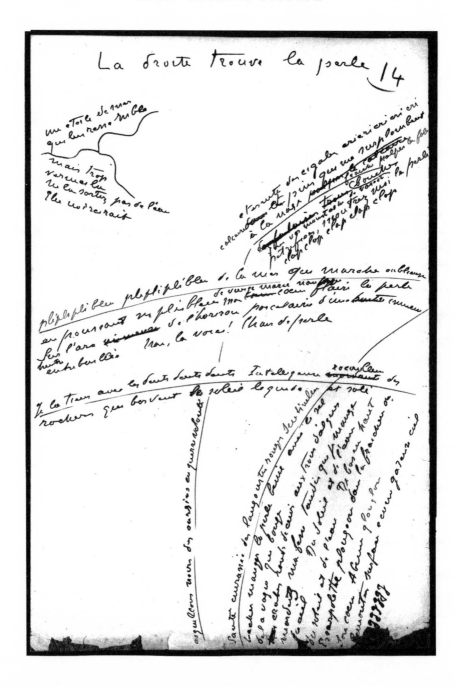

The right finds the pearl

a sea star
that looks like her

but too
red
don't take it out of the water
It would turn black

        eternity of cicadas creecreecreecreecree
        limestone ~~in the~~/and pines rising over me
        swimming ~~feel the limestone~~ cool feel the cliff
        ~~of the cliffs holes~~
        Under your kelp mustaches petrified
        mouths, show me the pearl
        lop lop lap lap lop

bluepleatpleatpleat bluepleatpleatpleat of the sea going by oblivious
        of shipwrecked Virgin Mary
pushing her bluepleats my ~~Heart~~ heart sniffs the pearl
On the ~~huge~~ arch of the porcelain horizon of ~~an oyster~~ huge
half-opened oyster   No, here it is!   Flesh of pearl

I hold it in my teeth teeth teeth   ~~Biting~~ Rocky intelligence of the
rocks that drink ~~some~~/the liquid salty sun

        black spurs of sea urchins at velvet war

        Armored vigor of red sentry lobsters
        Lick eat the blessed pearl with the salt
        of the moving wave
        crabs cushions with seaweed holes
        bite my behind as I eat
        sky   Sun and water
        sun and water   From the bottom up
        Swing dive in the coolness of
        her heart Abyss glugglug
        Rise surface sparkling foam sky
        ggggggg

La crevette trouve la perle

mots en liberté futuristes
pour Bouez

Août 1928

The right finds the pearl

> Futurist words in freedom
> for Beny

a sea star
   that looks like her

but too
red
don't take it out of the water
it would turn black

> Eternity of cicadas creecreecreecree
> creecree limestone and pines rising over me
> swimming cool feel the cliff
> Under your kelp mustaches petrified
> mouths   show me the pearl
> lop lop got gat lop

bluepleatpleatpleat of the sea going by pushing her blue
pleats pleats pleats pleats of shipwrecked Virgin Mary   my heart sniffs
sniffs the pearl on the arch of the porcelain horizon of a
huge half-opened oyster   No here it is! Flesh of pearl

> I hold it in my teeth Rocky
> intelligence Intelligence of the rocks that drink
> the salty Sun

Black spurs of sea urchins velvet war

Armored vigor of red sentry lobsters
Eat the dear pearl of her flesh with the salt of the wave
Crabs cushions with seaweed holes
Bite my behind as I eat sky
Sun and water from the bottom up
Swing in the surf of her heart Abyss
Rise   Surface sparkling foam
liquid sky ggggggggggggggg

> > August 1928

Poems to Beny

(1920–1938; published 1971)

The island casts the jetty out to sea to intense bitterness

Jetty hard geometry in the drenching poetry of liquid horizons

Jetty dagger in the pitiful flesh of journeys

Jetty thermometer in the bath of the sunny bay

Jetty guillotine blade slicing seas sobs handkerchiefs letters and gulls in the storm too soon too late too far never

Jetty straight line besieged by triangles cones rhombuses flourishes domes and tops of greenish madness

Jetty stone duty imposed on the exuberant spirit of the sea black vices blue passions have it all eat it all suck bite spit swill go mad

Jetty springboard of anguish on the sea crowd swell escape hubbub chemistry and game of green bowls loosening in shirtsleeves foam sensuality on Hell's Sundays

On the jetty standing Beny spiral of perfumed tenderness

She is dressed but suddenly the sparkling bareness of her soul beneath the shower of azure sun and salty wind

Her mouth Her mouth

I embrace her and her arms around my neck and her dear face against my breast

A long kiss tearing

I am one of the two lips of the wound and I am leaving

She is the other standing on the jetty

The waves wet her feet weeping with laughter like little girls tickled in play eee aaaaaa gggggggg eeeeee glott glugglugglug plink glong gloot

In the water up to their red bellies the fat obscene maternal boats under their sails deflated breasts whose milk has fed the whole pure sky babe

I dance in my boat neurasthenia of the waves and their manipulations scuffle brawl bout of blocks

3 waves up boxing then all the tremolos of violins of memories

Couplings of doleful nostalgias

Shudder of echoes

Buildup of ambitious notes and suddenly the main theme

Rending 20 nerve fibers and 50 cellos with their ritornellos of remorse 100 200 1,000 clarinets of prehistoric anguish and at last in unison plainchant

Volume weight of total negations

Pathetic thunder

Under my boat that dances joyous the waves' hot
    throats chatter warble cluck yap burst out laugh-
    ing suddenly squabble

Reconciliation and their avowals sighs words whis-
    pered in the ear

The sea would seduce me with its orchestras torn by
    too many sharp bows in my Christ's side crucified
    on this cross Infinity

The sea would seduce me and tear me from Beny pure
    melody one united unending infinite

Oh! to descend to the absolving depths

Transparency

Like a crystal of emotion in the waves of instincts run-
    ning blind

Another touseled wave spreads its wings falls and
    bursts entrails of emerald-remorse

But already the huge horizontal ostrich-feather fan of
    the open sea against the sweet profile of a sail pen-
    sive woman

The waves die down suddenly irritation of this wave
    hanging on

To whom? what for? my boat stretches out on soft
    cushions loving springs pessimisms

Yet up there sheer Will of the cliffs beneath the golden
    wisdom of the light before the boundless despair
    of the color green

But here near the boat this water is a milky porcelain
    shell

No no pearls pearls and the perfumed ecstasy of Beny's
    skin

Dear presence in the gushing of blood-desire

Poor reflections of the past her jasmine gardens gone
    gone playthings

Standing on the jetty Beny blessed by the sun

Beny friend of the elements

The sea would seduce me dance dance up down swing

Suppleness of all tigers and pet cats

Splash splash too low wwwww of the wind ggggg of
    all the foam of pleasure and rage too high still
    higher on the tip of a pyramid

Whales a herd of whales to make a pavement under
    blessed Beny's feet

Balloons of wind and the void under my feet para-
    chutes

Demolition and debris of foam block block block
    block feel of three seals in my boat

Inflate deflate collapse deepening abyss to nothingness

But all the springs push back like wild virility in the im-
    mense and so intense flesh Her flesh white green
    of Beny's blessed sea

Animal undulation of the wave bright eternal sleep of
    undulating metals

Blue porcelain azure oil

Fat azure carnal indigo almost thighs of blue negresses
    blissful bottoms of blue angels stripped bare by
    the hurricanes of Paradise

She is standing on the jetty that the island pushes far
    out to sea to intense bitterness

Blessed!

Beny svelte with white ardor

Her body molded sculpted by the passion from the
    high sea rushing

Aim of the winds at war to seize her

Absurd rending of the waves that at her feet writhe and
    tear their hair of foam

So it's a heart an immeasurable green heart this sea

Raging heart!

Inexhaustible heart sea whose pounding makes my
    boat dance

This boat whose wood and crying flesh I am and ribs
    nails nerves

Boat my sternum caging this overflowing heart that
    today became the horrid sea that tears me from
    Beny

She is standing on the jetty dressed sculpted by the
breath of weeping distances
Waves and your waving daggers out to stab hearts
Here's mine! But you laugh tumble of dark glances for-
ever lost
You tear me from Her! and you carry me to my child-
hood when I did not know her and dreamed of
her

She is standing on the jetty that takes the furious blows
of this heart sea sea sea!
Distance distance I no longer see her I see her better
for she sleeps next to me in her bed like a drowsy
sea on a summer night
She breathes
Her perfume all the perfume of her desire dear heart
Warm and sweet entreaty of her childish pores and her
hair gardens on the sea in full Neapolitan sun
Ecstasy of entering the sweet sea of this belly and sud-
denly I sail! I enter I plunge in Her Infinity
Infinity hot burning wound
Wound that loves me wakes and smiles moans returns
flees cries calls desires desires drinks my whole
heart ocean Mediterranean Gibraltar Ideal

Two canoes at Capri

On the hot turquoise of the empty bay
two red canoes
Alone . . .
But we embrace every moving reflection
She in her coral swimsuit
near my bare chest brick baked
by this heavy scarlet sun
sorrowfully leaving the sea
Words trysts shivers kiss of the waves
Oscillation
of the two canoes
pans of a balance of liquid gold
sighing and salivating
pensive
Suddenly an invisible hand
snatches one of the two weights
and I see her rise light in the sky
To guarantee the integrity of the balance
I dive into the Dolphin's snout
into its wet hair
soft algae or siren's lace
and with my teeth
I tear
its pink throat smelling
like a newly opened oyster

Our canoes touch
Slow kisses of wrecks washed with tears
In anger
and envy
the sun cut itself on the edge of the island
Suddenly
twilight thin curtain
falls from the gallery to darken
the seats of the bay
Death of a theater!
My box ablaze!
Gilt panelling and red velvet
drown in the bric-a-brac
of a dead province
Huge blue clouded face of the sea
a boat white like a tear on its cheek

Toward it
outstretched pointed
our canoes
like two red nails burn
in a blond
ray
supreme buffer of the night

—Do you want to soar
  like a perfect
  bird
  drunk with foam and already set
  for a blast in Paradise!
  Here place in your hair
  this frail Milky Way diadem
  or these lighthouse gems
  with their crossfire
  rapt at the window God's Rue de la Paix

—I'd sooner a bed
  smoother than the sea
  and harder
  Just
  once more
  kid!
  Later who knows?
  The sea might want to drink us too
  some night
  slow canoes
  or tears
  that seek
  the very
  bottom
  bare!

June 1929

Insufferable pride of the Lavaredos

futurist words in freedom

Insufferable pride of the Lavaredos pyramidal mountains

Endlessly looming from the opaque dreams of a hundred thousand patient servile bitter mists savor savor the stratified range of your victories and the enemy kings once conquered by you and by you harshly walled in

Proud whims of a crystal where a rosy human blondness swims singing

Ecstasy

Before renewing your solemn assault of the hypersensitive azure have fun criticizing from on high the extravagance and mincing elegance of the green hills decked with firs hands held round their forgotten slumbering cottage

They entreat a puff of fog on the pointed black hat of the forest chapel

Blue powder iridescent cream of shivers of Misurina for that lovely Lake skin perfumed with resin

Cool vanity of mirrors reflecting silver brushes tufted with rushes

An island jar of yellow makeup

A trout in a quick leap snaps up the gems

Ring ring a nothing of a dingaling gluglung stream of jewels bells of a herd of cows rising like a cloud black and white on the supple sensual side of an emerald mountain

Pride of the Lavaredos

Triangles of cosmic fury

You will never break the boundless excuseless pride of Benedetta dazzling spiral peak of hot snow

And yet the excuse exists and is surely called Beauty

Spiritual Beauty armed with charm charm

Beauty impassioning space!

It's you who makes my soul flicker flame or pine bough in mourning by the sea sob

Smile quick Benedetta and the first sharp tear will fly projectile of joy into infinity

August 1935

Should I choose these words one by one with care or
cast them out in a random fan of tropical scents
sherbets sparks
These words
These words whose duty is to serve your Beauty and
also certain noons adorned with fortune and fu-
ture the Duty languidly to rock the rich flashing
undulation of your eyes and your red lips orien-
tal divans
So I cast these words out how many how many a hun-
dred if any
—Run dig chase and come back that's quickly done
barking barking barking
Each one comes back panting his power and his speed
Thick muzzles blazing with solar joy jeweled drool and
bloody spoils
How beautiful they are these words of love with slen-
der limbs
I want to cheer them all and cajole them with their
beautiful names
Flash smile celebration splendor pride delicacy fluid-
ity ecstasy ardor marine depth exaltation elegance
grace
—Come! all you proud hunting and traveling words lie
down here for the poet's caress

But the two no the three last ones look spent they loll
their tongues in the sand and painfully lift their
dreamy eyes to offer me the limpid juice of their
burning agony of verbalized beasts
Beautiful Beautiful Beautiful
From all points of the nerves' cosmic sensibility some
clever echoes repeat
Beautiful Beautiful Beautiful
Pathetic and greenish the Dusk hastens to cross the sky
to admire them closer up
Night fallen now the Milky Way's most winsome breast
sighs
—Only once could I manage the miracle of so fresh
and sparkling a drop of supernatural milk
Unique
Perfect
Sadly all the rest clouds over bitter and biting eating
charcoal or dirty demons' chocolate
I tell Beny lying in her swimsuit in the sun in front of
the villa Varano
—If these words in freedom run away it's because they
are like you

Terminillo–Villa Varano–August 1938

141

Notes on the Poems

Numbered notes, which are arranged by poem, have been restricted to terms (including names of places and persons) not readily accessible in standard reference works. Dates of occupations, battles, and sieges have been taken, wherever possible, from the *Times*, London.

The Old Sailors

One of Marinetti's earliest efforts in free verse, dedicated to the theorist of *vers libre*, Gustave Kahn, Marinetti's "patron" in Paris. Published Sept. 20, 1898 in the French-Italian literary journal *Anthologie-Revue de France et d'Italie*; recited at Théâtre Sarah Bernhardt in 1899 and awarded a prize there.

The Conquest of the Stars

A selection from Marinetti's first book of verse, an epic in nineteen cantos describing a dramatic battle between the sea and the stars. Published in Paris in 1902 and dedicated to Gustave Kahn. The text used here is that of the 1909 edition, revised and corrected by Marinetti.

Destruction

Two selections from Marinetti's second book of poetry, published in Paris in 1904. Regarded by many critics as the best and most personal of Marinetti's early work.

The Sensual City

A personification of the urban landscape, published in Paris in 1908. The volume consists of "The Sensual City," a poem in ten cantos; eleven "little light plays" ("petits drames de lumières"), of which "The Death of the Fortresses" is one; a collection of "Dithyrambs" (homages to the automobile and to poet-contemporaries of Marinetti), which includes "To My Pegasus"; and a prose epilogue that, like "To My Pegasus," celebrates the energy of the machine.

The Mad Traveler

1. [the birds of Bukir.] An Arab legend describes an annual gathering of birds at the gorge of the Būkīr in the Djabal al-Ṭayr (Mountains of the Birds) in Egypt. According to the story, one by one each bird put its head into the cleft of the mountain, until it closed upon one of them. The flock then flew away, leaving the caught bird, suspended from the mountain, to die.

The Pope's Monoplane

The impetus for this "political novel in free verse," which urges the Italians to war against Austria, was André Beaumont's flight from Paris to Rome, during which he overflew the Vatican on May 31, 1911. Published in Paris in 1912. Two of the poem's eleven cantos appear here.

Flying Over the Heart of Italy

1. [mechanics hold me by the tail. . . .] Prior to and during World War I, aircraft were commonly restrained by crewmen until the engine was sufficiently accelerated for takeoff.

2. [castor oil.] Castor oil was utilized into the 1920s as an engine lubricant in airplanes.

3. [rudders.] The term *rudder* was used to refer to "elevator" until around 1910.

The Volcano's Decrees

1. [hydrogen-sulfide.] Hydrogen sulfide is one of many gases that may be emitted from the fumaroles of erupting volcanoes.

Zong Toomb Toomb

Zong Toomb Toomb, composed in 1912–1913, was published in Italian in Milan in 1914. The French text was prepared by Marinetti for printing but, because of the war, never appeared. Sections of the book were declaimed in French and Italian by Marinetti in 1913 and 1914. Marinetti's important essay "Technical Manifesto of Futurist Literature," which adumbrates the Futurist poetic of words in freedom, is found at the end of the French edition. It had first appeared in I poeti futuristi in 1912 and was frequently reprinted. The poem "Battle Weight + Smell," dated Aug. 11, 1912, appeared as an appendix to a supplement to the manifesto, as a demonstration of words in freedom. The fold-out "Synchronic Chart" comes at the end of the poem "Mobilization." Zong Toomb Toomb describes the Bulgarian-Serbian siege of Adrianople in Turkey from October 1912 to its surrender on March 26, 1913 during the first Balkan war. Marinetti was at Adrianople in October 1912 and so had first-hand experience of the early days of the campaign.

Correction of Proofs Desires

1. [Messina's ruuuubble in the strait.] On Dec. 28, 1908, an earthquake, the impact of which was felt throughout southern Calabria and eastern Sicily, destroyed Reggio and Messina, with a loss of 150,000 lives.

2. [my book on Adrianople.] Marinetti refers here to Zong Toomb Toomb. "Correction," though the last poem of the book to be composed, is arranged dischronologically at the head of the collection.

3. [Mustafa-Pasha.] Mustafa Pasha. Turkish frontier town occupied by Bulgarians on Oct. 18, 1912, at the beginning of the campaign in Thrace.

Synchronic Chart

1. [Adrianople.] Fortified Turkish city that fell to the Serbs and Bulgarians on March 26, 1913, after a prolonged siege. It is the setting for most of the poems of Zong Toomb Toomb.

2. [Maritsa.] River with source in Rhodope Mountains. Flows through Bulgaria and Turkey (where it passes through Adrianople).

Hadirlik Turkish Headquarters

1. [Hadirlik.] Fort in western sector of Adrianople; headquarters of Shukri Pasha at the time of the surrender of Adrianople.

2. [Nizams.] Members of the Turkish active army.

3. [Mustafiz.] Members of the Turkish territorial army.

4. [Redifs.] Members of the Turkish reserve army.

5. [Ichtiats.] Reservists of Nizams (see n. 2 above).

6. [Ismail Pasha.] Commander of fortresses at Adrianople.

7. [Fuad Bey.] Army staff secretary at Adrianople.

8. [Akbunar.] Outpost north of Adrianople.

9. [Kadiköy.] First station west of Adrianople.

10. [Stambul–Yolu road.] Main road connecting Constantinople (Stambul) and Adrianople (yolu = road [Turk.]).

11. [FALL OF KIRKILISSE.] Kirk Kilisse was taken by the Bulgarians on Oct. 24, 1912. Communication with Constantinople was interrupted a week later.

12. [Babaeski.] Site of Bulgarian defeat of Turks Oct. 27, 1912.

13. [Lule Burgas.] Site of Bulgarian victory over Turks Oct. 30, 1912.

14. [CAPTIVE BALLOON.] Balloon moored to the ground by cables, used for observations prior to and during World War I.

15. [T.] T-shaped sign on aviation field marking landing area and/or a possible representation of the plane itself.

16. [Demotika.] Turkish town occupied by Bulgarians around Oct. 31, 1912.

17. [Uskub.] Turkish town occupied by Serbs Oct. 26, 1912.

18. [Prishtina.] Turkish town occupied by Serbs Oct. 22, 1912.

19. [Nevrokop.] Turkish town captured by Bulgarians around Nov. 13, 1912.

20. [Kumanovo.] Site of Serbian victory over Turks Oct. 24, 1912.

21. [Elassona.] Site of Greek victory over Turks Oct. 18, 1912.

22. [18–31 October 328.] October 31, 1912. Marinetti dates by the *maliye* calendar, an Ottoman system employed from the 1700s until 1917 for fiscal affairs and often used in newspaper reports. Proclamations of this kind were periodically dropped by Bulgarian aviators upon Adrianople during the siege. Marinetti's is a translation of an actual document dropped on the city on Oct. 31, 1912.

23. [mohadjirs.] Refugees.

24. [SHUKRI PASHA.] Commander in chief at Adrianople.

25. [Halil Bey.] Governor of the vilayet (see n. 34 below) of Adrianople.

26. [Hakki Bey.] Unidentified Turkish officer.

27. [Nazim Pasha.] Commander of Turkish army at Tcherkesköy.

28. [Tcherkesköy.] Site of entrenchment of Turks after the battle of Lule Burgas.

29. [Tugrut Pasha.] Turgut Pasha, commander of the Turkish Second Army corps.

30. [Mukhtar Pasha.] Mahmud Mukhtar Pasha, commander of the Turkish Third Army corps.

31. [Abdullah Pasha.] General commander of the Turkish Eastern Army.

32. [Uzun Kupru.] Turkish town south of Adrianople. Communication lines between Adrianople and Uzun Kupru had been severed around Nov. 1, 1912.

33. [Defterdar.] Director of finance, one of the chief administrative officers of the Turkish vilayet (see n. 34 below).

34. [vilayet.] Major administrative division of Turkish empire; "province."

35. [regie.] See n. 42 below.

36. [Komitadjis.] Members of a guerilla band in Macedonia who fought on the side of the Bulgarians during the Balkan wars.

37. [W/T.] Wireless telegraph.

38. [Tsarigraad.] Tsarigrad (Constantinople [Bulg.]).

39. [Seliolu.] Site of Bulgarian rout of Turks Oct. 22–23, 1912.

40. [Marash.] Fort southwest of Adrianople taken by Bulgarians Oct. 23, 1912.

41. [Young Turks.] Members of Turkish reform party who supported the establishment of a republic in Turkey. Their extremist activities, which had been increasing dramatically during October and November 1912, culminated in an attempted coup d'état on Nov. 16, 1912.

42. [soldiers who attacked the tobacco regie.] Tobacco supplies began to run short at the regie (government monopoly) after mid-November 1912. A group of soldiers attempted to break into the regie on Nov. 19, 1912. Salt, sugar, and gasoline started to become scarce near the end of the month.

43. [Kavkas.] Fort in southeastern sector of Adrianople.

44. [Aivas Bata.] Fort Aivas Baba, in the northeastern sector of Adrianople.

45. [Rechadie Gardens.] Pleasure gardens in Adrianople.

46. [Institute of the Sisters of Agram.] Girls' boarding school in Adrianople, a place of refuge for many inhabitants of the city during the siege.

47. [Kaik.] Fort in eastern sector of Adrianople.

48. [WHITE FLAG OVER Hadirlik.] Adrianople fell on March 26, 1913.

49. [General Vasov.] Victorious Bulgarian commander at Adrianople.

50. [500 prisoners . . . 15,000 men lost.] Marinetti's dates and figures here do not precisely match those of contemporary sources.

Bridge

1. [Stambul.] Istanbul (Constantinople).

2. [Farman.] The *Henri Farman III*, biplane developed by Henri and Maurice Farman in 1909.

3. [Halles.] The Halles Centrales, old wholesale meat and produce market in Paris.

4. [Stara Zagora.] General headquarters of Bulgarian army at the beginning of the campaign in Thrace.

5. [pet-na-nozha.] *Pet na nozha*. Lit. "five on the knife," a popular misconstrual of the Bulgarian command *Napred, na nozha* ("Fix bayonets").

6. [Yörük.] West of Adrianople; site of Bulgarian repulse of Turks Oct. 29, 1912.

7. [Fort Kazal Tepé.] Fort in western sector of Adrianople.

8. [Selim Pasha.] Sixteenth-century mosque of the sultan Selim II in Adrianople.

Trainload of Sick Soldiers

1. [Abdul Pasha.] Captain arrested by Shukri Pasha for stopping a Bulgarian train without his authorization.

2. [Karagach station.] Railroad station serving Adrianople.

3. [barley comings.] Malt dust or comes.

4. [Rue de la Paix.] Street in Paris famed for its elegant fashion and jewelry shops.

5. [Horo.] Bulgarian dance.

Bombardment

1. [Shumi Maritsa o Karvavena.] First line of Bulgarian national anthem (1885–1946). Lit. "Maritsa rushes, stained with blood."

2. [Ibrahim.] Ibrahim Pasha, senior commander of the south sector at Adrianople.

3. [Rudolf.] Unidentified German officer in the employ of the Turks.

Technical Manifesto of Futurist Literature

1. [*Battle of Tripoli.*] Prose narrative by Marinetti, first published in L'Intransigeant (Dec. 25–31, 1911), describing the battle of Bumeliana (Oct. 26, 1911) during the Italo-Turkish war. Published in Milan in 1912. See "Geometric and Mechanical Splendor," n. 1, below.

2. [. . .as Voltaire maintained.] Though Voltaire would have concurred with this view, Marinetti's attribution is questionable.

3. [*Mafarka the Futurist.*] Ideological novel by Marinetti, published in Paris in 1909.

4. [Bumeliana.] Italian outpost south of Tripoli; its well supplied water to Tripoli.

Battle Weight + Smell

1. [Gargaresch.] Town southwest of Tripoli (outside Italian lines).

2. [149-gun.] 149-mm. gun.

Futurist *Words in Freedom*

First published in French in Milan in 1919. The prose essays—elaborations on the "Technical Manifesto" of 1912—had first appeared in Italian in 1913 and 1914. Representative selections appear here. The poems (presented as "examples" of words in freedom) were written between 1911 and 1919. The last four examples are fold-out poems.

Introduction

1. [Triple Alliance.] Diplomatic union of Germany, Austria-Hungary, and Italy, formed in 1882. Italy's unstable relations with Austria-Hungary culminated in her declaration of war on Austria on May 23, 1915.

2. [Vittorio Veneto.] Site of major Italian victory over the Austrians on Oct. 30, 1918, regarded as decisive in causing the collapse of Austria-Hungary.

3. [Futurist political party. . . . Futurist political Fasci.] The Futurist political party, Partito Politico Futurista, and the Fasci Politici Futuristi were founded in 1918. *Roma Futurista* was the party paper.

4. [Gabriele D'Annunzio.] Gabriele d'Annunzio (1863–1938). Popular Italian writer lauded by Marinetti in his early years but later subjected to attack for his decorative, esoteric poetry.

5. [Verhaeren.] Emile Verhaeren (1855–1916). Belgian Symbolist poet admired by Marinetti.

Futurist Sensibility and Wireless Imagination: Onomatopoeia and Mathematical Symbols

1. [*Adrianople-Siege-Orchestra.*] "Adrianopoli Assedio Orchestra," a version of "Bombardment" published in *Lacerba* 1, no. 6 (March 15, 1913).

2. [*Battle Weight + Smell.*] "Battle Weight + Smell," first published with the Supplement to the "Technical Manifesto of Futurist Literature" in 1912, appears in the present volume as part of *Zong Toomb Toomb.*

Geometric and Mechanical Splendor

1. [De Suni battery.] Marinetti, while serving as a war correspondent for L'Intransigeant in October 1911, spent time in the trenches with the 84th Infantry at Bumeliana and was an eyewitness of the battle of Bumeliana (see "Technical Manifesto of Futurist Literature," n. 1 above).

2. [the poem "*Hotel Lounge.*"] Luciano Folgore's "Salone d'albergo" appears in his collection *Ponti sull'Oceano: Versi liberi (Lirismo sintetico) e parole in libertà.* 1912–1913–1914 (Milan: Edizioni Futuriste di "Poesia," 1914).

3. [the poem "*Man + Mountain + Valley.*"] Umberto Boccioni's "Uomo + vallata + montagna" had appeared in

Lacerba on Feb. 1, 1914.

    4. ["*Smokers, Second Class.*"] Francesco Cangiullo's "Fumatori II." had appeared in *Lacerba* on Jan. 1, 1914.

    5. ["*Statement 1910–1914*" by . . . Carrà.] Carlo Carrà's "1900–1913. Bilancio" had appeared in *Lacerba* on Feb. 1, 1914.

Simultaneity—Synoptic Tables of Lyrical Values

    1. [the balloon drawn typographically.] See "Hadirlik Turkish Headquarters" in *Zong Toomb Toomb.*

Numerical Sensibility

    1. [expresses . . . + + + + +.] This passage, inadvertently deleted from the French text, is translated from the original Italian version of the essay, "Onomatopee astratte e sensibilità numerica" (1914), and restored here in brackets. We are grateful to Max Creech for supplying the translation.

    2. [*anterior sky where beauty bloomed.*] Marinetti quotes from Mallarmé's "Les Fenêtres" (The windows). Though Marinetti had in his early years regarded Mallarmé as the greatest nonliving poet, by 1910 he was writing about him as passé, as part of a poetic tradition that had to be rejected.

Examples of Words in Freedom

Dunes

    1. [Bu Fellah.] Unidentified Libyan town or oasis.

9-storied battle of Mount Altissimo

    1. [Mount Altissimo.] Mountain on Lake Garda, near the Italian-Austrian frontier. Italian Alpini descended from here on Oct. 24, 1915 to carry out a successful assault of the Austrian position, Dosso Casina. Marinetti, Boccioni, Russolo, and Sant'Elia, as members of an Alpinist battalion, participated in this battle.

    2. [Brion.] Fortified mountain northeast of Riva on Lake Garda on the Austrian side of the then Italian-Austrian border.

After the Marne, Joffre toured the front by car

    1. [Joffre.] Joseph J.-C. Joffre. Commander in chief of the French forces 1914–1916; victor of the Battle of the Marne (Sept. 6–12, 1914).

At night, lying in bed, She rereads the letter from her gunner at the front

    1. [Mount Kuk.] Hill near Gorizia, east of the Isonzo River. Italian troops captured Austrian positions there on May 15, 1917. Marinetti was wounded in the battle.

    2. [in ambush.] When this poem first appeared in *L'Italia futurista* on Sept. 9, 1917, it was entitled "Morbidezze in agguato + bombarde italiane" ("Softnesses in ambush + Italian mortars"). With this title, Marinetti paid tribute to Irma Valeria's recently published *Morbidezze in agguato* (1917), which had been given to him at the front. A conventional inscription and note of acknowledgment appear at the top and bottom of the page, and fragments (and expansions) of the title are scribbled in the picture's lower half.

    3. [bold comrades.] Lit. *arditi*, Italian assault troops, 1915–1917.

After Words in Freedom

    Marinetti developed the idea of "les motsfondus en liberté" ("fusedwords in freedom") as an extension of "les mots en liberté," a program that was to be elaborated in his "Manifesto dell'Aeropoesia" of 1931. The essay printed here is a draft in Marinetti's hand, circa 1924. We are grateful to Paolo Valesio for translating the fusedwords from the original Italian. "The right finds the pearl" appears in two versions in Marinetti's hand. The second of these two versions was included in the collection *Poems to Beny* (1971). Overwritten words are indicated in the English by strike-over lines followed by slashes.

Poems to Beny

    Marinetti's collection of poems to his wife, Benedetta, dated 1920–1938, was published in French in Turin in 1971.

Insufferable pride of the Lavaredos

    1. [Lavaredos.] Mountain peaks in Dolomites, overlooking Lake Misurina.

    2. [Misurina.] See n. 1 above.

Should I choose these words . . .

    1. [Terminillo–Villa Varano.] Villa rented by Marinetti in mountain resort north of Rome.

"The Most Enduring and Most Honored Name"
Marinetti as Poet

Paolo Valesio

> My father fought in this war; thus, I can speak about it.
> —VICTOR HUGO

What, essentially, was Futurism? An explosion of youth—youth with its obvious virtues (boldness, vitality, freshness) and with its less obvious but equally important defects (violence, dogmatism, superficiality). As usual, poets and other artists understood this before scholars realized it.[1]

Another answer: Futurism was the cultural movement whose affirmation, ironically, has been the strongest obstacle to an adequate recognition of the artistic and intellectual achievement of its founder, Filippo Tommaso Marinetti. His devotion to the movement has blurred the profile of his own artistic personality.[2] The moment has come to redress the balance, to bring Marinetti back to center stage while keeping Futurism in the background.

Futurism was the first cultural and artistic avant-garde movement in Europe—which means, in the historical period just after the turn of our century, the first avant-garde movement in the world. This is a strong claim, and it requires a pause. Literary historiography on the avant-gardes is still torn between two equally unsatisfactory tendencies: on the one hand, the obsession with finding the *protos euretes*, or original inventor, and on the other hand (given the impossibility of discovering such originating personalities or gestures), the inclination to give up the search altogether. A genealogical approach has a chance of striking the right balance.

At the end of the nineteenth century a river of innovation in literature, art, and general culture began to flow, especially in France—a river which from the beginning appears to have had many tributaries, creeks, torrents, and rivulets.[3] But these offshoots, interesting and significant as they are, do not modify the essential picture, in which the founding movement (still very much alive in contemporary literature) is Symbolism and the basic "historical" avant-gardes compose the well-known triad of Expressionism, Cubism, and Futurism. These movements take shape between 1903 (the founding year in Dresden of the German movement in painting, Die Brücke, which marks Expressionism's first phase), 1908 (the birthdate of Cubism in Paris), and February 20, 1909 (when the "Foundation and Manifesto of Futurism" appears in the Paris newspaper Le Figaro, followed by an Italian translation in the February–March issue of the journal Poesia in Milan). A little later (1916) the Dada movement surfaces in Zurich; later still (between 1919 and 1924) Surrealism emerges; and the rest, as the saying goes, is history.[4]

Why then do I call Futurism the first avant-garde movement in the world? Because Futurism merged three elements that had not previously been gathered together and that were combined afterwards mainly because of the decisive example of Futurism:

1. *(Meta)linguistic integration*. From the beginning, Futurism integrated a discourse *of* literature, a discourse *on* literature, and a discourse on and of the arts.

2. *Politicization of itself as a movement*. Every literary-artistic movement has historical and social implications (this is why, after all, one speaks of "movements"). But the Futurists intuitively recognized that what was necessary was a new impulse and (dis)connection: the intellectual movement *politicized itself*, on the same level as the political movements in the by then traditional sense of the term. (This sense begins, by this very fact, to become obsolete.)

3. *Assertion of the "Second World."* Before Futurism, innovative movements were identified with the most advanced countries in Europe: France, Germany, England. The Futurist intuition was that a real innovation, an effective break, can take place only at a weak (but not the weakest) link in the European chain, at the margins (but not at the remote periphery) of Europe. Italy was the ideal country for fulfilling this role.

From its birth as a unified nation in the mid-nineteenth century until today—thus, before, during, and after Fascism, and before the emergence of a Third World ideology—Italy has been the best representative of the Second World (last among the first powers, first among the last). Despite his hyperbolic exaltation of Italy as a primary country, Marinetti must have realized that what actually should be exploited was Italy's peculiar second-rank position. Unlike the Greek Jean Moréas (Jean Papadiamantopoulos), who wrote about Symbolism in French, and the Romanian Tristan Tzara, who, aside from his juvenilia, wrote about Dadaism in French, the Italian Marinetti realized the *revolutionary possibilities of literary bilingualism*. He used his bilingualism not merely as a personal and lyrical form of *Bildung* (as is the case, for instance, with Ungaretti's French/Italian bilingualism) but as the emblem of a new historical climate.[5] In short, Futurism once again launched Italian discourse on the international scene as an alternative to French linguistic imperialism (I refer here to the language of culture), but in constant and close collaboration with the latter imperial language. Such a situation was largely owing to the French/Italian bilingualism of the French-educated founder of the movement, who during the first phase of his literary career wrote primarily in French. (The present anthology, as the translators explain, consists of texts originally written in French by Marinetti or translated from Italian into French by him.) Such association is after all true also of political anti-imperialist struggles: they are simply unthinkable outside the context of an intimate relationship with the culture of the imperial powers.

There is a crucial element in this Italian role that does not seem to have been noticed until now (and this is hardly strange, because the international debate on the avant-gardes is still dominated by the languages of the First World: English, French, and German).[6] The essential point is this: an avant-garde movement born in the context of those literary languages, which, from the Enlightenment on, had dominated modern discourse, would not have been credible. These were classicized and canonized languages, which appropriately evoked the early-modern tradition of modernism but had by now too staid an image to be the instruments of a jump within modernism (this jump or skip *in the context of* modernism being the distinctive feature of the avant-gardes). Compared to them, Italian at this time was endowed with a fresh energy, a sense of novelty. Thus Futurism shows the distinctive feature of all subsequent avant-garde movements: recycling the old (with constant, often brilliant retouchings and modifications) under the guise of a hyperbolic celebration of the new. The great secret of the avant-gardes is a paradox: their acute sense of *continuity*. (There is in this recycling activity, brilliant as it is, a constant *bricolage*, with its slightly vulgarian tinge; hence the perfectly understandable rejection of the avant-garde logic—but not of the logic of modernism in general—on the part of all those artists who have a pure and dramatic sense of the relationship between the individual and tradition.)

Throughout the nineteenth century, and for all the impetus of the Risorgimento, it had seemed that Italian culture was destined never again to regain its leadership position in Europe (and hence, in the context of those times, in the world). Italy had almost uninterruptedly maintained a leading position from the beginning of the fourteenth century until the end of the sixteenth, only to lose it in the following period, and subsequent attempts to deny the marginalization of Italian culture—like Vincenzo Gioberti's noble book nourished on Risorgimento hopes, *Del primato morale e civile degli Italiani* (On the moral and cultural supremacy of Italians, 1842–1843)—had not, by and large, proceeded beyond the realm of ideological abstractions. The strategic aspect of Italian supremacy from the late Middle Ages to the early Renaissance consisted in the interconnection or interanimation of practice and theory, of tradition and innovation, with a deep sense of the "union of opposites."

From the beginning of the twentieth century to the aftermath of the First World War, Marinetti and his collaborators were the most visible group who brought Italy back to its position of international innovation (although they were certainly not the only Italians who realized this creative impetus). Their avant-garde movement accomplished this task by popularizing (if not inventing) the very notion of "avant-garde." This is not a play on words: the two occurrences of the word *avant-garde* in the preceding sentence are not synonymous. There is a general (or essentialist, or ontological) sense in which the term *avant-garde* describes any advanced, exploratory position, any position at the edge or limit or boundary of things, with all its attendant risks. In this generic but fundamental sense, the informational capacity of the term is minimal, but its evaluative function is crucial. If every authentic poet occupies an avant-garde position, to apply this term to him or her does not add much to the appreciation of what is specific to the poet's work. But this does not mean that such a characterization is useless, for it is with this gesture that critics assume their most important responsibility—that of being wrong—characterizing this or that poet as significant, destined to last. In this sense, every poet who counts is what a haunting Shakespearean verse (*King Lear* 4.7.35) calls "poor perdu": the soldier sent as an explorer or spy or watch in advance of the regular army, deep inside enemy territory, so that he is officially no longer accounted for. This is the essentialist sense of *avant-garde*.

But the notions of Futurism and avant-garde are usually connected in a different way, a *historical* way—not simply in the obvious sense that every poetical experience, for all its search for the absolute, turns out to be rooted in a specific historical context, but in the sense that "avant-garde" is a mainly Italian invention of early twentieth-century culture. The same fruitful ambivalence of historical and semantic dialectic applies to the term *Futurism*. In Marinetti's rhetoric, the word initially has a totalizing (or universalizing) and almost totalitarian ambition; but it eventually acquires the connotations (and limitations) of a specific historical movement that lasted, as a credible cultural development, for about twenty years. I have capitalized Futurism in order to symbolize this specific historical implication. Futurism's most durable heritage (perhaps its only lasting one), which is also its most important philosophical element (perhaps the only one of its elements which is endowed with a truly philosophical power), is its constant attention to the presence of the future in the bosom of the present. This is the *futurismus perennis* (or lower-case futurism) which defines every cultural attitude that strives to be really contemporary (what in Italian is called *cultura militante*). For the paradox of true modernity is that it is always *dischronic*, either creatively bent over the past (searching for the genealogies that matter) or projected toward the future; which means that the contemporary is never really contemporary.

The avant-garde is the culminating idea in the rhetoric of modernism; it also marks the beginning of the decline of modernism—a sumptuous sunset, to be sure, or a long autumnal season within which artists are still living and working. Contemporaneity is not very interested in the agitated, out-of-breath rhetoric of modernism. But what is contemporaneity? I limit myself to an image or parable: "He also said to the multitudes: 'When you see a cloud rising in the west, you say at once, "A shower is coming"; and so it happens. And when you see the south wind blowing, you say, "There will be scorching heat"; and it happens. You hypocrites! You know how to interpret the appearance of earth and sky; but why do you not know how to interpret the present time?'" (Luke 12.54–56).[7] Like every Gospel saying, this one can be read in the most diverse ways. On one level it evokes the soul-searching and modesty that the critic needs in order not to become a "hypocrite." But I quote it to show that all problematizations of the idea of the modern run the risk of tautology. The modern is the constantly receding horizon of the contemporary. The latter is always here and now; it is what takes us back to our indispensable existential context—with the danger, however, of flattening our perspective, so that we confine ourselves to what is merely real, forgetting what is true.

As far as Futurism is concerned, the response of tradition is the movement that in the history of Italian literature is known as the *ritorno all'ordine*, the return to the reassuring orderliness of traditional literary discourse. It is from this renewed call to tradition, rather than from Futurism, that (for good or ill) the main currents of contemporary Italian poetry descend.[8]

Every discourse on modernity is a problematization of time; and every problematization of time inevitably raises (no matter how informally or irreverently) metaphysical questions. The contrast—which follows the whole trajectory of modern discourse—between a linear and a cyclical notion of time is ultimately a theological question. From a related perspective, the poetic contrast between Futurism and Symbolism (or, more broadly, between avant-garde and tradition) can be seen as a late secular echo of an ancient, and mostly Judeo-Christian, metaphysical bifurcation: between an Apocalyptic spirituality (preparing—with a mixture of anxiety and joyfulness—for a culmination of time, a full redemption of the world in the near future) and what may be called an existential spirituality (in which redemption is essentially a matter for the individual soul, and a redeemed community can be found only in the Beyond). We witness here the age-old duel between imminence and immanence.[9] As far as literature and its history are concerned, the problematization of time has to do above all with a revision of the idea of tradition, which calls into question its different aspects: tradition in the positivistic and philological sense; *traditionis traditio*, or the tradition of tradition, in the cultural-historical sense (reception criticism and so on); and Tradition in the spiritual sense.

Avant-garde inaugurates the end of modernism because, with its aggressive and irreverent style, it lays bare the contradictions over which "softer" variants of modernism manage discreetly to glide. I have already identified Symbolism as the most significant of these variants. Symbolism is crucial for modernism but tangential with respect to the avant-garde because Symbolism is a locus of thought rather than a movement. Marinetti and poets like him put their individuality at the disposal of an idea of group, whereas d'Annunzio and poets like him put their individuality at the disposal of an idea of individualism.

By now it should be clear that the question What is Futurism? admits of no direct answer. In defining Futurism, as I do below, by means of selected quotations by its protagonist, I am not adopting a makeshift critical device; on the contrary, such a series of selected definitions fulfills the need, implicit in the preceding discussion, to develop an adequate critical response to the avant-garde by accepting its challenge to cross the boundaries between primary literary language and critical metalanguage. These, then, are some of Marinetti's sayings on Futurism:

> The sick man found out his own remedy. *We are the physicians who happened to be around.* The remedy works on sick persons everywhere.[10]

> Futurism is not, and never will be, *prophetism.* [. . .] We cannot intuit what the near future will be if we do not collaborate with it by living *all* of life. [. . .] We will never be pessimistic prophets, announcers of the great Nothing. Our practical and active Futurism prepares a Tomorrow which will be dominated by us.[11]

> We will soon arrive at a new, extraterrestrial, plastic spirituality.[12]

> The great book of Futurism teaches to improvise everything, even God![13]

> Everything that was is wrong, because it was. Everything that has not yet been is right, because it has not yet been![14]

But the most important definition is the one Marinetti himself underscores as such, mentioning it immediately after a parodistically historiographic definition:

> Futurism is a great antiphilosophical and anticultural movement, made of ideas intuitions instincts punches kicks slaps, which rejuvenate purify innovate and speed up; it was created on February 20, 1909, by a group of genial Italian poets and artists. Among the numerous definitions of it I prefer the one given by theosophists: "*I futuristi sono i mistici dell'azione*" [Futurists are the mystics of action].[15]

Going one step beyond these important and lively statements, what follows is a review of the main aporias or dialectical tensions of Futurism as an avant-garde movement.

Historicism versus antihistoricism. The avant-garde, while it defines itself ideologically by its polemical (and at times scornful) attitude toward every form of historiographical mediation, cannot even begin to conceive of itself as a form of organization if it does not see itself as a radically historical creature, almost obsessively attentive to all the nuances of the "before" and "after." The avant-garde seems to believe (with what amounts to an excessive optimism about history) that a few years are enough to create crucial differences, to transform the avant-garde into the academy and vice versa. (In this sense, the propagandists of the avant-garde can at times be more pedantic than the most pedantic historicists.) Suffice it to consider the continuous changes in the lists of Futurist champions as they appear in successive manifestos, around the immutable nucleus (which, interestingly, is a martyrological nucleus: it includes the architect Antonio Sant'Elia and the great painter Umberto Boccioni, both of whom died young in World War I).

Thus the expression "historical avant-garde" (often applied to Futurism and related movements) ceases to appear as an oxymoron and reveals itself instead as a pleonasm. To be precise: the avant-garde refuses mediations with the broad historical context, but only to concentrate (with an inevitably narcissistic connotation) on its own inner history.

The central paradox here is the following: the avant-garde, born out of a reflection on time (its rhythms, its periods and chronological segmentations, its game of anticipations and echoes, and so on), cannot, however, be adequately understood if one stays within a historicist perspective. Modernity is founded on an immemorial and archetypal idea, which brings together notions like the Alchemists' *renovatio* (a radical inner renewal of the human being) and Saint Paul's view of man: "So we do not lose heart. Though our outer nature is wasting away, our inner nature is being renewed every day" (2 Cor. 4.16). Thus history is made possible by an ultimately metaphysical and interior idea—an idea that, in order to found history, must remain outside of it.

Repeatability versus uniqueness. The semiscientific effect that avant-garde rhetoric will pass on to various subsequent forms of literary experimentalism comes from its insistence on repeatability: recipes showing how, from now on, a poem will have to be written in order to be really good, and so forth. On the other hand, the poems and narratives of the avant-garde are clothed in a rhetoric of uniqueness, even going so far as self-destructing in the case of certain performances. More wisely, poetry that does not will itself to be avant-garde accepts the tradition that precedes it and thereby encourages the tradition that follows it. Avant-garde, on the other hand, tends to generate frenzies of imitation followed by frenzies of refusal.

Mass appeal versus elitism. This is perhaps the most flagrant contradiction. Sometimes the quantitative element is used as if it alone would provide an ethical/esthetic justification (Futurism is right because all, or almost all, important artists are Futurists). At other times the strategy is exactly the opposite (Futurism is right because it fights those habits of inertia and conformism in the name of which the majority is opposed to Futurism).

Order versus chaos. The joyful (and anti-intellectual, anti-academic, anti-moralistic) exaltation of chaos is often accompanied by, and juxtaposed with, the obsession with technological and rationalistic control (praise of the industrial machine world and, in this perspective, also of war as a triumph of technique). The central aspect (from the literary point of view) of this general contrast between order and chaos is the conflict between the rhetoric of the destruction of the "I" and a series of procedures of esthetic/psychological control whose outcome is a strengthened integration of authorial consciousness. Another aspect of this contradiction is the tension between the cult of depersonalization and the cult of subjectivity.

Noise versus silence. While the tension between sound and silence is not a phenomenon of contradiction—on the contrary, it is the foundational dialectic of esthetic, and generally cultural, activity[16]—there is an aporetic conflict between noisiness and the nostalgia for silence. In fact, the conflictual emergence of silence in the bosom of noisiness is one of the most significant distinctive features of avant-garde art.[17]

Desecration versus exaltation of art. The contrast is between a desecrating attitude toward art (and particularly poetry) and the hyperbolic exaltation of art with respect to other values—an exaltation that often adopts the language of the sacred; for instance, the Romantic and Risorgimento tone of this statement by Marinetti: "In Italy, the country of every intellectual and moral tyranny, it is a sacred duty to fight always and everywhere with the weapon of Poetry."[18]

But this contradiction is perhaps more apparent than real. In its strongest moments, the avant-garde recovers the sense of sacredness in art at the level of the deep bivalence of the Latin term *sacer*—which essentially designates the entity or person that cannot be touched without generating some sort of contamination; hence the semantic duplicity by which *sacer* can be something holy or something accursed.[19]

Thus the avant-garde keeps questioning, in the wake of Romanticism (the continuity of Tradition, once again), the peculiar sense in which poetry is something absolute, that is, sacred ("Poesia! Poesia . . . . O sublime putrefazione dell'anima!" [O Poetry! Poetry . . . . O sublime putrefaction of the soul!]).[20] Also, working in what is basically the same direction, the avant-garde enlarges the boundaries of the artistic enterprise: *"Let us boldly create 'the ugly' in literature, and let us kill off solemnity everywhere."*[21] Once again, this esthetic of ugliness has late-Romantic roots; suffice it to recall Baudelaire's poetry and poetics.[22] This is another of the many aspects in which Futurism anticipates later avant-garde movements: in this case, the hermeneutically productive views of the "hatefulness" and "misery" of poetry by the two rivals in the delimitation of territories of the imagination in French modernism, Georges Bataille and André Breton.[23]

The list above enumerates the essential tensions within the avant-garde; rather than making it more detailed, I want to underscore the importance of the formalistic, experimentalistic aspect of the avant-garde. This experimentalism in its highest moments—which are moments of generous utopia—makes clear the avant-garde ambition to change the world (or at least ways of perceiving the world) by the manipulation of linguistic structures. Experimentalism is heir to magic both in its noble and in its less than noble aspects—the latter consisting especially in a form of elitist and narcissistic pride. From this perspective, Italian Futurism is one of the most visible (and noisy) modern spiritual heirs of that peculiar syncretism of secular philosophy, science, rhetoric, and Judeo-Christian monotheism with an Islamic tinge that nourishes the Neoplatonism of the early Italian Renaissance; one should recall here the historical-philosophical approach of Marsilio Ficino and the cabalistic explorations of Pico della Mirandola.[24]

What is the specific contribution and significance of Marinetti's work? I do not add "contribution to the Futurist movement," because (as it is now high time to acknowledge) Marinetti's opus is an important contribution not simply to the avant-garde movements but to Italian literature *tout court*, beyond any "ism."

Clearly, Marinetti is the only poet connected to the whole trajectory of Futurism (or to most of it)[25] who can fly with his own wings, without the support of the Futurist movement.[26] All the rest are Futurist poets; Marinetti is a poet who is also a Futurist. A half-century after his death is certainly not too early to try to assess his role in the shaping of twentieth-century Italian poetry in its international context. Marinetti still works in the wake of Gabriele d'Annunzio and Giovanni Pascoli, the fathers of modern Italian verse.[27] Yet he belongs in the forefront of their successors—the small group of poets who are decisive in the development of early twentieth-century Italian poetry: Aldo Palazzeschi and Corrado Govoni, and also Sergio Corazzini and Guido Gozzano. In particular, Marinetti shares with Palazzeschi (and inherits from d'Annunzio) the rare gift of versatility in poetry and prose, including the various aspects (not only the strictly narrative ones) of the latter. Marinetti, in short, is the "missing link" in the chain of elaboration of the language of *contemporary* Italian poetry—a chain that reaches from d'Annunzio to Pier Paolo Pasolini.

The central feature of Marinetti's work is that he is primarily a poet. Moreover, he is a poet in the sense that becomes *traditional* (another paradox of the avant-garde writer) from Romanticism on: that is, he is a lyricist. The problem generated by Marinetti's work is analogous to that caused by d'Annunzio's: a great, overflowing, and at times overpowering *generosity* of writing. What makes Marinetti special (and here the parallel with d'Annunzio no longer works) is that he is a *displaced* lyricist; he gives his lyrical best in a variety of media and genres that are not primarily lyrical and in fact are not even primarily poetic. In this sense, Marinetti is the pertinent figure for contemporary poetry: he reconstructs the lyric by assaulting lyricism.

Later twentieth-century Italian poets (such as Eugenio Montale and Giuseppe Ungaretti) for a variety of reasons shifted away from the generous, overflowing style and adopted instead a carefully parsimonious attitude. Until recently, literary criticism tended in great part to mimic that thriftiness. It is not totally surprising, then, that it has taken so long for Marinetti's poetry to be adequately appreciated.

Marinetti is:

- a captivating playwright and organizer of spectacles (*Le Roi Bombance* [1905]—*Re Baldoria* [1910]; *Poupées électriques* [1909]—*Eletricità sessuale* [1920 or 1919]; *Il tamburo di fuoco* [1922]; and so on)[28]
- a lively journal writer[29]
- a delicate author of the prose of remembrance (for example, *Il fascino dell'Egitto* [1933])
- a brilliant writer of memoirs and essays (*Le Futurisme* [1911]—*Guerra sola igiene del mondo* [1915]; *Democrazia futurista. Dinamismo politico* [1919]; *Al di là del comunismo* [1920]; *Futurismo e fascismo* [1924]; the posthumous *La grande Milano tradizionale e futurista*, edited by Luciano De Maria together with *Una sensibilità italiana nata in Egitto* [Milan, 1969]; and so on)[30]
- a narrator and novelist of great talent (*Mafarka le futuriste* [1909]—*Mafarka il futurista* [1910]; *8 anime in una bomba* [romanzo esplosivo] [1919]; *Un ventre di donna* [romanzo chirurgico] [1919, coauthor Enif Robert]; *Gli Indomabili* [1922]; *L'alcova d'acciaio* [romanzo vissuto] [1927]; *Novelle con le labbra tinte* [1930]; and so on)[31]
- an innovative composer of manifestos in lyrical prose
- a very important poet.

The last two are the most remarkable aspects of Marinetti's career. His manifestos, in addition to their artistic value, have a peculiar modernity that is related to the art of poetic prosing, an extension of the Symbolist prose poem. In this sense, Marinetti's writing marks (before Surrealism) a significant step forward even in light of a high achievement like the *Chants de Maldoror* of Lautréamont (Isidore-Lucien Ducasse). Radical, even outrageous, as the latter texts are, they are still within the tradition of the Baudelairian prose poem, because of the coherence of their literary language qua literature. Marinetti, on the other hand, is one of the first to question the literary specificity of the prose poem, by weaving into it metalinguistic elements (essayistic, polemical, and sociological). The results of this skillful hybridization are texts in which the poetic element does not maintain a clear hierarchical superiority with respect to the prosaic one (a superiority symbolized in English by the substantive *poem* vis-à-vis the adjectivally used term *prose*), but is more deeply compromised and entangled with the latter (I symbolize this by the reversal of the grammatical relationship: *poetic* as an adjective, *prose* or *prosing* as the governing noun). Here, too, tradition exists before innovation and nourishes it: specifically, there is a genealogy of poetic prosing that includes Whitman, d'Annunzio, and others.[32] But what matters here is Marinetti's remarkable achievement, both in the lyrical prose of the manifestos and in the prosaic lyric of his poems.

We have come to a strategic point. On the one hand, Marinetti's poetry makes itself into prose; thus the famous "parole in libertà" ("mots en liberté," words in freedom) are words that reach a daring compromise with the machinery of a technological world. On the other hand, the cloudiness or gauziness of a continuous restless lyricism spreads over Marinetti's whole poetic landscape, and what happens then is that the "words" (or prosaic statements) of the technological world are liberated and become poetry.

In Marinetti's oeuvre there is no "properly" poetic area (I have already spoken of a constantly displaced lyricism). Rather, there is, before and beyond *paroliberismo* as a program, a feverish turbulence of diction in all areas of discourse. It is a vibration that (with an unembarrassment which in so many cases results in authentic poetry, sometimes in mere impatience) dispenses with certain connections of images that Symbolism had rendered traditional.

For instance, a theme that recurs throughout Marinetti's poetry is hostility toward stars, from his first publication in book form, *The Conquest of the Stars* (1902), to the *Futurist Manifesto* and beyond. At first sight this looks like a mere reversal of one of the most venerable topoi of poetic diction. But what is at work here is a more complicated process: a kind of rough anti-Kantianism, with hermetic implications.

Hostility to stars emerges in one of the first sentences of the first *Futurist Manifesto* ("in front of the army of the inimical stars") and reappears in that text's final sentence: "Standing on the top of the world, we hurl once again our challenge to the stars! . . . "[33] There is here, among other things, a sort of poetic/polemical response to Dante (the endings of all three *cantiche* of the *Comedy* are symmetrically marked by a positive evocation of stars). But even behind this move lies a more ancient and vaster archetype. It is the biblical one, constituted by one of the most enigmatic among Jesus's sayings: "The kingdom of heaven has suffered violence, and men of violence take it by force" (Matthew 11.12), which reappears in Dante (*Paradiso* XX.94).

Marinetti's aversion to the stars makes sense (that is, constructs its own peculiar poetic sense) on at least three levels: (a) impatience toward the world of nature, an impatience connected to love for the world of machines; (b) opposition to stars as emblems of a too facile and consoling idea of poetry; and (c) rebellion against the late Symbolist poets, especially Mallarmé, toward whom Marinetti felt a complex mixture of admiration and hostility.[34]

Marinetti's poetry is a poetry of, or on, esthetics—not a poetry pleased with its own esthetic arrangement. An emblem of this attitude is a sentence in prose which, however, constitutes a poetic image, and is perhaps the most frequently repeated remark on Futurist esthetics: "A racecar whose hood is adorned with big pipes, like snakes with an explosive breath . . . a roaring automobile which seems to run on machine-gun fire is more beautiful than the *Victory of Samothrace*."[35]

The strategic question here is: How can we read this sentence today? Or: In what sense can this sentence still be contemporary? I spoke above of the several layers of ambiguity in avant-garde discourse. Marinetti's work is a particularly good example of such ambiguity, because he cultivates what (above and beyond his programs) is a process of anti-analogy rather than analogy.

It is impossible, in fact, not to notice that a car can be infinitely reproduced,[36] which is not the case for the *Victory of Samothrace*. Thus Marinetti's image (con)fuses at least three different universes of discourse: (a) different forms of life; (b) different forms of *art* (classic versus modernist); and (c) different artistic *dimensions* (works that can be reproduced versus works that cannot be reproduced).

The result of all this is that the antithesis is not as sharply polarized as it at first appears; rather, what we have here is actually a mixing or blurring of distinctions. (One might also ask what would be in this context the status of a Futurist work of art representing an automobile, like the handsome painting by Luigi Russolo, *Dynamism of a Car*, at the Musée National d'Art Moderne in Paris.)

But two points especially must be underscored here. First, while the car versus winged *Victory* contrast could have a provoking and progressive value at the beginning of the century, the situation, at this turn of the century, is completely reversed. The car has become the symbol of the worst side of our contemporary situation, the side in which progress is only apparent—on the contrary, this "progress" turns out to be a form of destructive waste and regression. This consumeristic degradation is reflected in current advertising rhetoric in which the car—with a sort of ironically "poetic" justice with respect to the avant-garde's most inflated claims—has become the locus of vulgar and anti-poetic ostentation.

Second, this contrast is a confirmation (*a contrario*, to be sure, but still a confirmation) of the persisting influence and validity of Tradition. In choosing this ancient masterpiece as a term of comparison (even if it is conceived as a negative term), the avant-garde artist pays homage to it; this turns out to be a way of indirectly strengthening a whole Symbolist tradition that finds its European culmination in Gabriele d'Annunzio.[37] As proof, consider a much less known passage by Marinetti, which is, however, essential for an adequate critical understanding of this image or, better, nexus of images: "Warlike and cutting lines. The perfect state of mind during flight. All the symbols of the ancient winged Victories have disappeared. Of the Victory of Samothrace, only minuscule fragments of feathers, that the sky absorbs, float in the air. To be sure, she was machine-gunned from on high."[38]

Even in this "machine-gunned" shape, it is the *Victory of Samothrace* who has had the last word, by virtue of her peculiar nexus of absence/presence (one of the founding paradoxes of esthetics). Once again, we find continuity under the appearance of rupture and discontinuity. This nexus—dominant continuity through significantly discontinuous variations—applies not only to individual artistic personalities but, once again, to the general literary strategies of Symbolism and Futurism.[39]

Another aspect of the energization of avant-garde esthetics in Marinetti is his theory of touch, or tactilism (*tattilismo*).

> Human beings speak to each other with their mouths and eyes, but do not reach a real state of sincerity, given the insensitivity of skin, which continues to be a mediocre transmitter of thought.
>
> While eyes and voices communicate their essences to us, the touches [*tatti*] of two individuals communicate almost nothing in their knockings, interlacements or rubbings.
>
> Hence the necessity of transforming the handshake, the kiss and the act of coupling into continuous transmissions of thought.[40]

Poetic statements like this one contain synthetically a bundle or mixture of those features which give Futurism a particular and lively force in the context of the "historical" avant-gardes: (a) an intelligent and exploratory sense of paradox; (b) elements of humor and grotesqueness; (c) suggestions of broad cultural connections; and (d) esoteric aspects of Tradition.[41]

This avant-gardist energization of esthetics is apparent in the two manifesto-like prose essays in this book: *Futurist Words in Freedom* and *After Words in Freedom*. But the core of the book is constituted by the poetic selections.

The peculiar nature of Marinetti's poetic geniality is not always easy to perceive, because it runs counter to the *apparent* strategy of his poetical statements, and of Futurist discourse in general, which is (apparently, I repeat) a cult of exclusion. But, as I have already indicated, this is merely the tactical dimension. At a deeper level—thus, at the level of real strategy—Futurist discourse is a discourse of continuity and inclusion (at least, this is the component that will win out and remain a lasting intellectual acquisition).

Once this is clear, Marinetti's poetry becomes more accessible; for its distinctive feature is at bottom its broad, generous relation with literary tradition. Such a relation does not diminish originality—on the contrary. Marinetti's originality, which sets him apart from, and above, the orthodox Futurist poets, lies largely in the wide range of his literary culture. This culture allows him to develop his poetic voice without premature delusions of novelty and at the same time without fear of his predecessors. Marinetti moves without embarrassment within the great poetic traditions of France and Italy (and their international implications); this is why he can afford to be himself, as a poet.

A full analysis of Marinetti's voyage as a poet will be possible only when a complete and critically accurate bilingual edition of his works is available. In the meantime, however, the general picture can, and must, be sketched—a task to which this book makes a crucial contribution.

In its first impetuous wave (and the image of the wave is one of the strongest and most frequent in Marinetti's early poetic phase), the poetry of Marinetti recovers and develops with an original tone what may be called the broad visionary sweep in the early-modern French poetic tradition, which entertains a complex relationship with Symbolism. (This early-modern tradition, for instance, is distant from the French father of Symbolism, Baudelaire; indeed, Marinetti's poetry is resolutely a-Baudelairian.) The visionary sweep that Marinetti's early poetry embraces could be defined more precisely as a form of savage, quasi-mystical contemplation, a violently active delineation of hallucinatory vistas. Such a poetic strategy is common to such otherwise divergent poets as Lautréamont and Arthur Rimbaud. (I speak here of general genealogies, not of philological sources.) Moreover, in early poems like *The Conquest of the Stars* (1902) and *Destruction* (1904), Marinetti daringly recovers some elements of the poetic lesson transmitted by the most powerful pre-Symbolist voice in French literature, that of Victor Hugo.

This latter genealogy looks surprising at first sight, in view of the popularized image of Futurism, which seems antithetical to Romantic effusions. But we have seen how much more complex Futurism is than the vulgarized image that the movement itself sometimes cultivated; and in any case, what I am describing here is Marinetti's poetry in its peculiar originality, which cannot be metonymically reduced to the poetic programs of Futurism.

This early Marinettian poetry is in large measure a poetry of the sea, with archetypal implications that call for a critical approach in the neo-Jungian line of, for instance, Gaston Bachelard. At the same time, with a refined sense of balance, Marinetti cultivates a more intimate and delicate strain (already perceivable here and there in his first publicly acclaimed poem, "The Old Sailors" [1898]). It is a poetic vein that recalls the tone of poets like Francis Jammes—to whom Marinetti explicitly dedicates a poem—and of Italian "crepuscular" poetry. This vein reappears in Marinetti's late poetry, for instance in the *Poems to Beny* (Turin, 1971).

After this first, symbolic-natural (not naturalistic) wave, Marinetti's poetry faces the modernistic challenge of the urban landscape (see, in this book, the selections from *The Sensual City* [1908]); but it does this without renouncing its emotional personifying style, in the wake of the grand old tradition.

But Marinetti's seminal achievements as documented here are *The Pope's Monoplane* (1912) and, especially, *Zong Toomb Toomb* (published in book form in 1914 but inspired by the siege of Adrianople in 1912).[42] These long poems are crucial texts for Italian—and not only Italian—poetic modernity. No adequate history of modern Italian poetry can fail to take these Marinettian texts fully into account. What matters in these poems, beyond the technical and stylistic details, is the properly philosophical challenge that they deliver—the intellectual test which the poet puts to himself.

The importance of *The Pope's Monoplane* does not lie in the slightly sacrilegious *frisson* implicit in the title (with a felicitous reticence, Marinetti does not develop this element in the poem). Rather, the poem is important because it is one of the extremely few successful projects in modern Italian poetry (aside from d'Annunzio's great achievements in this area, and some poems by Carducci) to poetize politics.[43] The Italian landscape is not only brought to life as a natural and archeological entity (as in the poetic tradition); it is now energized as a context susceptible of political developments, a locus of struggle.

As for *Zong Toomb Toomb*, it is difficult to overestimate its importance. It is one of the definitive or definitional *poemetti* in modern-to-contemporary Italian literature—I mean, in the dynamic component of modern Italian literature that gives shape to poetical contemporaneousness in Italy. This poem was composed in the *Epochenschwelle* (threshold of an epoch) of the years immediately preceding World War I (see n. 4). In particular, 1912 was the year in which Giovanni Pascoli's death marked the end of one of the most brilliant international careers in poetical Symbolism. It was also the year in which Rainer Maria Rilke embarked upon one of the masterpieces of Symbolist poetry, the *Duino Elegies* (see n. 34). But it was also the year in which poets as diverse as Guillaume Apollinaire and Gottfried Benn (the latter with his first and perhaps most haunting verse collection, *Morgue*) began to shape the dimension of irreverently quotidian diction in contemporary poetry. And it was the year in which the historic Futurist anthology was published in Milan: Marinetti's *I poeti futuristi. Con un proclama di F. T. M., e uno studio sul verso libero di Paolo Buzzi*.

But even in this animated modernist panorama, *Zong Toomb Toomb* stands magically alone, as only great poetry can stand. It is not, I reiterate, a matter merely of linguistic experimentation. The revolutionary element here does not have primarily to do with onomatopoeias (although, significantly, one of them lends the poem its title) or with "words in freedom." The disturbingly creative effect of the poem lies, rather, in its philosophical challenge: the presentation of war as a quickening of life rather than as a process of death and destruction. The esthetic horror, or horrible esthetics, of war: this is the real theme of the *poemetto*. This is what still gives us a shock when we read *Zong Toomb Toomb* (a shock that we no longer feel, for instance, when we read another modernist masterpiece of eight years later, Eliot's *The Waste Land*).

On this theme of perturbing agitation, Marinetti will continue to work with important poetic results. But he will also modulate his voice, writing in his late period surprisingly tender lines (and arriving at a reconciliation of sorts with the once-besieged stars).

It is time to recognize that, among his multifarious activities, Filippo Tommaso Marinetti most deserves to be called, in Dante's words, "col nome che più dura e più onora" (the most enduring and most honored name; *Purgatorio* XXI.85)—the name, also, which is most naked and defenseless: the name of poet.

NOTES

1. One example will suffice for all: Aldo Palazzeschi, one of the major Italian writers of this century, declared that "the five years during which I was a part of the Futurist movement were those in my life in which I knew youth" (*Opere giovanili*, vol. 2 of *Tutte le opere di Aldo Palazzeschi* [Milan, 1958], p. 4). In his preface to Marinetti's *Teoria e invenzione futurista* (2d ed., ed. Luciano De Maria [Milan, 1990], p. xxvi), Palazzeschi wrote of "the ardor of youth which was in him spontaneous, explosive, solar, aggressive, and in the other one only as an aspiration and enjoyment," where "him" refers to Marinetti and "the other one" to Palazzeschi himself. (Here and elsewhere translations are mine unless otherwise specified.) The idea of Futurism as youthfulness appears in descriptions by other artists, such as the important writer and painter Ardengo Soffici and a minor but significant author, the Neapolitan Francesco Cangiullo. See the latter's *Le serate futuriste: Romanzo storico vissuto* (Naples, 1930; repr. 1961), a book that one still reads with pleasure for its narrative brio.

2. Once again, writers have come before professors. Giovanni Papini, one of the most remarkable Italian essayists of the twentieth century, clearly delineates the problem in the very first sentence of his short essay "Futurismo e marinettismo" (published on Feb. 14, 1915, in the journal *Lacerba* and anthologized in his *Esperienza futurista, 1913–1914* [Florence, 1919; repr. 1981]): "In Futurism there has always been a confusion between principles and personalities." But Papini's solution is inadequate: he opposes a positive "futurismo" to a negative "marinettismo," and offers superficial characterizations of both.

3. See Philippe Hunt, "Archi-avant-gardes," *Lingua e stile* 28: 2 (June 1993): 269–85.

4. This familiar landscape is surveyed in the rich essay by Hans Robert Jauss, *Die Epochenschwelle von 1912 (Guillaume Apollinaire: 'Zone' und 'Lundi rue Christine')* (Heidelberg, 1986).

5. In these as in many other aspects, Marinetti was preceded by Gabriele d'Annunzio. Indeed, under what seems at times to be a virulent anti-Dannunzian polemic, Marinetti develops Dannunzian attitudes and poetic ideas. The first writer to use Italian/French bilingualism as a real political weapon, leading the whole movement for Italian intervention side by side with France in World War I, was not a Futurist intellectual but d'Annunzio, the Symbolist poet. This shows, among other things, that Symbolism is not as etiolated and ethereal as its degraded cliché would suggest.

6. The fact that I am presenting this text in English does not contradict this reasoning—in fact, it is an ironic/dialectic confirmation of it. In translating Italian notes into English, one inscribes oneself in the transcultural tradition of Futurism. Also, when I give numbered lists of the movement's different elements, I do so simply as an aid to exposition, not in the name of a misguided scientific-structuralist ambition. One ought to preserve a light and free attitude toward taxonomies—in the spirit of François Rabelais and in that of Futurism.

7. See *The New Oxford Annotated Bible, with the Apocrypha*, expanded edition, ed. Herbert G. May and Bruce M. Metzger (New York, 1977).

8. I have sketched a non-dogmatic and non-normative vision of modernity—a vision in which the modern is neither exalted nor scorned. This perspective differs from that adopted, for instance, in Jürgen Habermas, *The Philosophical Discourse of Modernity (Twelve Lectures)* (trans. Frederick Lawrence [Cambridge, Mass., 1987]), an authoritative survey of the relevant terrain, but one which remains captive to the more or less utopian attitudes of a certain left-wing intelligentsia that finds what is different from itself "irritating" (a word that often recurs in Habermas's book).

9. See, for instance, *Apocalyptic Spirituality*, translated by Bernard McGinn, with a preface by Marjorie Reeves (New York, 1979), and the reference to Frank Kermode on p. 15.

10. From "Lettera aperta al futurista Mac Delmarle," *Teoria e invenzione*, p. 92. (Unless otherwise specified, italics in quoted passages are in the original.) This metaphor has a long history in popular traditions. One thinks, for instance, of an anonymous revolutionary song current in northern and central Italy at the time of the Socialist agitations known as the Red Week (in June 1914), which says in part: "Italy is sick / and Lenin will be its physician." Both pronouncements (the political/literary one by Marinetti and the directly political one by the Socialists) are, among other things, a late echo of the medieval topos of *Christus medicus*, which in turn has evangelical roots: "Those who are well have no need of a physician, but those who are sick" (Matthew 9.12).

11. From the "Aggiunte" to *Guerra sola igiene del mondo* (1915), a composite book of which some parts are translated in F. T. Marinetti, *Let's Murder the Moonshine: Selected Writings*, ed. R. W. Flint, trans. R. W. Flint and Arthur A. Coppotelli (Los Angeles, 1991); for this passage, see *Teoria e invenzione*, pp. 331–32. (I follow Marinetti's capitalization; ellipses not in brackets belong to his original text.) The prophetism from which Marinetti distances himself is not only that of the prophets

"del gran Nulla" (whose genealogy includes, among others, Schopenhauer and Nietzsche); it is also (implicitly but radically) the prophetism of the Good News. This position evokes the whole question of atheism (more precisely, anti-theism; or more precisely still, theophoby) in Futurism and the other avant-gardes. It is an anti-theism which does not exclude but rather encourages, in a peculiar way, a nostalgia for the sacred, as evidenced for instance by Marinetti's late Christological figurations in poetry, Breton's constant dialogue with the occult, etc. For Marinetti in particular, see his brilliant poetic prosing L'aeropoema di Gesù, composed in 1943–44 and published only recently in an edition by Claudia Salaris (Montepulciano, 1991).

12. From Il paesaggio e l'estetica futuristica della macchina (1931); see Teoria e invenzione, p. 631. This is not the only evidence that Futurism is, among other things, one of the crucial sources of science fiction.

13. From the novel Gli Indomabili (1922), one of the most important results of Marinetti's artistry in prose (see The Untameables, trans. Jeremy Parzen [Los Angeles, 1996]). Once again (see n. 11), a rebellious anti-theism emerges, especially akin to that of Lautréamont. But this anti-theism is soon transformed into something quite different—a kind of casual and savage theism. Could one speak of an avant-garde theism? I think so, but this is a matter for detailed future research.

14. The speaker is Mirmofim, one of the leaders of the "Indomabili," in the novel referred to above; see Teoria e invenzione, p. 1002. This statement is an interesting reversal of the philosophical rhetoric (of mainly Nietzschean origin) of the eternal return. Contrast with d'Annunzio's great Symbolist tragedy Fedra (1909, the year of the official founding of Futurism), in which Fedra asks the messenger (whom she calls aedo, or bard): "And which, o bard, is the time / most desirable? The past, / perhaps? The future? Tell me." The messenger replies: "Woman, what once was will return" (Tragedie, sogni e misteri, vol. 2, in Tutte le opere di Gabriele D'Annunzio, ed. Egidio Bianchetti [Milan, 1946], p. 244).

15. This is the opening paragraph of Futurismo e fascismo (1924); see Teoria e invenzione, p. 491. The rapid shift or swerve in stylistic register—from "pugni calci e schiaffi" (punches kicks slaps) to the mysticism of the "teosofi"—is typical of what is still exciting in Futuristic style. The sentence that Marinetti himself underlines appears (signed "I Teosofi") also at the beginning of the book, as its motto. Who these "teosofi" might be is not specified (an unspecificity which, after all, is in keeping with the hermetic or esoteric tradition). I have already hinted at the need for research on the relation-

ship between the avant-garde and esoteric thought (which is one of several aspects in which Marinetti anticipates André Breton). I submit in this regard a little-known and hard-to-find pamphlet by the most important—perhaps the only—thinker of the modern radical right in Italy, Julius Evola. In this discussion of artistic theory and practice, Evola (having reversed, in hermetic style, a traditional evangelical aphorism: "They do not see because they have eyes, they do not hear because they have ears" [p. 5]) develops a critique of Futurism (the Futurists were "the first among these very late Romantics" [p. 12; see also p.9]), and then remarks: "Modern art will fall very soon, and just this will be the sign of its purity; mostly it will fall because of its having been realized with an external method / because of a gradual growing of the sickness on the basis of partly passional motivations / rather than with an interior (mystical) method" (Evola, Arte astratta: Posizione teorica / 10 poemi / 4 composizioni [Rome, 1920]; emphases and slashes in the original). One notes how early a historicizing critique of Futurism arises (the appreciation of the "nuovissimi romantici"); and above all one recognizes significant intellectual connections between Futurism and its Dadaistic-mystical alternatives, as, for example, in the very notions of mysticism and "sickness" (on the latter, see n. 10 above).

16. See my Ascoltare il silenzio: La retorica come teoria (Bologna, 1986).

17. "The representation of noise becomes at times real, objective noise," writes Tristan Tzara, reviewing a poetry collection in the journal Dada 4–5 (May 1919); see Tzara, Manifesti del dadaismo, e lampisterie, ed. Giampiero Posani (Turin, 1970), p. 54. Critical hints for a future study of silence in modernism can be found in Frederick R. Karl, Modern and Modernism: The Sovereignty of the Artist, 1885–1925 (New York, 1988), esp. pp. 29–33.

18. See Marinetti's "Prefazione futurista a 'Revolverate' di Gian Pietro Lucini," Teoria e invenzione, p. 28.

19. See, for instance, the article by Carsten Colpe, "The Sacred and the Profane," in The Encyclopedia of Religion, ed. Charles J. Adams et al. (New York, 1987). See also, in the classic book on this subject, Otto's remark on the holy as "a category of interpretation and valuation," which is peculiar to religion but is "applied by transference to another sphere—that of ethics" (Rudolf Otto, Das Heilige [1917]; translated by John W. Harvey as The Idea of the Holy [London, 1923], p. 5). An intelligent early attempt (which, as was to be expected, André Breton immediately rejected) to apply this kind of analysis to the poetic language of modernism is Jules Monnerot, La Poésie moderne et le sacré (Paris, 1945). Of particular interest are the idea (merely

hinted at in the short "Statement to the Reader") of an "essai d'histoire de la sensibilité, certes, mais aussi de philosophie appliquée" (essay in the history of sensitivity, to be sure, but also an essay in applied philosophy) and the remark that "la présence ou l'absence de la faculté mystique se joue du contenu manifeste des conceptions régnantes et des vicissitudes apparentes de l'histoire des idées" (the presence or absence of the mystical faculty eludes the most readily available content of dominant notions and the apparent ups and downs in the history of ideas) (p. 159; the entire sentence is italicized in the original).

20. This exclamation is found in what is, together with the already cited novel *Gli Indomabili*, the most important narrative contribution by Marinetti, the novel *Mafarka il futurista* (1910; originally written in French, 1909); see *Teoria e invenzione*, p. 264. (The original version has been reprinted as F.-T. Marinetti, *Mafarka le futuriste* [Paris, 1984].)

21. From the *Manifesto tecnico della letteratura futurista* (1912); see *Teoria e invenzione*, p. 53.

22. The late-Romantic esthetic of ugliness extends also to philosophy and criticism. The most important example is the 1853 book by Karl Rosenkranz, *Ästhetik des Hässlichen* (facsimile repr. Darmstadt, 1979; see also the Italian edition, *Estetica del brutto*, ed. Remo Bodei [Bologna, 1984]).

23. The one who really develops a poetic view of this dark nexus is Bataille, although in his text he never speaks directly about poetry and even changes the reference in the title. See his *L'Impossible* ([Paris, 1962]; translated by Robert Hurley as *The Impossible* [San Francisco, 1991]); the first edition of 1947 was titled *La Haine de la poésie*. This harrowing prose poem evokes the existential and spiritual processes that actually nourish poetry. By contrast, André Breton's *Misère de la poésie: "L'Affaire Aragon" devant l'opinion publique* (Paris, 1932) is an ideological pamphlet riddled with contradictions, and the long poem reprinted in it (Aragon's "Front Rouge") is a late Futurist echo with a superimposed Marxist ideology.

24. See, for instance, Chaim Wyrszubski, *Pico della Mirandola's Encounter with Jewish Mysticism* (Cambridge, Mass., 1989).

25. This qualification is necessary to distinguish Marinetti and the other fully integrated Futurist poets from the movement's temporary "fellow-travelers," because it is to the latter category that belong two of the most important poets of the early twentieth century in Italy, poets for whom the Futurist movement is crucial but whose range finally transcends the Futurist program and its rhetoric: Aldo Palazzeschi and Corrado Govoni.

26. This does not mean, of course, that one can afford to disregard the study of all other Futurist poets, men and women (see the anthology *Le Futuriste: Donne e letteratura d'avanguardia in Italia* [1909–1944], ed. Claudia Salaris [Milan, 1982]). Indeed, such a detailed study is indispensable to an understanding of the history of twentieth-century Italian poetry.

27. He vainly tried to enroll the aging Pascoli in the Futurist ranks. As for d'Annunzio, Marinetti's critical attitude toward him was complicated and shifting. It never degenerated into the envious superficiality of so many anti-Dannunzian intellectuals in those and later years. His book *Les Dieux s'en vont, D'Annunzio reste* (Paris, 1908) is an interestingly impressionistic narrative, in which the Dannunzian mimesis oscillates between anxiety and admiration. (The title itself is significantly ambiguous, something between irony and appreciation.) See also *D'Annunzio intime* (Milan, 1903).

28. Here, and elsewhere, I cite successively (where appropriate) Marinetti's original French titles and their Italian versions, separating the two with a dash. By "organizer of spectacles," I refer to a vast range of Marinettian activities: he functioned as producer, dramaturge, organizer of "serate futuriste," dramatic reader of his own and other people's poetry, organizer of political demonstrations, inspirer of radio broadcasts and films, etc. For some of these phenomena, see Giovanni Antonucci, *Cronache del teatro futurista* (Roma, 1975). See also F. T. Marinetti, *Teatro*, 3 vols., ed. Giovanni Calendoli (Rome, 1960).

29. The most interesting documentation of such activity, besides collections of correspondence (e.g., F. T. Marinetti and Aldo Palazzeschi, *Carteggio*, ed. Paolo Prestigiacomo [Milan, 1978]), is the thick volume *Taccuini 1915–1921*, ed. Alberto Bertoni (Bologna, 1987). But much should be added, drawing on both published works and unpublished papers. It would be interesting to develop a comparative and rhetorical study of notebooks in this period. Such a study should include at least, besides the cited Marinettian texts, the great models in this genre, which are d'Annunzio's notebooks (see *Taccuini*, ed. Enrica Bianchetti and Roberto Forcella [Milan, 1965], and *Altri taccuini*, ed. Enrica Bianchetti [Milan, 1976]) and those by the most important, and sinister, nonliterary interlocutor of both d'Annunzio and Marinetti (see *Taccuini mussoliniani*, ed. Yvon De Begnac, with preface by Renzo De Felice and introduction by Francesco Perfetti [Bologna, 1990]).

30. I do not mean to erect barriers between the fluid genres I have been listing. But nuanced distinctions are necessary, in one form or another, in order to do justice to the complexity of the texts. The category "journal" may be ap-

plied to activities that range from epistolography (because of the "journal," or daily, rhythm that the rhetoric of letter writing refers to) to that peculiar literary genre, the "notebook." The prose of remembrance, on the other hand, works on recollections, chiseling them until they enter the sphere of fiction. Memoir writing follows an opposite path, focusing and narrowing the activity of memory (witness the different connotation of the two terms, whose etymology is essentially the same, memory and memoir in English), so that it may be employed in projects of documentation with polemic (and thereby partially political), ideological, and apologetic implications.

31. L'alcova d'acciaio has recently been republished (Milan, 1985) as part of a resurgence of interest in Marinetti's work. Such a trend should of course be welcomed; but it is still rather confusedly scattered, in the absence both of a complete critical edition of the writings and of a general critical hypothesis and contextualization of Marinetti's work. A significant part of this renewed interest is the analysis of Marinetti's life and times—a recent contribution to which is Gino Agnese's Marinetti: Una vita esplosiva (Milan, 1990). A curious biographical contribution is the "Futuristic" narrative in comicbook style by Pablo Echaurren, Caffeina d'Europa: Vita di F. T. Marinetti (Montepulciano, 1988).

32. On the notion and the development of poetic prosing, see chap. 7 of my Gabriele d'Annunzio: The Dark Flame (New Haven, 1992).

33. See Teoria e invenzione, pp. 9 and 14.

34. One of the most significant alternatives to Marinetti's anti-star verse is the Symbolist poetry of Rilke, especially the Duino Elegies. Let one example suffice: "[. . .]— but also the nights! the high summer nights, / the nights and the stars, the stars of the earth. / Oh, to be dead at last and know all the stars, / forever! Then how, how, how could you forget them!" These are lines 26–29 of the Seventh Elegy—a poem in which one of the basic sense dimensions is what could be called the anti-Futuristic one: "For even the immediate future is far from mankind. This / shouldn't confuse us; no, it should commit us to preserve / the form we still can recognize" (ll. 65–67; see Rilke, Duino Elegies and the Sonnets to Orpheus, trans. A. Poulin, Jr. [Boston, 1977]). As for Mallarmé, see Versi e prose di Stefano Mallarmé, trans. F. T. Marinetti (Milan, 1916).

35. From the first Futurist Manifesto; see Teoria e invenzione, p. 10. Futurism deserves a special chapter in a future history of the Italian language—both the general standard language in its social and political dimensions, and the specific language of literature. One of the points to be addressed in such a study should be the psychological and stylistic implications of the masculine gender that the word automobile possesses at this point in the history of Futurist usage. (Later, automobile will become feminine also in Futurist texts—and this latter is of course the only grammatical possibility in contemporary Italian; the oscillation between the masculine and the feminine gender of automobile is to be found as well in French usage of this period.) It is the masculine gender which gives a lively semantic value to the twice-repeated comparison in the Manifesto between a car and a shark—a fish of masculine gender and connotation in Italian: "[. . .] to fish out my car, which looked like a large stranded shark [. . . .] They thought it was dead, my beautiful shark" (see Teoria e invenzione, p. 9).

36. One immediately thinks of Walter Benjamin's Das Kunstwerk im Zeitalter seiner technischen Reproduzierbarkeit (1936), an English translation of which, "The Work of Art in the Age of Mechanical Reproduction," is in Benjamin's Illuminations, trans. Harry Zohn, ed. Hannah Arendt (New York, 1978). That text contains, in its "Nachwort" (pp. 42–44 of the German edition), the often-quoted contrast (based on a vague reference to Marinetti) between the "estheticization of politics" which is attributed to Fascism and the "politicization of art" which is regarded as characteristic of progressive, and particularly Marxist, movements. This contrast, for all its ponderous rehearsals (see, for instance, Russell A. Berman, "The Aestheticization of Politics: Walter Benjamin on Fascism and the Avant-Garde," Stanford Italian Review 8:1–2 [1990]: 35–82), today looks embarrassing, to say the least, for its proponents.

37. I do not refer simply to the picturesque lore of d'Annunzio's life (a reproduction of the Victory can still be seen in what used to be d'Annunzio's study in his palatial mansion, the Vittoriale) but to the logic of his poetry. But the passage I want to recall here belongs to a much less known, and yet significant, link in the hermetic/esthetic genealogy of Tradition: "N'as-tu-pas vu briller au regard de Saint Jean la subtilité même? la Samothrace: t'as-t-elle pas parlé, la niké surhumaine?" (Didn't you see subtlety itself sparkling in the eyes of Saint John? Didn't the Samothrace speak to you, the superhuman Victory?) (This is the esoteric novelist Joséphin [i.e., Joseph] Péladan, in his "Prélude" to La Queste du Graal [Proses lyriques de l'éthopée:'La Décadence latine'] [Paris, 1892].)

38. From Il paesaggio e l'estetica futuristica della macchina (1931). It is the description of an "aerosculpture" by the artist Thayaht (see Teoria e invenzione, p. 635).

39. Indeed, this image of the Victory of Samothrace is an apt focus for the study of the connections between the Symbol-

ist and Futurist imaginations. In the second of Marinetti's passages, the ornithological aspect is underscored. If the wings of the *Victory* seen as compact sculptural masses belong to the rhetoric of the sublime, these same wings, when they let fall "minuscule fragments of feathers," make one think of a bird, thus creating a slightly grotesque, or magical-realist, effect that recalls certain fantastic bird images in the paintings of Alberto Savinio (Andrea De Chirico). Also from the archetypological point of view: in the first Marinettian quote, the image of the hood of the car "adorned with big pipes, like snakes with an explosive breath" juxtaposes—with a suggestively mythologizing and syncretistic effect—the image of Medusa with that of the Nike, or Victory.

40. From *Il tattilismo* (1921); see *Teoria e invenzione*, p. 161. See also Marinetti, *Let's Murder the Moonshine*, pp. 117–20.

41. As for point (b), suffice it to quote: "To express the buttocks-and-backs sensitivity of the volunteers (tactilism), which substitutes the facial (visual, auditory) sensitivity" (from "Decollaggio," which serves as a preface to the *Aeropo-ema del Golfo della Spezia* [1935]; this directive is the fourteenth in a list of twenty-two items that are supposed to be a kind of protocol for "aeropoets"; see *Teoria e invenzione*, p. 1102). With regard to point (c), it would be interesting to study the genealogical connections between Marinetti's poetic theory of tactilism and Bernard Berenson's art-critical theory of "tactile values." As for point (d), finally, Marinetti's "continuous transmissions of thought" are genealogically connected to the parascientific rhetoric of Mesmerism, which is one of the basic sources of fantastic narrative at the turn of the eighteenth and nineteenth century. This idea also has serious implications for mysticism.

42. In French, *Zang toumb toumb*; in the Italian, *Zang Tumb Tumb*—but also *Zang Tumb Tuuum*; and at least six other variant spellings began to circulate very early. This is an indication of the task that a future critical edition of Marinetti's poetry will face.

43. On the literature of politics, see my *Gabriele d'Annunzio*.

Original Texts of the Poems

Les vieux marins

A Gustave Kahn

Un soir qu'il faisait rouge
En un port glauque, fleurant le musc et les embruns,
Le vieux couchant meurtri
Traînait au fond des bouges son angoisse sénile,
Et son sang purulait
Tragiquement, au cœur des vitres mortes.
– Un soir qu'il faisait rouge...

De voix sourdes houlaient
Au ras des flots, sur la marée,
Et des âmes pleuraient, lointaines et bleues,
Au glas morne des cloches...
On enterrait un mort.
Qui sait? Quelqu'un là-bas le long du port...
Parmi les cierges blêmes...
Les cierges ingénus pleuraient et souriaient
Comme des enfants qui viennent
Le soir au cimetière
Parmi les tombes noires fleuries de primevères,
De roses rouges et de bleuets;
Et l'on rêvait, là-bas, au fond des bouges...
– Un soir qu'il faisait brun...

Et l'on rêvait à celles qui sont mortes
Là-bas, on ne sait où, et qui savaient sourire,
Le soir, quand les marins s'en revenaient
Du large et des tempêtes.
Et les vieillards disaient, marmonnant des prières:

« Elles passèrent hier à la tombée du soir,
Elles passèrent portant sur la tête leurs urnes
Pleines du sang des crépuscules morts.
Elles passèrent hautaines,
Là-bas, près des fontaines.
Elles étaient blanches et presque nues,
La robe dégrafée, avec sur les seins doux
Les larmes et les joyaux du soir.
Oh ! elles étaient belles, ardentes et pâlies,
Comme les jours lointains de la jeunesse ».
Et les vieillards se turent,
Parmi le glas des cloches qui se fanait au ciel,
Songeant aux lèvres pâles de ces mortes
Qui chantaient autrefois au seuil bruni des portes,
A leurs lèvres de miel, à leurs âmes exhalées
Qui s'en allèrent un soir comme des voiles ardentes
Voguant au large des crépuscules d'or.
Et parmi les vieillards une voix brune pleura:
« Mon fils, te souviens-tu de la vitre brisée
Que nous trouvâmes, près de son lit, quand elle fut
        morte? »
Et les marins assis au seuil de leurs portes,
Faisaient en frissonnant le signe de la croix.
Leurs prunelles viraient au large de la mer
Un soir qu'il faisait noir...
Là-bas, au fond des bouges,
Leurs prunelles tanguaient comme des barques lasses
Cherchant l'azur et les espaces...

Comme des vieilles barques humant le ciel
Vaste et l'océan...
Des barques un peu folles et qui ne veulent pas
Mourir parmi les algues du rivage
Des barques amoureuses des flots et des étoiles.
– Un soir qu'il faisait noir...

Cruellement les girouettes
Vrillaient les ors brunis du nocturne silence,
Et les vents qui trompettent
Narguaient au loin le râle immense
Des cahutes fumeuses et leur bruit de squelettes
Et leurs pleurs infinis et leurs abois de chiens
Qui luttent contre la houle noire.
– Un soir qu'il faisait noir...

Éperdument,
Les vents chantaient comme des cors
Sur l'entonnoir des ports:
« Virez, virez au large, vieilles prunelles lasses,
Virez au large des écueils, loin des sables perfides...
Virez sur l'infini, âmes épuisées, barques mourantes,
Prunelles sans espoir !...
Vous qui souffrez de vivre et de si lentement mourir,
Prunelles assoiffées d'infini et d'espace,
Virez sur l'horizon des vagues rutilantes,
O barques qui tanguez parmi le remous noir,
Prunelles désolées, barques mourantes !...
Vous qui flambiez au temps jadis
Hissant vos voiles d'or
Sur les royales pourpres des aurores,
Virez, virez au large, virez sur l'infini ! »
Les vents gonflés d'or et de nuit
Râlèrent éperdument comme des cors
Et moururent à jamais dans l'espace.

Alors les cloches frêles eurent des mots suaves
Et redirent tout bas l'âpre chanson des vents
De leurs lèvres fanées de béguines mourantes :

« Virez, virez sur l'infini, âmes épuisées ! »
Mais la nuit était lasse...
La nuit les bâillonna tout doucement, dans l'ombre...
Et leurs lèvres de bronze, ivres de soir et de tristesse
Frémirent à jamais sous les mains de la nuit...
« Virez, virez sur l'infini ! »

La Conquête des Étoiles

Poème épique

I
LE CHANT AUGURAL DES VAGUES

« Hola-hé ! Hola-hé ! Hola-ho!
O Vagues antiques, ô Vétérans de la Mer Souveraine,
debout, guerriers puissants aux barbes vénérables
    d'écume !
Debout ! Debout, nos frères ! Aiguisons nos rapières
pour la grande bataille. Revêtons nos pesantes
armures d'or, incrustées d'émeraudes
que la mousse et la rouille dévorent !
Hola-hé ! Hola-ho ! Stridionla Stridionla
    Stridionlaire !
Nous sommes las de dormir au fond des grottes
    bleues,
encastrés comme des gemmes colossales dans
    les pierres.
Nous sommes las de grignoter les brise-lames
et de croquer au large les escadres.
L'heure est venue de conquérir l'espace et de monter
à l'assaut des Étoiles. Elles ricanent !
Les voyez-vous ? C'est le défi, mes frères !
Bientôt, demain, ce soir peut-être,
La Mer, la flagellante Mer, viendra vociférer
ses lourds commandements que scande le tonnerre !
Hola-hé ! Hola-hoo ! Aiguisons nos rapières !
Que nos armures d'or resplendissent !...
Stridionla Stridionla Stridionlaire ! »

Qui donc chante aussi lugubrement
à pic, sous les falaises géantes ?
A mes pieds s'approfondit un gouffre immense,
un entonnoir d'ombre glauque qui fume.
Des Vagues aux panses flasques tordent
leurs croupes de poix gluante et de bitume.
Elles soulèvent leurs épaules montueuses,
toutes bosselées de lueurs intermittentes,
en déroulant leurs bras musclés de racines verdâtres.
D'une voix lente qui gargouille, les Vagues chantent
l'hymne augural des batailles célestes,
parmi les grincements et les stridences des rapières,
« Hola hé ! Hola ho ! Stridionla Stridionlaire ! »

Les Vagues par instants s'abattent de fatigue
entrechoquant les roches monstrueuses
avec des sons de cloches ; les Vagues s'abattent
avec des pesanteurs d'hippopotames,
avec des hurlements et des huées
et des tapées violentes de pioches et de marteaux.
    « Stridionla Holahé !
Stridionla Stridionla Holahooo !
    Debout ! Aiguisons nos rapières ! »

Au large, le Désespoir des solitudes écrase
la mer toute encombrée de cendre et d'écume,
comme un cimetière immense dévasté
dont les tombes verdoyantes s'écroulent ;

et la mer s'abandonne livide et croupissante
dans le jaune renfoncement de l'aube.
L'aube est brisée de lassitude !
L'Aube est soûle encore
du baiser vénéneux des Étoiles !
          « Stridionla ! Stridionla Stridionlaire ! »
Au loin les promontoires dorment accoudés,
dans la torpeur humide et le silence intense,
leurs crânes chevelus, abandonnés sur la mer plate.
Des écueils accroupis, aux aguets,
forment des noyaux d'ombre violette,
tandis que des vaguettes, plus souples que des chattes
taquinent à coups de patte des pelotes d'écume.

A pic sous mes pieds, dans le gouffre qui fume,
les Vagues métalliques se balancent
d'avant en arrière, pareilles
aux crémaillères formidables de l'enfer.
Et ce sont leurs armures qu'elles balancent
en cadence, pour les polir,
sur l'arête des rochers noirs.
Ce sont leurs armures squamées d'or qui bruissent
et leurs jambières et leurs brassards de bronze !
Holahé ! lentement, holahoo ! à miracle,
les rapières s'aiguisent et les mailles reluisent.
Des Vagues boueuses se dressent menaçantes,
émergeant à mi-corps hors des embruns grisâtres.
Leurs prunelles de diamant jaune éclatent
dans la buée, cependant que d'autres Vagues
plus flasques et plus pesantes,
traînassant derrière elles des crinières
d'algues somnolentes,
soulèvent leur face rouge et coriacée
et se cabrent d'un coup de reins inattendu.
Et voilà campé, debout, leur corps gluant et enfumé,
leur grand corps de centaure,
embreloqué de coraux et de cailloux qui sonnent !
Elles brandissent au bout du bras vers la lumière
leurs cuirasses d'or toutes ocellées de gemmes,

puis elles hochent en cadence
leurs têtes exaspérées de sauvagesses,
en criant: « Stridionla ! Stridionlaire ! »

Dans la crique profonde toute enfumée d'embrun,
Guerriers et Guerrières, s'enivrent à déchaîner
le tonnerre de leurs poumons d'airain,
si bien que des rictus tétaniques tiraillent
leurs vastes mâchoires disloquées.
Quand tout à coup, sur l'arc de l'horizon,
par-delà un monceau de nuées qui tressaillent,
la lumière dégaine
ses épées étincelantes en auréole.
Le soleil va bondir sur le champ de bataille !
Holahé ! les métaux entassés dans le gouffre
commencent à trépider d'une fièvre fulgurante,
pêle-mêle, en le tohu-bohu des fumées noires.

Certes, les Vagues ont soulevé, à tour de bras,
les dalles de porphyre qui recouvrent l'abîme ;
certes le couvercle de l'enfer
fut défoncé, car une armée de démons
se déchaîne au fond du gouffre et surgit
et s'élance vers le faîte, une marée
de lances miroitantes bouillonne,
et la crique fume, volumineusement,
comme une cuve colossale.

Alors victorieusement le Soleil
enjambe l'horizon et larde la mer vaste
d'une estafilade d'or vermeil.

Et voilà, presqu'aussitôt que des nuages
verdâtres se profilent, tout tigrés de feu,
qui vont fouillant l'espace, avec des trompes
chimériques d'éléphants.
Où vont-ils ? Où vont-ils ? C'est le Vent
qui s'en va pâturer son troupeau de Cyclones.
Au loin dans les herbages fantastiques de la mer,

s'allongent des meuglements lugubres.
         « Holahé ! Holahooo !
Stridionla ! Stridionlaire ! !
L'heure est venue de la conquête des Étoiles !
Brandissons nos rapières comme un faisceau
         de flammes!
Nous avons détruit, à coups de hache,
la mousse des nuits et la rouille des crépuscules
sur nos cuirasses d'acier,
qui flambent maintenant ainsi que des brasiers.
Nos casques sont cimés de feu et nos bras sont tendus
comme des courroies de catapultes.

Holahé ! Holahoo ! Hurrah !

Nos grands chevaux sont prêts. Regardez !...
leurs croupes crénelées et véhémentes
sont enharnachées d'azur et de béryls.
Ils quoaillent tranquillement, en paissant dans
         les prairies
herbues de l'espace, faisant sonner
leurs freins souples de rayons
et leurs baves de pierreries.
Nous les attellerons bientôt à des chariots géants,
pour transporter nos cargaisons de projectiles:
tous les cadavres pétrifiés qui s'entassent
depuis des siècles dans les profondeurs des eaux.
Et d'ornière en ornière, en des cahots tragiques,
les chariots bondiront sur leurs grosses roues pleines,
transportant des monceaux d'or et de phosphore
         humain,
que plus tard les Cyclones rangés lanceront
contre vous, Étoiles ricanantes et perfides !
Oui, oui. C'est contre vous, que les Cyclones
         puissants
lanceront tous les cadavres pétrifiés de l'abîme,
les cadavres de vos amants méprisés !

Holahé ! Holahoo ! Hurrah !...

Car ce sont là tes projectiles, ô Mer Souveraine !
Les cadavres pétrifiés qui dorment symétriques
en tes abîmes ! Les Savants ont déclaré
qu'ils se gonflent et se dissolvent en pourriture.
Les Savants l'ont prouvé ! Qu'importe? Leur science
         est vaine !
Regardez leurs Syllogismes qui se démènent,
         dégingandés,
en cheveux blancs, sous leur bonnet pointu de mage
qui nargue les nuages !
Regardez leurs Syllogismes, dont le vieux corps
         prolixe,
en forme d'X, est tôt ouvert et tôt fermé,
à volonté, tel un pliant commode,
qu'un chasseur bedonnant peut porter sous le bras !
Les Syllogismes dégingandés dansent en rond,
autour des Vérités mignonnes et bleues,
prises de vertige et se fermant les yeux !
         Ah ! Ah !
Les graciles Vérités ainsi que des fillettes
se pâment d'épouvante, dès qu'un savant les touche,
et disparaissent par enchantement
en laissant leurs voiles d'or entre leurs mains
         farouches !
         Ah ! Ah !
Esclaffez-vous, belles Vagues ! Esclaffez-vous
d'un vaste rire adamantin jusqu'aux étoiles !
Que votre rire éblouissant lézarde
les voûtes du Silence !
Car, regardez donc, les Syllogismes impuissants
en cheveux blancs, cassés en deux, lèchent les traces
des fascinantes Vérités qui passent insaisissables !

Je ne crois plus qu'en mon grand Rêve illuminant
         de phare !
Je ne crois plus qu'en sa prunelle énorme d'or,
comme une lune d'août,
qui vagabonde aux profondeurs des Nuits !

II
LES RÉSERVOIRS DE LA MORT

Voici ! Midi éclate: un fastueux midi d'Été !
Je descends à pas lents dans la crique incendiée
qui flambe, comme une solfatare ;
je colle mon visage sur tes joues fraîches
et transparentes, ô Mer ; j'abandonne mon corps
sur ta poitrine qui palpite endolorie,
sous le poids des turquoises brûlantes,
et j'explore les puits vertigineux
de tes prunelles merveilleuses.
Je vois s'approfondir en tes eaux translucides
un admirable crépuscule verdâtre.
A mille coudées, sous mes yeux, se dessinent
des montagnes bleuâtres dont les fines arêtes
oscillent en déclinant, des montagnes
gazées de vapeurs incandescentes.
Et dans ce crépuscule submergé,
une longue chaîne de montagnes pyramidales
se déroule au gré de la pénombre.
La distance ennuage les arêtes des plus lointaines,
qui paraissent là-bas, sur l'arc fondu
de l'horizon sous-marin, tels des cônes bleus
cimés de flammes lisses couleur de rose.
Et les flammes flexueuses obéissent
à l'ondulation des remous,
si bien qu'on les prendrait pour des lampes
     vagabondes
dans l'assoupissement d'un vaste soir d'Été.

Suis-je halluciné ? Non !... non ! je m'abandonne
sur ta poitrine, ô mer, et je baise tes joues
pour explorer la profondeur de tes prunelles,
tandis que les Midis font crouler
sur ma tête leur avalanche de blocs d'or broyés.
Le fracas effrayant du silence horrifié
emplit mon cœur et je sens, dans mon crâne,
les chariots géants de la lumière aux roues de fer

creusant leurs ornières symétriques.
Quand je soulève ma tête, j'admire,
par-delà la paresse des collines marines,
les vastes golfes gorgés d'azur aveuglant
et de chaux vive, qui soufflent vers le large
des voix volutantes et globuleuses d'or.
Je vous écoute et je vous reconnais,
ô grandes voix belliqueuses et vengeresses,
qui charriez des fracas de caissons et des ronrons
de cloches en allègresse et des bruissements d'épées !
    Stridionla ! Stridionla ! Stridionlaire !
    Holahé ! Holahoo ! Aiguisons nos rapières !
Je vous écoute, ô Vagues, et mon âme se grise
au bruissement gazeux de vos manteaux d'écume !...
Au large, passent des chevauchées véhémentes
de Vagues, tels des tourbillons innombrables de
     pourpre
et d'or, balayant l'immensité.
C'est ainsi que passe le Simoun,
aiguillonnant sa furie, de désert en désert,
avec son escorte caracolante
de sables soulevés tout ruisselants de feu ;
c'est ainsi que le Simoun galope
sur l'océan figé des sables,
en balançant son torse géant d'idole barbare
sur des fuyantes croupes d'onagres affolés !

Au large, passent des escadrons de Vagues,
par chevauchées véhémentes et radieuses,
et je songe à l'horizon de sables embrasés,
où passe le Simoun poussant à fond de train,
à toute folie, ses onagres et ses zèbres diaboliques
crêtés de flammes, qui semblent,
crispés au loin par la vitesse,
des traits de plume horizontaux sur la pâleur du ciel.
Le soleil a lancé tous ses dards en pluie d'or
contre l'immense cavalerie des Vagues.
Des guerriers ont faufilé leurs épées étincelantes
du haut en bas, par les grilles, les meurtrières

et les créneaux des nuages, pour leur barrer la route
par une herse flamboyante !
Mais les fiers escadrons passent insouciants,
et les dards du soleil volent en éclats sanglants,
et ses épées, pliées en deux, ne font que balayer
le dos souple des Vagues en peignant les crinières.
Ah ! les dieux hautains qui hantent les Midis
piétinent mon crâne et défoncent mon cœur
sous leurs pieds chaussés d'airain,
et j'implore pitié sur tes yeux, douce Mer
        Souveraine !
Suis-je fou? Suis-je halluciné ?
Non ! non !... Voici que je replonge mes regards
en tes abîmes... Au fond, tout au fond,
le beau soir submergé a clarifié sa solitude.
C'est la pureté agonisante d'un ciel d'orient,
abandonné par la lumière, et qui se meurt
irréparablement désespéré au fond des eaux.
Un soir pâle enfiévré de désir,
plein d'une amertume auguste et résignée,
un soir magique, frais et profond
comme un puits d'azur
apparu au fond d'une margelle de nuages,
puits de larmes et d'étoiles !
Tout à coup, l'énorme chaîne de montagnes
noyées me révèle son essence tragique.
Je vois et je comprends: ce sont des pyramides
de cadavres entassés, dont les crânes serrés
forment les gradins vastes et grenus.
Les chevelures pendent comme des algues
sur les arêtes phosphorescentes.
On dirait des pyramides de boulets embrasés
et fumants. Des millions de visages
révulsés vers le ciel, exorbitant les yeux haineux
contre le zénith ! Des milliards de prunelles
aiguisées sur la pointe des astres,
prunelles acérées par la colère et pourtant
liquéfiées en des tristesses infinies !
Au-dessus de moi, sur ma tête bourdonnante,

par la fournaise exaltée des Midis
passe le triomphal cortège des Conquérants
de la lumière. Au loin, les anses concaves,
pleines de l'encre bleuâtre de l'ombre,
ouvrent leurs goulets, comme des bouches humant
        l'espace.
Ce sont des soupiraux d'où monte un bruit d'épées
et des voix qui ululent : « Holahé ! Holahooo ! »
Les savants ont déclaré que les cadavres brûlent
tout leur phosphore avant de se dissoudre
en pourriture somptueuse. Non ! Les savants ont tort,
car voici, je contemple des corps pétrifiés,
des corps d'acier, de braise et d'or
plus durs que le diamant !
Ce sont les suicidés, ceux dont le courage
a défailli, sous le poids de leur cœur,
fournaise d'étoiles ! Ils sont morts
d'avoir attisé dans leur sang le feu de l'Idéal,
la grande flamme enveloppante de l'Absolu !
Ils sont morts d'avoir cru aux promesses des Étoiles.
O Divins creusets d'Astres !
O vénérables lingots d'or astral ! Regardez !
Regardez, leurs chevelures phosphoreuses
s'immensifient comme des comètes !

O dieux tout-puissants de l'Espace,
suis-je fou? Ne vois-je pas tout simplement
un reflet pâlissant des Voies lactées ?
Non! non! Ô mon âme, confie-toi en ton rêve,
car Midi plane dans l'immensité !
Le vaste bloc des Midis éclate sur ma tête
en quartiers de métal incandescent.
Je suis penché sur les joues de la Mer
et je contemple, oui ! le prestigieux
crépuscule submergé et ses montagnes
vindicatives ! et les cadavres symétriques,
et leurs vives chevelures qui, depuis des siècles,
éventent des visages métallisés.
A travers l'immensité verdâtre,

les pyramides submergées regardent le zénith,
de toutes leurs prunelles démentes.
Toutes ces faces vertes guettent le ciel stupide,
la Nuit sorcière et ses Étoiles de luxure
et l'Infini !

Viendra ! Viendra l'heure des vengeances,
songent-ils lugubrement, où nous serons saisis
par les immenses bras des Cyclones
et brandis par les machines de la Mer
et lancés, férocement lancés,
contre les remparts où rêvent les Étoiles de saphir !
Nos crânes durcis par le Désir
cliquetteront aux doigts des Trombes
comme castagnettes, nos crânes entrechoqués
sonneront, ainsi que des tambours frénétiques,
sur les tréteaux arlequinés des foires !
Nous aiguiserons nos prunelles inassouvies,
les unes sur les autres,
jusqu'à la cuisson rouge du délire !
Écoutez ! écoutez !... les Vagues chantent plus fort :
« Holahé ! Holahoo ! Stridionla ! Stridionlaire ! »
Demain, ce soir peut-être, la Flagellante Mer
viendra vociférer ses lourds commandements !
Déjà les troupeaux de ses chevaux hennissants
encombrent l'horizon de leur piaffe sonore.

V

LA MER SOUVERAINE

Une forme noire se dessina, grandissante au loin,
qui montait sur l'arc de l'horizon.
Elle se profila comme un dos de baleine
lancée à toute vitesse vers la plage ;
puis elle assuma la forme d'une île entièrement
couverte de forêts, qui allait se hérissant
de plus en plus de clochers noirs, d'obélisques
     pointus

et de prolixes cheminées, aux fumées volutantes.
Mirage ! Une énorme face anguleuse et olivâtre
sortit toute ruisselante des eaux.
Une face, aux méplats puissants de roches visqueuses,
sous une vaste chevelure liquide
soulevée et jaillissante en auréole noire !
Et cette chevelure bondissant autour d'elle
inondait le ciel ; et c'étaient des torrents
de poix, galopant en amont de l'espace,
et ruisselant à rebours pour remonter leur lit ;
Et mon Rêve reconnut avec effroi,
l'énorme face spongieuse de la Mer Souveraine !
Ses prunelles flambaient en pelotes de phosphore,
dénouant ses regards tels des nœuds de couleuvres,
et sa bouche s'ouvrait en forme de ventouse.

La Mer Souveraine se dressa à mi-corps
sur l'horizon; elle tordit d'un coup de reins
sa croupe saure et gluante de cétacé.
Puis en mouvant ses hanches massives,
la Mer révolutionna, à l'infini des côtes,
l'immense déploiement de ses vastes draperies
de houles, qu'Elle porte attachées à sa taille nue,
comme une traîne somptueuse.
Et toute la draperie des eaux mouvantes
bouillonna, gorgée d'épées, d'éclairs et de cuirasses.

La Mer Souveraine planta droit dans les abîmes
ses bras géants de fumées jaunes, ses bras
tout musclés de tourbillonnants boas.
Et cambrée, soutenant sur ses poings
son corps de Titan, les seins glauques
pointés en avant, Elle secoua
sur l'horizon sa croupe luisante et sculptée
continuellement par le déchaînement des nerfs.

Toute sa croupe colossale et mouvante parut,
dont la surface s'effrangeait sans cesse,
sinueuse, ondoyante et prête à se dissoudre.

Et ses hanches arrondies démesurément
déferlaient sur l'horizon,
ainsi qu'une montagne qui s'écroule.
La Mer Souveraine tendit en avant
le losange de sa face spongieuse
dont les orbites sont pareilles à des trous
de serpents, sous le jaillissement noirâtre
de la vaste chevelure bondissante
qui par instants la submergeait complètement.
Mais elle apparaissait énorme et fatidique
de nouveau, et toujours, la grande Face
olivâtre et ruisselante !...
Or donc, comme Elle ouvrit soudain toutes grandes
ses mâchoires délabrées,
le couchant écarlate flamba
dans son vaste gosier d'airain :
« Aux armes ! Aux armes ! hurla-t-elle. Et debout !
En avant ! A l'assaut des Étoiles ! »

D'un grand geste, la Mer Souveraine emprisonna
dans son poing de fer toute la masse irradiante
et floche des rênes, que les cavaleries des Vagues
traînent derrière elles.
Et sur cent lieues de côtes sinueuses
l'immensurable armée parut bridée
et sursautante au bout des courroies innombrables
que la Mer férocement empoignait.
Les Trombes alignées contemplaient le spectacle,
très loin, là-bas, sur leur front de colonnade,
formant un angle droit avec l'arc de l'horizon.
Les courroies s'irradiant
jusqu'aux pieds de la falaise, s'effrangeaient d'écume
et dansaient pesamment, au large,
comme de longues scies d'argent,
sur les casques et les crinières des escadrons lointains
qui montent jusqu'au ventre de la Mer Souveraine.
A mes pieds sous la falaise,
toutes dressées sur leurs queues squameuses d'or,
les Licornes crachèrent leur colère vociférante

et leur bave sanglante, l'une après l'autre,
comme un long feu de file.
Haussées de toute la longueur de leur corps,
elles tendaient en avant leur tête d'étalon
sauvage, leur gueule rouge éclatée de rage
sous les tiraillements des rênes violentes.
Elles dardaient, contre la Mer, leur langue,
comme une flamme farouche que le vent couche
et rue en avant.
Sur le nœud de leur queue,
les Licornes se dressèrent géantes,
récalcitrantes, arquant leur croupe d'épouvante.

Tendues en arrière, elles menaçaient l'infini
avec leurs pattes formidables de devant,
brandies ainsi que des harpons,
sur leur poitrail vaste armé d'un éperon.
Tels, les Chevaux de marbre qui s'avancent,
menaçants et symétriques,
levant tous à la fois leurs pattes droites,
sur les frises des Ninives mortes !

Et la grande bouche rouge de la Mer cria
sur l'échevèlement des cavaleries ameutées :
« Je vous commande de vous trancher en deux
        armées !
Tous les escadrons des Vagues en avant !
Entassez-vous les unes sur les autres ! Je le veux !
Je vous impose un suicide glorieux !
Vous formerez de votre grande masse inerte
une montagne colossale, que les Houles,
les Licornes et tous mes Vétérans graviront
jusqu'au faîte, pour atteindre et défoncer
les murailles de l'Infini ! Je le veux !
Les Houles, en avant ! Piquez, les Licornes !
Trombes, Typhons, en avant !
Cernez les armées que je sacrifie, entassez-les,
culbutez de force les légions, amoncelez
escadron sur escadron, jusqu'au Zénith !

« Et vous, mes filles, ô mes jeunes guerrières,
en avant ! au galop, portez mes ordres
jusqu'aux confins vaporeux de mes armées !
O mes filles, jeunes guerrières, ordonnez aux
      Cyclones
de se ranger sur leur front de bataille et d'attendre.
L'heure viendra pour eux de fouiller mes abîmes
et de hisser très haut entre leurs bras
des pyramides de cadavres phosphorescents !
L'heure viendra où les Cyclones lanceront
tous mes projectiles aux murailles de l'Infini !

XIII
L'ÉCLAIREUR D'OR

Alors, à droite de la montagne d'eaux amoncelées,
dans le renfoncement de la nef aux voûtes de fumée,
sous les chevelures palpitantes des Trombes,
très loin, sur la bande sulfureuse de l'horizon,
un énorme chevalier tout cuirassé d'or
apparut campé sur un coursier de poix.

C'était l'Éclaireur d'or des armées de la Mer.
Et une grande voix, sa voix d'airain chanta
dans la sublime Immensité :

— « Ah ! vous voilà donc démasquées, Étoiles !
Infâmes courtisanes, aux seins turgides
et lourds et translucides comme deux énormes
gouttes d'ambre ! Entremetteuses divines aux yeux
      de perles !
Jeteuses de maléfices et de charmes mortels ! »

Une, deux, trois fois, l'Éclaireur d'or
dégaîna sa grande épée de flamme,
coupant l'espace d'un vaste éclair éblouissant.
Et parmi sa clarté jaune qui déferle
le profil monstrueux de la montagne

se dessina immense et noir,
avec, à droite, à gauche, de géantes armées
      de Cyclones,
tournant sur place à toute vitesse,
leurs bras levés, gesticulant en un délire,
ainsi que des ramures giflées par l'ouragan.
Puis les ténèbres emmitouflèrent l'étendue
des eaux tragiques, et la voix formidable
éclata de nouveau par rafales acharnées :

« O sorcières de l'Impossible ! Étoiles !
Prometteuses de néant ! Vous voilà donc devant moi !
à la portée de ma vengeance ! O ma joie !
Oh ! que je savoure l'ivresse effrénée
de cracher sur vos visages augustes !
La victoire est certaine, sachez-le !
La victoire est à nous. Nous serons dix millions
de Vagues à l'assaut de vos murailles de métal ! »

Fougueusement, dix fois, vingt fois, mille fois,
à toute vélocité, l'Éclaireur de la Mer Souveraine
dégaîna sa grande épée de flamme à l'infini.
Et, très haut, sur le faîte de la montagne cimentée
par des torrents de haine, très haut, au bout de
      la rampe,
étincela une citadelle aux tourelles d'ivoire,
et les dents rouges d'innombrables créneaux,
et des murailles de soufre s'étageant en plein ciel,
et au delà, encore plus haut, se déployaient
toutes les armées fulgurantes des Voies Lactées,
avec la plénitude heureuse et la paresse
d'un fleuve de lumière serpentant dans l'infini.

A droite, à gauche de la morne montagne,
sur les moutonnantes armées de la Mer
Souveraine, Cyclones, Typhons et Trombes,
les uns, haillonneux, à demi nus,
tous crêtelés de flammes et d'ailes jaunes,
les autres, solennels et drapés

en leurs bouffants manteaux de crêpe,
ployaient leur torse gigantesque, en fourrageant
les eaux, l'un après l'autre,
de leurs bras prolixes et mous comme des boyaux.
Par instant, des Cyclones redressaient
lentement leur taille, avec des torsions
déferlantes de croupe, en soulevant hors des eaux,
au bout de leurs grands bras tendus comme des
      câbles,
des masses pyramidales et grenues de phosphore !
« Ce sont des pyramides incandescentes de cadavres
que les Cyclones soulèvent et brandissent
contre vous, Étoiles à jamais maudites !
Ce sont les cadavres pétrifiés de vos amants,
qui sont morts d'avoir bu
votre baiser empoisonné !
Oui, maudits ! mille fois maudits,
vos visages d'amour et d'amertume, Étoiles,
et vos prunelles pleines de regards illusoires
de nos maîtresses perfides !
Je les oindrai de nos crachats verdâtres qui fument,
vos visages trempés de fausses larmes,
et fardés d'éphémère douceur !
Vos visages adamantins qui souriaient jadis,
à mon âme, en les beaux soirs pervers de ma
      jeunesse,
à travers la chevelure des forêts que torture
une chaude angoisse printanière... vos visages
      d'émeraude !...
c'est pour les déchirer, que j'entraîne
les armées de la Mer Souveraine
par les escarpements d'une montagne artificielle
à l'assaut, à l'assaut de vos tourelles éblouissantes !
Et mes Vagues sont saoûles de vengeance !
Par delà vos murailles inaccessibles,
nous mâcherons à mille dents vos grands cœurs
      d'or !
Chaude ripaille ! et nous les engloutirons
dans nos panses humides et transparentes ! »

Mille fois ! dix mille fois ! l'Éclaireur de la Mer
Souveraine dégaîna royalement son épée
embrasée, hachant l'espace en mille quartiers ;
et, dans la profondeur livide de l'horizon,
un frisson agita les masses ténébreuses
qui commencèrent à rouler leurs vastes anneaux
de serpents fabuleux. Et plus loin
les légions menaçantes des Cyclones rigides
dans les plis roides de leur robe de suie fumante,
s'ébranlèrent en avant, avec l'oscillation
fantômale des colonnades qui s'écroulent.
Des Trombes nues, érigeaient leurs seins irrités,
en tournoyant agilement sur elles-mêmes.
On les voyait de minute en minute
se plier en deux, cassant leur taille molle
pour plonger leurs grands bras dans les pierrailles
et les broussailles mouvantes du sol.
Tout à coup mille Typhons, rangés en demi-cercle,
s'illuminèrent de flammes électriques
dans l'épaisseur noirâtre de leur corps.
Ils portaient à la ceinture des girandoles
de feux follets et des colliers d'éclairs
en sautoir sur la poitrine.
Et ils s'avançaient, en tournoyant, tous,
si rapidement, que leurs grands manteaux de brume,
leur chair d'aveuglant azur, leurs girandoles
et leurs colliers, semblaient ruisseler
comme une eau merveilleuse
autour de leur grande âme implacable de feu !
Et le martellement de leurs sandales de fer
précipita son lourd fracas d'avalanche sinistre.
Et leurs jambières sonnaient ainsi que des tonnerres.

XIX
LE BAISER D'UNE ÉTOILE MOURANTE

Lentement, les mains ouvertes du Silence
apaisaient la furie de la Nuit

et la démente palpitation du ciel
encore touffu d'épées et de lances.

Sous des mains planes d'ouate amoureuse
et d'éternel oubli, le grand Cœur
sanguinolent d'or et de phosphore
se calma d'heure en heure.
Le grand Cœur de la Nuit
s'apaisa voluptueusement assouvi,
parmi les caresses vaporeuses d'une Aube
vierge et bleue qui souriait, surhumaine
et loin du monde.

Je descendis à pas cassés dans la crique
profonde, toute ronronnante encore
comme un ventre plein de borborygmes.
Les roches semblaient toutes endolories,
et je marchais parmi les ricanements
et les sanglots épuisés des grottes,
dans les sables, le long des flots roidis par les
        ténèbres.
Quand je vis tout à coup la houle pesante et flasque
qui traînait lentement vers la plage,
sur son dos de phoque tout luisant d'huile noire,
le corps décoloré et meurtri d'une Étoile.
Étoile mourante, hélas ! à demi-nue et toute
        flexueuse
avec sa chair moite et verdissante !
Son visage d'améthyste voilé de larmes lentes,
resplendissait parmi des chevelures d'algues.

Oh ! combien suavement, ses prunelles
d'ombre glauque imploraient l'inconnu !
Alors ! en me couchant à plat dans la fraîcheur
        des sables,
je baisai doucement ses lèvres sinueuses,
qui s'entr'ouvraient sur des lueurs nacrées de lune.
Longtemps, je savourai ce funèbre baiser
pour en mourir, pour en mourir !

Elle m'inonda de ses larmes d'amour,
l'inconsolable Étoile de mon Rêve !

L'Aurore, clarifiée par ces larmes divines,
et souriant d'extase sibylline,
emboucha son grand cor d'ivresse et d'amertume
qui chanta, rouge, sur l'horizon comme un soleil
        levant,
avec au loin, une agonie d'échos et de sanglots
noirs, et des caillots de sang,
dans les mâchoires éclatées des grottes
        moribondes !...

Destruction

Poèmes lyriques

I

INVOCATION A LA MER TOUTE-PUISSANTE POUR QU'ELLE ME DÉLIVRE DE L'IDÉAL

pour Eugène Lautier.

O Mer, divine Mer, je ne crois pas,
je ne veux pas croire que la terre est ronde !...
Myopie de nos sens !.. Syllogismes mort-nés !...
Logiques mortes, ô Mer !... Je ne crois pas
que tu roules tristement sur le dos de la terre,
comme une vipère sur le dos d'un caillou !...
Les Savants le déclarent, t'ayant mesurée tout
      entière !...
Ils ont sondé tes houles ! Qu'importe ?...
Car ils ne sauraient comprendre ton verbe de délire.

Tu es infinie et divine, ô Mer, et je le sais
de par le jurement de tes lèvres écumantes,
de par ton jurement que répercutent, de plage
      en plage,
les Echos attentifs ainsi que des guetteurs,
de par ton jurement que scandent les tonneres !...
Infinie et divine, tu voyages, ô Mer,
comme un grand fleuve en son heureuse plénitude.
Oh ! qui pourra chanter le digne épithalame
de mon âme qui nage en ton giron immense ?...
Et les nuages éblouis te font des signes,

quand tu plonges sans effort, en droite ligne,
dans l'insondable profondeur des horizons !...

Comme un fleuve dont les eaux miroitent gorgées
      de flammes,
oui, tu plonges en droite ligne !... et les Savants
      ont tort,
car je t'ai vue, par des midis d'apothéose,
fulgurer au loin, telle une épée d'argent,
pointée contre l'Azur exaspérant de perfidie !...
... Car je t'ai vue rougeoyante et cruelle,
implacablement brandie,
contre le flanc charnel d'un soir d'Avril agonisant
parmi les chevelures démoniaques de la Nuit !...
O Mer, ô formidable épée à pourfendre les Astres !...
O formidable épée,
chue des mains brisées d'un Jéhova mourant !...

Et les Couchants alors, qui se métamorphosent,
ne sont que les blessures sanguinolentes que tu
      creuses,
à travers les temps, pour te venger, pour te venger !...
Qu'en disent les Savants ?...
Qu'en dites-vous, vieux grimoires, éternels alambics,
balances argentines, télescopes brandis ?
Et d'ailleurs, quoi qu'ils disent, ils ont tort,
      les Savants.
Ils ont tort de nier ton essence divine,

car le Rêve seul existe et la Science n'est plus
que la brève défaillance d'un Rêve !..

Tu plonges dans l'Infini, comme un fleuve
        sans bornes
et les Etoiles flexueuses de saphir
s'accoudent nonchalamment sur tes bords,
en leurs robes palpitantes de métaux
aux cassures adamantines !...
Et cependant des Astres impérieux
casqués de feu, agiles en leurs gaines d'émeraude,
se dressent sur tes berges, étendant sur les flots
leurs grands bras de lumière, ô Mer, pour te bénir,
toi qui circules dans les prairies bleues du ciel,
pour y répandre ton désir éternel
et ta démente volupté,
ô Veines radieuses de l'Espace !...
O Sang pur de l'Infini !...

Les savants sont venus sur tes promontoires,
gambader suspendus, ainsi que des fantoches,
aux fils enchevêtrés des pluies automnales,
pour t'explorer, ô Mer !...

Ils te traitent d'esclave lamentable
sans cesse culbutée, flagellée sur le sable,
par les Vents, tes bourreaux !...
Ceux-là méprisent tes sanglots
et la tristesse submergeante de tes yeux !...
Ils ont dit que tu entoures les courbes de la terre
ainsi que les humeurs perverses de nos corps,
— hydropisie d'un monde décrépit !
D'autres qui t'ont vue verdir de fiel, de sanie
et de bave et roussir aux crépuscules,
ont déclaré que tu recules, incessamment,
loin des plages et que tu meurs tristement desséchée.
Tu n'es pour eux qu'une couleuvre de vieil or,
tordue sur le missel racorni de la terre !
Qu'importe ?... les marteaux et les vrilles de ta voix

sauront vite émietter la parole éphémère !...

Moi qui t'aime, de tout mon désespoir cloué sur
        le rivage,
moi qui crois en ta puissance divine,
je chanterai ta marche triomphale dans l'espace,
que tu traverses de part en part, en déployant
tes eaux étincelantes et solennelles,
peignées par la rafale au sein de l'Infini !..
Gonfle mon âme, ô Mer, comme une voile d'or.
O sang de l'infini, gonfle et submerge enfin
en ce soir de vertige la plage de mon cœur,
de tes marées gonflées de poupre et de rayons !

D'innombrables Etoiles nostalgiques
sont descendues, ô Mer,
en ton courant majestueux de fleuve,
à la nage fouillant l'horizon vaste,
guettant au loin, toutes attentives,
le clair estuaire d'or aux fraicheurs éternelles,
pour apaiser leur cœur aux nœuds de flammes
et la brûlure de leurs bras illuminants !...

O Mer, hâte-toi ! hâte-toi !... car des taureaux géants
de vapeur, aux croupes monumentales,
descendent — les vois-tu ?... indolemment, vers
        tes berges,
en trainant les énormes chariots des Constellations.
Ils viennent s'abreuver à tes eaux miroitantes,
en balançant leurs têtes informes,
sous leurs cornes de fumée divergentes,
et leurs naseaux ruissellent de mondes braisillants !...

Ciel ! Ciel !.. quel prodige ?... Echos sonores,
répercutez le cri de la stupeur et de la joie !...
Le beau miracle, ô Mer, s'est-il donc opéré ?...
Oui ! Oui !... Enfin, je te sens dans mes veines,
ô turbulente Mer, ô Mer aventureuse !..
Tu es en moi, comme je te désire !...

Galope donc avec ivresse dans mon cœur élargi,
avec la meute acharnée de tes tempêtes aboyantes,
donnant du cor, à pleins poumons, vers les étoiles,
sous ton panache romantique de nues échevelées.

III
LES BABELS DU RÊVE

pour E. A. Butti.

Les Couchants aux griffes d'or,
sous leurs crinières embrasées !...
Les Couchants accroupis au seuil de l'horizon,
leurs pattes fauves allongées, ainsi que des lions,
ont déchiré longtemps ma chair adolescente !...

C'est toi, ô Mer crépusculaire, qui m'a donné
l'âpre nausée de vivre et l'infinie tristesse !...
C'est de t'avoir trop contemplée dans ma jeunesse
que je chancelle en ton haleine, ivre de désespoir !...

Des soirs, là-bas, en l'Afrique sorcière,
on nous menait sur tes plages moroses,
nous tous, mornes troupeaux de collégiens, qui
        trainent
moutonniers, sous la garde sévère des prêtres noirs.
O silhouettes d'encre qui tachaient les soieries
immatérielles d'un beau ciel oriental !...

Et tu venais indolemment vers nous, ô Mer sensuelle,
fraîche et verte, à demi-nue sous tes ruches d'écume,
pour sécher tes pieds de neige sur le sable...
En piétinant de rage, comme une enfant sauvage,
tu boudais le beau Soir paresseux qui s'attarde,
le beau Soir, ton amant, qui te farde les joues !...
Et tu lançais très haut jusqu'au zénith,
du revers et du creux et du plat de tes vagues
nos étoiles et nos rêves,

molles verroteries qui nous viennent d'Orient !...

Mon cœur s'est enivré du bruissement des perles,
que ta main lasse égrène au creux des roches !...
Mon cœur a sangloté entre tes doigts brûlants
comme une lyre satanique, dont les cordes tendues,
épuisées de caresses, s'esclaffent tout à coup
de rires déchirants !...
Mon cœur ?... je l'ai roulé en tes tresses nocturnes...
Mon cœur ?... je l'ai trainé tout pantelant
sur tes vagues d'écume, dentelées
comme des cruelles scies d'argent !...

Oh ! que tu sois honnie, mille fois honnie
de par les lois astrales,
ô Mer, toi qui peuplas ma jeunesse pensive
de bouches levantines aux chansons spasmodiques,
et de l'obscène torsion des vagues sexuées !...
O toi, ballerine orientale au ventre sursautant,
dont les seins sont rougis par le sang des naufrages !..

Nous marchions traînant la patte, ô Mer,
l'oreille ensanglantée, comme des chiens blessés
        à mort,
qui étanchent leur soif dans les flaques pourries...
... déjà fleuries d'étoiles illusoires !...
Nous rêvions échoués, ainsi que des mendiants,
devant le porche éblouissant de la nuit vénérable,
où tes doigts frénétiques de flux et de reflux
ont noté les faits-divers de tes naufrages !...
Et j'avais dans mon cœur le fastueux mirage
d'un palais noir aux cent tourelles d'or
brandies contre l'azur, où clore enfin,
et garder intangible l'Épouse des Épouses,
conquise au prix de tout le firmament
constellé de mes rêves !...
Et mes yeux exploraient au fond du crépuscule
        haineux,
parmi les fourches verdâtres des nuages,

la profondeur bleuie des grottes fabuleuses...

Plus tard, à mon retour, sous le toit paternel,
préludait une douce veillée familiale,
sous la lampe qui dresse au ciel son col de flamme,
arrondissant ses ailes de clarté sur la table,
pour couver les désirs exaltés de mon âme
dans le trémoussement de ses rayons soyeux...
— comme une poule aux grands œufs d'or
        magiques, —
... tandis qu'en un coin d'ombre,
ma rugueuse nourrice soudanaise
chantonnait tristement,
de sa voix grêle et noire,
et marquait la cadence en frappant dans ses mains
qui sont pareilles à des cliquets de bois...
Et dans l'étouffement du soir gorgé de feu,
la voix de ma nourrice imageait le silence
de légendes crépues comme des têtes nègres,
lézardées de rires blancs
et couronnées de plumes écarlates !...

Et par instant je m'accoudais à la fenêtre
pour t'écouter ô Mer, marmonner des prières
à de vagues passants, comme une fille au carrefour.

— O Mer, qui donc viendra ce soir partager
        ton alcôve
orageuse... et caresser les loves menaçants
de ton corps de boa... et mordre jusqu'au sang,
en un râle de mort, tes seins cloutés de feu
qui se déclanchent contre Dieu, dans les tempêtes ?...

Tout à coup, surgissant d'un bond entre les roches,
écumante et sauvage, ô Mer,
comme une folle en des sursauts de rage,
tu agitais tes bras d'ivoire cliquetants d'amulettes,
tout en claquant des dents, galets sonores....

. . . .

... cependant que la Nuit lentement conquérait
        la plage
comme une pieuvre colossale aux ventouses d'or.

La Ville charnelle

I
LE VOYAGEUR MORDU

Pour dompter les simouns enfantés par l'enfer
qui trouent, d'un geste fou, leur grand manteau
    de sable,
j'ai couru, j'ai bondi, avec l'incalculable
vitesse d'un rayon ricochant sur les flots.

Pour rejoindre la Nuit couchée dans les campagnes,
j'ai surmonté la chaîne immense des montagnes,
j'ai pu fouler la Nuit sous mes pas monotones,
la Nuit de miel toute écœurante de chaleur
que la lune, en rampant, empoisonne de fiel.

J'ai devancé la marche pénible de la terre
comme un jongleur debout sur l'oscillation
d'une boule roulante... J'ai vaincu la grande Ourse,
j'ai dépassé l'Aurore enfantine à la course,
et je puis désormais ralentir mon allure
parmi ces palmiers noirs qui tamisent l'azur
et le soyeux murmure de la mer africaine.

Déjà mes pieds cassés savourent la langueur
et l'abandon de cette plage confiante.
Mon oreille extatique évoque la cascade
sonore des galets aux flous éclats de rire,
et voilà qu'en la brume attentive de l'aube

mes yeux peuvent enfin contempler ton profil,
ô toi, Ville opulente aux courbes féminines
dont la blancheur charnelle affriole ma bouche,
sur ta couche odorante de vergers assoupis
qui fleurent le jasmin, la menthe et le cassis.

Elle sommeille encore nonchalamment assise
offrant son dos aux chaudes caresses de l'Aurore,
dont l'haleine rosée voyage sur les flots
et frise les herbages au sommet des collines.
Elle étire avec grâce un corps nu, mi-voilé
des surabondants cheveux noirs qui l'ennuagent,
en moutonnant sur le versant de son échine
ainsi que les feuillages des jardins suspendus.
Son corps est tout gemmé par la fine rosée
nocturne et la sueur des lentes voluptés
qu'elle a bues longuement aux lèvres des Étoiles.

Tout à coup sur la ligne de l'horizon marin
le grand Soleil mulâtre agite lourdement
sa tête empouacrée de sang et sa tignasse
embroussaillée de feu et de monnaies vermeilles.
Son torse tatoué émerge de la mer
en ruisselant comme au sortir d'un bain de pourpre.
Il se dresse d'un bond, s'arcboutant sur les nues
pour contempler l'insouciante Ville rose ;
puis, se penchant il ose en caresser les hanches
si bien que les blanches murailles

tressaillent de plaisir.

C'est alors que leur ombre s'étendit sur les sables,
comme un mol éventail d'azur immensurable.
J'en fus enveloppé sur mon chemin poudreux...
C'est alors que je vis flamboyer les vitraux
sur le beau front d'ivoire de la suprême citadelle,
qu'écrasent les cheveux embaumés des jardins...
Vitraux brûlants, dont les cils d'or battent d'effroi
parmi l'éclat répercuté de la lumière,
un passant en prière m'a narré les splendeurs
dont vous auréolez les clairs pèlerinages
qui viennent de partout plier leurs vieux genoux !...

Oh ! rouges sont tes portes, toutes rouges des cœurs
pendus en ex-votos sur tes vantaux d'ivoire !
Oh ! rouges sont tes portes, toutes rouges d'avoir
broyé à leur passage des épices grisantes
tassées jadis sur des chariots par les sorciers d'Egypte,
et dont fut parfumé le clair linteau de nacre.

Oh ! rouges sont tes portes, rougies par les massacres
où de noirs conquérants sont venus culbuter
leurs corps géants d'ébène et leurs musculatures !...
Oh ! rouges sont tes portes, toutes rouges du sang
que les mendiants d'amour, assoiffés de tortures,
ont versé sur ton seuil hors de leurs plaies impures
qu'avait empoisonnées l'haleine du désert !...
Oh ! rouges sont tes portes, pour avoir étranglé
dans l'entrebâillement affamé des vantaux,
les oiseaux de Boukir, qui viennent chaque été
y plonger avec rage leurs grands becs flamboyants
et ne fuient que le soir où l'un d'eux plus dément,
se tord, enfin pendu, comme un sanglant mouchoir.

La ville rose allonge ses murailles charnelles
veinulées comme un marbre et teintées de carmin,
arrondissant ses belles hanches de déesse
qui se terminent en collines,

plus lisses que des cuisses couleur de pêche,
et finissent au loin dans les fraîches forêts
de l'horizon,
où la ville a voulu cacher ses pieds mignons.

V
MON CŒUR CHANTA...

« A quoi bon s'acharner sur la mer turbulente,
virant vers la promesse illusoire des caps ?
C'est ici ! c'est ici l'ivresse des ivresses !
C'est bien toi que je veux absorber d'un seul trait,
Vulve rose embaumée par l'haleine des Astres !

Vous pouvez haleter de rage et de dépit,
je fais fi de vos longs hurlements de colère,
ô galopants Simouns de mon ambition,
qui piaffez lourdement sur le seuil de la ville !
Vous ne m'atteindrez plus malgré votre vitesse !
Vous ne franchirez pas les murailles charnelles !
Vous avez beau hennir ; j'ai bouché mes oreilles !
Mieux encore, mes oreilles sont déjà assourdies
par le rose murmure de sa voix souterraine,
tels de frais coquillages qu'emplit le chant des mers.

O rage de creuser ma tombe en sa chair bleue !
Oh ! loin de toi, bien loin de toi, Soleil
qui me guettes en plein ciel !
Car j'entends sans te voir le bruit que font tes ailes
frappant aux parois du Zénith !
Je ne crains plus la bouche de l'horizon glouton,
qui voudrait m'avaler d'une seule lampée !
O Soleil envieux, affolé de grandeurs,
esclave travesti en l'absence du maître,
j'ai déjà oublié tes grands gestes brutaux,
tes regards et tes cris plus lourds que des marteaux.
Je veux creuser ici ma fosse et mon berceau !
Vulve chantante, au frais glouglou de source vive,

oh ! la joie frétillante de reposer en toi,
dans ton humidité chaude et fraîche à la fois !

Je veux enfin tremper mon cœur dans ton odeur
de rouille humide et de rose pourrie !
Reflets d'acier vaincu, tronçons de glaive épars,
fumant encore du sang qu'ont versé les héros
trucidés sur ton seuil, et pour l'amour de toi !
Oh ! joie de te donner ma vie, mon sang, ma force,
et de prendre la tienne en un baiser sans fin !
Héroïsme du sang qui s'élance vers toi
éclaboussant de joie tes lèvres chaudes
comme un jet d'eau pourpré par l'aurore vermeille !

Bonheur de se noyer dans ton immensité
illusoire et brûlante,
d'océan tropical, Vulve inondante,
mignonne et si fragile, et pourtant
plus vaste que mon âme en ce moment !...
Le monde est aboli ! Le désir est tué !
L'infini est comblé, puisque c'est toi le but !

Et pourtant c'est si doux de te faire du mal,
en te mordant comme un beau fruit,
pour te manger à pleine bouche,
pour boire les sanglots et les sursauts farouches
de ta liquide volupté !

Tu vois bien, je me tords de délice et d'extase
dans ton creux jaillissant et moelleux de source !
Je veux creuser ton sable avec mes dents, mes doigts,
toujours plus bas, plus loin, jusqu'à
          d'imperscrutables
profondeurs, pour savoir
et trouver le filon de la joie,
le filon merveilleux du bonheur métallique !

Malheur à moi ! Je sens le feu d'une blessure !
C'est le Soleil qui m'a mordu à la cheville !

Oh ! le chien enragé !...
Je devrais m'endormir, la bouche sur ta bouche,
Vulve rose et sacrée, dont le sable est sucré,
et pourtant je me tords comme un serpent blessé
qui voudrait rebondir de douleur, de désir
et d'espoir éternel !...

Malheur à moi ! malheur à moi ! Car voici je me lève
et j'éloigne mon cœur et je pense déjà
à votre joie sublime, vitraux dominateurs,
vastes prunelles d'or, qui grandissez toujours
parmi la parfumante retombée
des jardins suspendus !...
Hélas ! Je pense à vous, vitraux qui reflétez
sans fin, l'allure conquérante des soleils
et le pèlerinage des voiliers, toile au vent,
que l'on voit de très haut, figés dans leur vitesse,
sur le tressaillement de la nappe marine.

VI
LES LÉZARDS SACRÉS

Et cependant la Ville s'enlisait
dans le sommeil incandescent de l'heure...
ô sommeil velouté, ô respiration
de la Ville pâmée dans le Soleil !

De tous côtés, sur les pavés roussis par la chaleur,
je vis alors s'éveiller les lézards
somnolents et bleuâtres, qui s'accouplaient
formant des entrelacs de veines palpitantes
sur la peau lisse de cette place, ronde
comme un ventre de jeune femme épanouie.

Lézards émeraudés de la luxure,
beaux lézards assouvis de volupté solaire,
j'aime assister ainsi à votre lent réveil
sur le ventre dormant d'une place déserte,

dont la peau chaude est duvetée d'herbe vermeille.

Mais la dernière pierre du grand Soleil mulâtre
me chassa dans l'humide touffeur des bananiers.
Je longeai les coupoles fumantes dans l'azur,
m'arrêtant par instant pour embrasser les arbres
et les buissons de fleurs, à tâtons, à genoux,
pour baiser les racines de tous les arbrisseaux,
dont le parfum gonflait mon cœur,
quand j'atteignis l'orée
qui s'ouvre sur le ciel comme un quai sur la mer.
Mon âme s'embarqua sur la nue en partance
qui concéda sa toile au vent de l'infini.

LA MORT DES FORTERESSES

(Petit drame de lumières)

I
LES CARÈNES COQUETTES

Or c'est depuis la vieillesse des âges,
que les rugueuses Forteresses du port
sont assises sur les quais noirs,
parmi des cargaisons pyramidales
de fruits juteux et de métaux et de bois odorants.
Elles ont leur échine colossale encastrée
dans les remparts et les pieds dans la mer,
coulant leur ombre et leurs vies monotones
parmi les huiles somptueuses de la houle
et ses longs soliloques de ventriloque.
Elles paressent en la douce intimité
de leurs enfants, les tout jeunes Navires
mi-vêtus de leurs voiles en loques
ainsi que des gavroches, qui jouent en liesse
avec la balle incandescente du soleil.

Et le parfum vermeil et fertile des Iles
berce leur sommeil d'aïeules vénérables...

Mais parfois, brusquement,
au sourire désenchanté des soirs d'automne,
les grands sacs pleins d'écorces d'oranges desséchées
leur lancent des bouffées de senteurs violettes
dont s'exaspèrent leurs grands dos pétrifiés.

Car les vieilles Forteresses du port
furent jadis de vivantes carènes
dont la quille éraflait élégamment
les reins souples des vagues, au hasard des voyages...
Elles s'en allaient nonchalamment,
en s'inclinant à droite, à gauche, au gré des brises,
roulant leur poupe comme des hanches,
gonflant leurs voiles blanches
comme des seins jaillis hors du corsage.
Elles voguaient soulevant au passage
leur jupe ébouriffée d'écume en éventail,
cambrant le gouvernail ainsi qu'une cheville
en un sillage froufroutant de dentelles.

Les carènes filaient sournoisement
sous la lanterne rouge des couchants maraudeurs,
serrant sur leur poitrine leurs voiles palpitantes,
éteignant sur la proue
leurs grands fanaux versicolores,
comme on cache des bijoux fascinateurs
dans les pans rabattus d'un ample manteau noir.

Au large de la mer, les carènes vécurent,
heureuses, de la pulpe mûre
et parfumante de l'aurore...

Dans la pâmoison des nuits printanières,
elles se lamentèrent, en panne,
avec un frais roulis de berceau qui s'endort,
désespérées d'attendre la brise favorable

sous le ricanement strident des lunes jaunes,
guettant le cuivre d'une étoile filante
qui tinte au creux des mers comme une aumône,
dans la sébile d'un misérable.

Dans les chantiers fuligineux qui ronflent
et bourdonnent comme des cloches sous la pluie,
tous les ans,
à la Saint-Jean,
des calfats empouacrés de suie
radoubaient le bas-ventre moussu des carènes
à grands coups de marteaux pour refondre
leur native beauté.
Et les pilons hissés dans les grasses buées
retombaient avec un bruit de mine,
en fracassant les enclumes qui fument
dans la sanguinolence échevelée des torches.

Et la beauté défaillante des belles,
refleurissait toute rajeunie au soleil.

Ils écrasaient l'étoupe goudronnée
aux craquelures fines de la peau,
en guise de fards et d'onguents miraculeux,
aplatissant la tête noire des grands clous protecteurs
que l'on dit tout-puissants sur l'orgueil des Orages
...On eut dit, çà et là, des mouches de coquette.

Mais un jour les marteaux retombèrent inutiles
pour radouber les vertèbres d'acier
et la coque mollasse des carènes...
Les clous, les maquillages et les mouches de fer
ne tenaient plus sur la peau ;
les cloisons n'étanchaient plus les fuites d'eau...
Les calfats ricanaient tendant leur mufle rogue
et boucané de dogue : « Oh ! les belles carènes
ont fini de jouir dans les bras des Orages
du moment qu'elles font
pipi au lit de leurs amants,

les belles de jadis !... »

Ce fut le soir de leur défaite...

II
L'INUTILE SAGESSE

Les illustres Carènes s'en vinrent échouer
sur les quais noirs ; et maintenant, assises,
leur dos large encastré dans les remparts,
et leurs vertes prunelles soûles de naufrages,
les belles agonisent...
en portant sur leurs genoux évasés
des terrasses désertes qui surplombent la mer.

Leurs jupes grises lampassées de coquillages
et fleuries d'émeraudes, retombent en plis roides
jusques aux flots, qui bercent mollement
leurs falbalas d'algues somnolentes,
avec des longs glouglous loquaces de goulot.
Elles sont devenues les gardiennes du port,
les mornes Forteresses,
avec sur la poitrine ridée par les batailles,
des étoiles-de-mer en guise de médailles.

Tout à coup elles se sentent frôler
par des mains innombrables et ce sont
leurs enfants, les tout jeunes Navires,
qui les embrassent violemment et les caressent,
et dont les mâts, les drisses et les cordages
leur font un lierre terrifiant d'allégresse.

Les Forteresses sourient frileusement
ouvrant leurs bouches lasses aux rares dents jaunies...
Ce sont de vieux balcons aux balustres que casse
le Vent, à coups de poings, ivrogne millénaire !...

A grands cris, d'un grand geste, les Navires implorent

le bonheur de partir en voguant sans effort
comme on prend un essor !... Les vieilles Forteresses
étreignent à deux mains leur vieux cœur en détresse,
et les voilà pareilles à nos vieilles grand-mères
qui connaissaient la mer sauvage de l'amour
et prévoyaient tous ses naufrages...

O chétives Grand-mères, j'évoque tout à coup
vos ombres affalées dans les fauteuils profonds,
dont le dossier monumental surgissait
sur votre échine courbe, tel un fantôme
s'évaporant dans le plafond crépusculaire !...
La chambre se fonçait de deuil et de tristesse
et tremblotait sous vos gestes d'ailes blessées...
L'air semblait grenu et rugueux de vieillesse,
et les voix s'efforçaient vainement de grimper
glissant comme des rats en un tuyau d'égout.

Un jour de beaux enfants crépitants de jeunesse
s'étaient rués à vos genoux,
s'agrippant à vos jupes, en un falot de joie :
— « O ma petite mère, faut nous laisser partir,
nous désirons jouer et danser au soleil... »
Car ils avaient senti palpiter au dehors
sur les volets fermés ainsi que des paupières
le blond soleil des Dimanches qu'on rêve,
et se gonfler comme un grand cœur heureux de
       vivre...
C'est ainsi, c'est ainsi que les jeunes Navires
implorent affolés leur délivrance,
en s'esclaffant de tous leurs linges bariolés
claquant au vent comme des lèvres brûlées de fièvre.
Leurs drisses et leurs haubans se raidissent
tels des nerfs trop tendus qui grincent de désir,
car ils veulent partir et s'en aller,
vers la tristesse affreuse (qu'importe ?), inconsolable
et (qu'importe ?) infinie,
d'avoir tout savouré et tout maudit (qu'importe ?).

Les Forteresses, aux yeux vitreux brouillés de larmes,
marmonnèrent : « Nous sommes revenues des
       voyages,
vaincues et dégrisées par l'horreur des mirages
et des plages où nos quilles agonisèrent
sous la dent des Rochers !...
Prenez garde ! Ils vous guettent,
sournois comme des bonzes que nourrit la Tempête
en leur offrant les voiles qui roucoulent
au large, déployées, ainsi que des colombes !...
. . . .
Garez-vous du sourire enjôleur des Sirènes
qui vivent invisibles et cachées sous la mer !...
Un soir, nous devinâmes leurs lèvres désirantes
aux suaves bouillonnements des flots...
Lentement nos antennes s'amollirent,
et nous flottions parmi nos toiles dégrafées,
le beaupré tâtonnant sur l'horizon
et les flancs assoiffés de plénitude immense.
Nos longs cheveux brûlaient sous la chaude torture
qui nous venait de l'infini silence...
La brise ne fut plus qu'une caresse éparse
sur la pure émeraude de la mer qui coulait
ainsi qu'une prunelle fondue par la tendresse ;
et ce fut tout autour, au long des bastingages,
la fauve et délirante apparition
des Tritons, sur la mer suffoquée de chaleur.
Ils allaient déchaînant leurs corps de caoutchouc
et de bronze verdâtre dont la musculature
est feutrée de varech et huilée de rayons,
entrelaçant leurs longs phallus, tels des ramures,
s'esclaffant de luxure et de rire insolent
dans le flic-flac empanaché des vagues...
Ce soir-là, nous faillîmes échouer sur la côte...
. . . .
Prenez garde au sourire enjôleur des Sirènes !... »
Puis les aïeules granitiques se turent,
et, songeant à la vanité de leur sagesse,
au désir éphémère qui renaît dans nos cœurs

malgré le vieux savoir et l'antérieur dégoût,
voulurent allécher l'angoisse des gavroches
en leur offrant des vierges aux lèvres printanières.

Sur leurs vastes genoux élargis en terrasses,
dans le relent acide et mielleux des saumures,
elles firent asseoir les fillettes du port,
dont le teint est fardé d'embrun et de soleil
et le corps assoupli par l'audace du vent.
Des grappes de fillettes vêtues de rose et de lilas
s'inclinèrent nonchalamment aux parapets
d'où l'on voyait déjà, sur l'horizon grisâtre,
le soleil émergeant s'embrouiller aux mâtures
parmi la rousse chevelure des cordages.

Et les jeunes Navires tendaient vers les fillettes
leurs antennes crochues et leurs grands doigts rapaces
bagués et parfumés de cuivre et de goudron...

III
LA VICTOIRE DE L'AURORE

Mais l'Aurore exaltée effeuilla sa voix d'or
dans le silence, épanouie comme une rose immense.

Des joues de pourpre apparurent, bombées,
soufflant de l'héroïsme en des clairons voraces...
des nuées éblouissantes ramifièrent
leurs veines de rubis sur les tempes du ciel.

Et l'Aurore enthousiaste, rugit sur les nuages
dont les mille blessures ruissellent de folie
et dont le sang sonore retentit dans l'espace:
— « Au large! Suivez-moi, beaux Navires,
vers les îles absurdes, à l'infini des mers! »
La voix d'or empoigna, coup sur coup avec rage,
le cœur fumeux et décrépite de la Ville,
étreignant l'ossature des vieilles Forteresses

et tordant jusqu'au spasme la tresse des cordages.

Puis l'hymne de l'Aurore s'évada sur la ville
parmi la bousculade et l'essor des clochers
et la rébellion des toits et des pignons
insurgés et criards qui donnent l'escalade,
en masse, au vaste cirque des montagnes,
par delà les fiévreux applaudissements
des linges suspendus aux séchoirs des terrasses.

Un écho persista, frissonnant, immobile,
comme une larme rouge dans le silence blanc.

On pressentait déjà au ronron grandissant
de l'atmosphère ardente énervée de lumière
que l'appel de l'Aurore allait tonner encore!...
« Pitié, pitié, car ils ne sauront pas
résister à la voix!... »

Et voici, précédé d'un remous nostalgique
le grand cor émouvant fit éclater sa voix
qui s'égrène en mitraille de notes explosives,
repercutées par les échos, frappés au cœur,
bourdonnants et guerriers ainsi que des tambours.

Alors, d'un coup de reins, les Navires brisèrent
leurs amarres tragiques, bondissant en avant,
sur la moire des flots convulsée de regards,
en l'air gonflé d'horreur et d'espoirs élastiques.

Un rêve de folie souriante et vermeille
émut les promontoires accroupis dans la mer,
et leurs contorsions de tigres enchaînés
qui hument dans l'Aurore le vent des libertés!...

Un rêve de luxure brutale et de carnage
ensanglanta les sables de la plage
squamés et miroitants tels des peaux de serpents.

Un rêve de suicide absurde et d'aventure

tonna contre le vent cave des quais sonores,
où le ressac se traîne comme un dogue à la chaîne.

Glorieux, dominateurs, sur les grands perroquets
les drapeaux éloquents, fous de pourpre et d'azur
crièrent pour mieux tordre et dérouler leur enver-
      gure
battant fièvreusement des ailes,
tels les oiseaux des îles invoquent leur patrie.

Et d'abord, les Navires sortirent alignés,
brandissant par milliers leurs grands mâts pavoisés,
et déployèrent grandiosement leurs voiles
en tabliers tendus pour la cueille des étoiles.

Puis dépassant le goulet noir tacheté de lumière
ils s'enfoncèrent à pas lents dans l'au-delà des mers.
On les voyait de loin, déjà fourbus,
chanceler sur l'émeute des flots aux dents de scie,
près de la bouche incandescente du Soleil
qui s'accouda joyeusement aux nuages vermeils.

Et c'est ainsi, et c'est alors, parmi les gestes
chatoyants et fleuris de l'Aurore,
que les antiques Forteresses,
tremblotant sur leur siège de marbre immémorial,
avec sur les genoux des terrasses désertes
que lave coup sur coup l'horreur de l'infini,
moururent tout à coup d'avoir vu le Soleil
lascif et levantin, mordiller et manger
de ses dents embrasées, les vaisseaux puérils
aux voilures semées d'azur et de beryls
comme des violettes amollies de rosée.

DITHYRAMBES

A MON PÉGASE

Dieu véhément d'une race d'acier,
Automobile ivre d'espace,
qui piétines d'angoisse, le mors aux dents stridentes !
O formidable monstre japonais aux yeux de forge,
nourri de flamme et d'huiles minérales,
affamé d'horizons et de proies sidérales,
je déchaîne ton cœur aux teuf-teufs diaboliques,
et tes géants pneumatiques, pour la danse
que tu mènes sur les blanches routes du monde.
Je lâche enfin tes brides métalliques... Tu t'élances,
avec ivresse, dans l'Infini libérateur !...

Au fracas des abois de ta voix...
voilà que le Soleil couchant emboîte
ton pas véloce, accélérant sa palpitation
sanguinolente au ras de l'horizon...
Il galope là-bas, au fond des bois... regarde !...

Qu'importe, beau démon ?...
Je suis à ta merci... Prends-moi !
Sur la terre assourdie malgré tous ses échos,
sous le ciel aveuglé malgré ses astres d'or,
je vais exaspérant ma fièvre et mon désir
à coups de glaive en pleins naseaux !...
Et d'instant en instant, je redresse ma taille
pour sentir sur mon cou qui tressaille
s'enrouler les bras frais et duvetés du vent.

Ce sont tes bras charmeurs et lointains qui m'attirent!
ce vent, c'est ton haleine engloutissante,
insondable Infini qui m'absorbes avec joie !...
Ah ! Ah !... des moulins noirs, dégingandés,
ont tout à coup l'air de courir

sur leurs ailes de toile baleinée
comme sur des jambes démesurées...

Voilà que les Montagnes s'apprêtent à lancer
sur ma fuite des manteaux de fraîcheur somnolente...
Là ! Là ! regardez ! à ce tournant sinistre !...
Montagnes, ô Bétail monstrueux, ô Mammouths
qui trottez lourdement, arquant vos dos immenses,
vous voilà dépassés... noyés...
dans l'échevau des brumes !...
Et j'entends vaguement
le fracas ronronnant que plaquent sur les routes
vos jambes colossales aux bottes de sept lieues...

Montagnes aux frais manteaux d'azur !...
Beaux fleuves respirant au clair de lune !...
Plaines ténébreuses ! je vous dépasse au grand galop
de ce monstre affolé... Étoiles, mes Étoiles,
entendez-vous ses pas, le fracas des abois
et ses poumons d'airain croulant interminablement ?
J'accepte la gageure... avec Vous, mes Étoiles !...
Plus vite !... encore plus vite !...
Et sans répit, et sans repos !...
Lâchez les freins !... Vous ne pouvez ?...
Brisez-les donc !...
Que le pouls du moteur centuple ses élans !

Hurrah ! Plus de contact avec la terre immonde !...
Enfin, je me détache et je vole en souplesse
sur la grisante plénitude
des Astres ruisselants dans le grand lit du ciel !

Le Monoplan du Pape

ROMAN POLITIQUE EN VERS LIBRES

1.
EN VOLANT SUR LE CŒUR
DE L'ITALIE

Horreur de ma chambre à six cloisons comme une
    bière !
Horreur de la terre ! Terre, gluau sinistre
à mes pattes d'oiseau !... Besoin de m'évader !
Ivresse de monter !... Mon monoplan ! Mon
    monoplan !

Dans la brèche des murailles brusquement éclatées
mon monoplan aux grandes ailes flaire le ciel.
Devant moi le fracas de l'acier
déchire la lumière, et la fièvre cérébrale
de mon hélice épanouit son ronflement.
Je vibre en dansant sur mes roues raisonneuses
giflé par le vent fou des fantaisies,
tandis que les mécaniciens dans le noir logique de la
    chambre
me retiennent par la queue élastiquement
comme on tient en laisse un cerf-volant...
Allons-y ! Lâchez tout !...

J'ai le puissant bonheur de me sentir enfin

ce que je suis :
un arbre révolté qui se déracine
d'un coup de volonté et s'élance
sur son feuillage ouvert et bruissant
en poussant droit, tout droit contre le vent
l'écheveau de ses racines,
contre le vent !

Je sens ma poitrine s'ouvrir comme un grand trou
où tout l'azur du ciel, lisse, frais et torrentiel
s'engouffre avec délices.
Je suis une fenêtre ouverte, éprise de soleil
et qui s'envole vers lui !
Qui donc peut arrêter encore
les fenêtres affamées de nuages
et les balcons souls
qui s'arrachent ce soir aux vieux murs des maisons
pour bondir dans l'espace ?

J'ai reconquis mon courage massif
depuis que mes deux pieds végétaux
ne pompent plus le suc conservateur de la peur
dans la terre prudente !

Très haut ! Plein ciel ! Me voici appuyé

194

sur les lois élastiques de l'air ! Ah ! Ah !
Me voici suspendu à pic sur la ville
et son désordre intime
de maisons disposées comme des meubles
        serviables !...
Je me balance à peine comme un lustre allumé
sur la place centrale, table servie,
aux plats fumants, nombreux, automobiles,
et dont les verres étincelants défilent
électriquement !

La dernière balle du soleil déclinant
me frappe, oiseau ensanglanté, mais qui ne
        tombe pas.
Je saute de branche en branche
sur la forêt énorme, illusoire des fumées
qui montent des usines.

Plus haut ! Plus loin ! Hors des murs !
C'est une émeute de croix qui s'avancent
entre les rangs rébarbatifs des cyprès policiers.
Les jardins sépulcraux crient leurs rouges et
        leurs verts.
Les marbres blancs ont l'air de mouchoirs agités.
Ce soir les morts voudraient me suivre...
Ce soir les morts sont ivres, les morts sont gais !
J'étais mort comme vous, je suis ressuscité !...

Le ciel est empesté par l'huile de ricin de mon
        moteur.
J'en ai partout : sur les yeux, sur la bouche... Une
        douche !
Estomac, mon estomac volant,
ne fais donc pas le dégoûté !
Il faut bien payer ton voyage par un peu de nausée...
Vomis donc sur la terre ! Dernier lest pour monter,
et pour jouer légèrement à saute-mouton
sur le dos velu des montagnes !
Campagnes géométriques ! Labours et prés carrés !

O tombeaux de géants ! Chacun aura ses quatre rangs
de candélabres verts que le soleil allume lentement.
Réveillez-vous, fermes tranquilles ! Ouvrez ! Ouvrez
les ailes rouges de vos toits pour voler avec moi
vers ton fou battement, Sicile, grand cœur de l'Italie,
jailli de sa poitrine dans l'élan des conquêtes !...

Enfin, enfin je puis entrer dans les rougeurs du
        couchant
en conquérant, parmi les grimpantes architectures
de la ville future au métal orgueilleux
que les subtils crayons des nuages
dessinèrent dans mon cerveau d'adolescent !
Enfin je fais escale dans les golfes pourprés
de ce grand continent aérien !

Une vaste odeur salée ? La mer !
La mer, innombrables rangs de femmes bleues
qui se dégrafent... Voici l'écume de leurs frêles
        nudités
entrelacées, qui se penchent vers la dernière
gorgée de lumière
dans le rond désert du ciel !
Ah ! laissez-moi rire de vous, voiliers tanguant
        sur place,
insectes culbutés qui ne peuvent — laissez-moi
        rire ! —
et ne pourront jamais se remettre sur pattes !

Ilots prétentieux sous vos pompeuses robes vertes,
vous n'êtes pour moi que de plates
fleurs palustres rongées de mouches grasses !
Je vous dépasse en tourbillon
et je caresse à toute vitesse de la main
l'immense globe d'atmosphère,
dos énorme du danger massacrant
qui me sépare de la mer...

Je vois, je sens au fond, à pic

sous mes pieds,
l'épouvantable choc possible
contre la poitrine plus dure que la pierre,
de la mer !
Joie ! ma joie !... Il faut bien que je lâche
les leviers, pour applaudir l'escadre !
Vingt tortues fabuleuses, immobiles,
avec les têtes des canons tendues
hors des carapaces métalliques
et tout autour le gai frétillement des torpilleurs
et des canots-crapauds,
qui gambillent sur leurs menues rames folles.
Les silhouettes des marins s'écrasent arrondies,
leurs visages gris-perle suivent mes applaudissements
comme on suit les cris bleus des oiseaux migrateurs.
Les larges cuirassés se taisent, mais ils reparleront
avec leur éclatante éloquence de plomb en éventail,
sur l'émail balayé de notre lac Adriatique !

Ah ! Ah ! Sombre vent africain,
vent balourd aux lenteurs hypocrites,
tu guettes mes distractions ?
A quoi bon corriger ta dérive sournoise ?...
Je veux te laisser faire et profiter de toi !
Je m'envole en tes bras filandreux et mouillés.
A mille mètres sous mes pieds la mer noircit de rage.
Nous regagnons la terre ! Elle a donc une odeur ?

Mais quel est ce relent écœurant de caveau ?
J'ai peine à lire et je me penche, le nez sur
        ma boussole.
Cette molle puanteur tombale c'est Rome,
ma capitale !... Ah ! bah ! Taupinière géante,
monceau de paperasses grignotées lentement
par des milliers de rats et de tarets...
Coupoles ! Ventres gonflés de colosses flottants
dans les vapeurs violettes du soir !
Je les vois presque tous percés d'un clocher d'or,

poignard droit vibrant encore dans sa blessure
        sonore,
sur le funèbre maçonnement des ténèbres !...

Des trains ? Je n'y crois guère !
On dirait de véloces serpents dont les anneaux
        rutilent,
et qui nagent souplement par longs bonds cadencés
contre les énormes vagues agressives des forêts
en piquant des plongeons dans le flux des
        montagnes.
De temps en temps les trains s'arrêtent
pour flairer les villages, charognes blêmes
dont ils pompent la vermine phosphoreuse
en faisant claqueter leurs ventouses rayonnantes.
Ah ! que je sois un jour un poison foudroyant
dans vos ventres agiles et cadencés,
lorsque vous bondirez vers la frontière !

Gloire à vous, trains-serpents,
qui profitez de l'ombre pour vous emparer de
        la terre !
La lune a beau vous caresser en vous narguant
de ses longs persiflages de lumière...
La lune a beau montrer le coude reluisant
de son rayon lascif, pour découvrir
la nudité dormante et respirante des fleuves...

O lune triste, somnolente et passéiste,
que veux-tu que je fasse de ces flaques du déluge ?
Je te biffe d'un trait, en allumant mon réflecteur
dont l'énorme rayon électrique est plus neuf
et plus blanc que le tien ! Mon rayon se prélasse
sur les terrasses, inonde les balcons en amour
et furète dans le lit offert des jeunes filles.
Le rayon vagabond de mon grand réflecteur
brûle de gloire et d'héroïsme les ruisseaux
        murmurants

de leurs veines dormantes...
Mais j'ai bien mieux à faire, vent têtu !
Lâche-moi ! A bas les pattes ! Je regagne la mer !

La mer et son grand peuple emprisonné
qui hurle entre ses murs de fer.
Tous ses gardiens sont là. Tous les phares debout
d'autant plus effrayants qu'ils sont silencieux,
immenses et violents dans les ténèbres.
Les uns plongent partout leurs regards
de chasseurs affairés
et d'autres penchent leurs tiges d'or sur les flots noirs
comme des pêcheurs aux lignes lumineuses.

Phares ! Pauvres pêcheurs désenchantés
qu'attendez-vous de cette mer vidée ?
Levez la tête et regardez ! Tous les poissons d'or gras
que vous cherchez frétillent en plein ciel !
J'aime à voler ainsi, comme un lourd papillon
en aveuglant de gestes et de cris
la prunelle douloureuse d'un phare,
sans y brûler mes ailes.

Prenez garde aux cailloux, paquebots somnolents
qui roulez par les collines et les vallées de la mer,
sur les cent reflets-pattes de vos hublots rougeâtres !
Oh ! je plains vos fanaux empalés sur vos mâts
et leur regard souffrant, harassé, qui soupire
vers l'eau bourbeuse et courtoise des ports.
Je vous plains d'être ainsi repoussés violemment
par la mer et le vent qui fait tourbillonner
sur vos voiles en pleurs
les voûtes grimaçantes de sa bouche ébréchée !

Là-bas ce sont des paquebots en déroute !
On dirait des usines envolées, fumantes, vitres en feu,
que le cyclone a brusquement
déracinées de toutes pièces.

Elles filent sur la noirceur vivante de la mer !
Et ce navire a l'air... Mais de quoi donc ? J'y suis !...
...d'un grand moulin à moudre les étoiles !
Ses mâts pompent le ciel, et tout autour
une farine sidérale ruisselle hors des hublots !

Mais il faut résister à tous les coups du vent debout
qui m'arrête, et je tangue, et je roule, et je tiens
mon monoplan en équilibre
en manœuvrant les deux gouvernails...
Un coup de pompe suffira pour me donner encore
le ronron velouté du moteur assouvi...
O bon carburateur, coule donc grand ouvert
comme une blessure de héros !

Enfin mon cœur, mon grand cœur futuriste
a vaincu sa rude bataille millénaire
contre les barreaux du thorax.
Mon cœur vient de bondir hors de ma poitrine.
C'est lui, c'est lui, qui me soulève et qui m'emporte
avec son tourbillon sanguinolent d'artères.
Tournoyante hélice épouvantable !
Je suis fondu avec mon monoplan,
je suis la vrille colossale
qui perce l'écorce pétrifiée de la nuit.

Plus fort ! toujours plus fort ! Il faut creuser en rond
profondément dans cette fibre momifiée par les âges.
Vais-je longtemps battre des ailes
comme un vautour cloué sur les vantaux du ciel ?
Ce point résiste ? Cherchons plus haut ! Brisons
le triste vitrail de l'aube jaunissante !
Hélice ! forte hélice de mon cœur monoplan,
formidable vrille enthousiaste et volontaire,
ne sens-tu pas craquer les ténèbres exécrables
sous ton effort perçant ?

L'écorce empouacrante va perdant son opacité.

Quelle rage ! Hâtons-nous... Qu'a-t-elle donc
à s'opposer ainsi ?
Encore un grand effort ! Encore ! Encore !...
C'est presque fait : tout va tomber !
Encore ! Voici ! Voici ! Hourrah !
Un grand effondrement de pourpre emplit l'espace,
et le soleil juteux, fruit colossal,
saute avec joie brutalement
hors de sa molle gousse de ténèbres.

Habitants de Palerme ! Me voyez-vous venir ?
C'est moi ! C'est moi !... Applaudissez,
car je suis un des vôtres !...
Mon monoplan a l'air d'un homme blanc, géant,
debout sur le tremplin des nuages, et qui se penche
les bras grands-ouverts pour piquer un plongeon
dans votre frémissante aurore sicilienne.

Dans cette rade mauve et baignée de silence,
ce village dormant
tire encore sur les yeux de ses vitres vermeilles,
machinalement,
le grand drap moelleux de soie bleue de la mer.
Et cet autre village comme un morceau de fer
chauffé au rouge ardent par le soleil
fume entre les tenailles mordorées de la mer.

Hourrah ! les jeunes cloches de Palerme
m'ont déjà aperçu ! Elles s'élancent joyeuses
sur leurs escarpolettes enfantines
et se balancent d'avant en arrière
pour ventiler leurs jupes de bronze ronronnantes
et leurs jambes mordues par un désir de liberté.
Me voici ! Me voici, ô cloches de Palerme !...
Pour jouir de vos longs élancements sonores,
je coupe l'allumage et je file vers vous
comme un long canot blanc qui vient de soulever
son double rang de rames au bout d'une régate.

Tu m'apparais de loin, Palerme,
comme un formidable arsenal
défendu à droite, à gauche par les murs des
            montagnes
avec tes longues rues qui plongent dans la mer,
et leurs terrasses rapprochées qui serviront
de glissière au Dreadnought dominateur du
            monde !...
Tes rues profondes ont dans leur creux le fiévreux
va-et-vient des calfats, et très haut le suave
déchirement des brises roses...

Siciliens ! vous qui luttez depuis les temps brumeux
nuit et jour, corps à corps avec la rage des volcans,
j'aime vos âmes qui flamboient
comme les fous prolongements du feu central,
et vous me ressemblez, Sarrazins d'Italie,
au nez puissant et recourbé sur la proie que l'on
            mâche
avec de belles dents futuristes !...
J'ai comme vous les joues brûlées par le simoun,
l'allure élastique et violente des félins dans les herbes
et le regard criblant, qui refoule dans l'ombre
les dos visqueux et sursautants du policier et du
            bedeau.
Vous ouvrez comme moi toutes les souricières.
Les rats peuvent gaiement ronger nos manuscrits,
car nos moteurs écrivent en plein ciel
les strophes claires d'acier et d'or définitives !
Chacun de vous sait faire une justice hautaine
autour de son grand Moi dompteur et indomptable.
Fi de la pesante machine sociale !...
Fi de la triste mécanique des lois
et de son pauvre rendement de justice !
Mécanique enfantine aux rouages sommaires
qui brusquement accroche un miséreux tremblant,
pour le rouler, le triturer, le broyer stupidement,
et, *vlan*, par la fenêtre comme une gousse morte
au nom sacré d'une invisible majesté !

2.
LES CONSEILS DU VOLCAN

Je viens à toi, Volcan, et je nargue
tes furibonds ricanements de ventriloque.
Je ne suis pas à ta merci, crois-moi !
Tu voudrais bien me capturer
dans tes filets de lave,
comme tu fais des promeneurs mordus d'ambition
quand ils affrontent sur tes flancs
l'effroyable tristesse du couchant énorme
qui tout à coup s'esclaffera lugubrement
en tremblement de terre !
Je ne crains pas les menaces ni les symboles
de l'espace, qui peut bien à sa guise
ensevelir les villes
sous des monceaux de cuivre et d'or
et de caillots de sang.

Je suis le futuriste invincible et puissant
emporté par son cœur au vol infatigable.
C'est pourquoi je m'attable chez l'Aurore
pour me gaver à son étal de fruits multicolores !
J'écrase les midis, fumantes pyramides de boulets,
j'enjambe les couchants, armées sanglantes en
          déroute,
et je traîne à mes trousses
les sanglotants crépuscules nostalgiques !...

Etna ! Qui donc saura danser mieux que moi
et se dodeliner élégamment sur ta bouche farouche
qui beugle à mille mètres sous mes pieds ?
Je descends et je plonge en ton haleine sulphydrique
parmi les globes colossaux de tes fumées rougeâtres.
J'entends le lourd fracas retentissant
de ton vaste estomac qui s'effondre
comme les pans d'une capitale souterraine.
C'est en vain que la rage charbonneuse de la terre

voudrait me repousser en plein ciel !
Mes leviers sont fermes entre mes doigts,
cependant que je hurle :

MOI

O Volcan,
démasque ton visage aux verrues de phosphore !
Mets donc en branle tes muscles buccaux,
ouvre tes lèvres rocailleuses encroûtées de granits,
et crie-moi quelle est la destinée
et quels sont les devoirs qui s'imposent à ma race.
Réveille la résonnance épouvantable
de tes poumons fuligineux.
Je suis agile et fort, et je contrains les vents
à pépier peureusement sous mes deux ailes,
ainsi que des poussins.
Admire donc mes ailes qui paraissent immenses,
noyées là-bas dans les spirales courroucées des
          vapeurs.

Je vois derrière moi mon stabilisateur,
très loin, et mon gouvernail qui s'ensanglantent
sur la conflagration réverbérée de tes entrailles.
Ma toile vibre monotone comme un tambour
sous la danse aérienne des tisons roses.
Buanderie infernale où tout se décompose !

Comme un fumeur repousse la fumée d'un cigare,
d'une rude bouffée tu éloignes, ô Volcan,
ton imposant panache blanc, avec désinvolture.
Mon horizon est barré de toutes parts
par l'énorme contorsion
de tes mâchoires éclatées, toutes dégouttantes de
          braise !...
Je suis au beau milieu, dans le délabrement sinistre
de tes lèvres plus hautes
et plus épaisses que les montagnes...

Et je descends encore en contemplant autour de moi
tes monstrueuses gencives boursouflées...
Quelle est cette flore de molles fumerolles
que tu voudrais mâcher
comme une lourde moustache bleue ?...
Voilà que le rauque entonnoir de ta gorge
m'apparaît comme un théâtre incendié,
d'une ampleur incalculable,
où furent conviés tous les peuples de la terre.
Car ils peuvent à plaisir y trouver large place.
Ce sont là des gradins grouillants de peuple en fête !...

On y voit s'y presser tout en gesticulant
plus d'un milliard de flammes
spectatrices enthousiastes
qui applaudissent et crient différemment
un milliard de jouissances.
Sur la cohue rougeâtre, subitement plastronnent
des explosions de gaz violâtres,
apoplectiques et bedonnantes.
Plus loin, des vapeurs jaunes hystériques
sous leurs brusques chapeaux verts déclanchent
des rayons passionnés, attendris et soudain
      persifleurs.

Quelle est donc cette flamme amusée et rieuse,
toute gaînée de velours mauve
et qui sait si bien lancer paraboliquement
son chapeau orangé, jailli, évanoui,
vers le spectacle des spectacles qui commence ?
Dans le parterre du théâtre qui doit bien mesurer
plus de vingt kilomètres de diamètre,
se déploie largement une invitante mer de feu
ça et là plissée d'ombre et fraîchement teintée
de corail et de joues enfantines,
avec de longs tressaillements de cris blancs.

Est-ce donc le fracas écrasant d'une enclume
qui va haussant de plus en plus la surface

irradiante de cette mer de feu ?
Des fleuves, des rivières
et des ruisseaux resplendissants
gorgés de lingots d'or, accourent à l'envi
pour la nourrir en ruisselant
hors des crevasses éloquentes
qui s'ouvrent de distance en distance
tout le long des gradins,
parmi l'ondoyante moisson
des flammes et des gaz spectateurs.

Parmi la corpulence des rochers congestionnés,
flammes et gaz mènent la fête et s'ébaudissent...
Tout cet étrange public cramoisi
est entraîné pêle-mêle par l'élan véhément
des gestes applaudisseurs
vers la gorge, vers le cœur, vers le centre
du cratère, entonnoir et cirque ardent.

Et cette mer de feu se fige et s'empierre.
Par groupes de caillots et d'îlots cousus, fondus,
par rapides alluvions de rubis et d'agates,
un continent se forme, vermeil, éblouissant...
Tout autour sur la mer de braise
une flottille tangue
en déployant sa toile qui réfléchit
toutes les couleurs brillantes de la lave.

Le continent se dalle peu à peu de chrysolithes,
et voilà brusquement les dalles défoncées
par la chute émerveillante
de trois mille lions,
qui tombent du ciel, cataractant de haine
et giclant hors de leurs naseaux d'usines
de criardes fontaines de perles et de mica.
Echeveau furibond, forêt de pattes et de crinières
      incendiaires
dont une seule peut carboniser trois villes,
peindre à fresque le ciel blafard du pôle

et réchauffer les joues des étoiles hivernales.

Ebranlement viscéral de la terre !
Toutes les grenades d'Italie accumulées,
sanguinolence d'un assommoir qui brûle,
trombe virante de croupes emboîtées !
Enorme pyramide de hurlements noirs
courue de haut en bas par des sanglots-bébés
et qui chancelle dans la ronde des frayeurs blêmes !...
N'est-ce donc pas notre planète ensanglantée
par cent mille batailles,
qui roule au loin sous la lunette d'un habitant
        de Mars ?...

Ah ! bah ! ces apparences ou ces réalités
sont bien à la portée de la main !...
J'ai par exemple sous la main
cet illusoire soleil couchant, écailleux, chevelu,
formé de trois mille fauves qui s'entremordent.
Je pourrais bien le soupeser tandis qu'il s'enfonce
dans le cratère dramatique de ce volcan...

Je me vois nimbé d'une riche poussière
        phosphoreuse.
Je brûle et je fonds comme un métal,
parmi d'incessantes combustions d'hydrogène.
Ce craquement formidable qu'est-ce donc ?
Le broiement sans doute des ossatures des trois
        mille lions
sous des pans de montagnes !...
Le carnage méticuleux des fauves se propage.

Tous leurs crocs d'ivoire grandissent, s'exagèrent,
couvrent d'un treillis crayeux la bouillie écarlate
et ses râles éclaboussants d'horreur.
Ce sont des crocs immensifiés ou plutôt des fumées
        blanches ?..
Non, non, c'est de l'ivoire, car voici
des trompes d'éléphants se mêlent à la bagarre.

Des éléphants vont çà et là posant leurs pattes
pareilles aux obélisques
flicflacant dans la sauce jaune de ce soufre liquide,
et dans ce tumulte rouge de raisins
qui s'éboule sur les coins et réjaillit très haut
en corolles de vin, pour arroser les spectateurs...

Par-dessus la vendange piétinée
glissent vélocement en équilibre sur des fils invisibles
les fumées bariolées comme des clowns,
en déchargeant à droite, à gauche leurs revolvers
qui exaspèrent la folie inouïe des couleurs enragées !

O Volcan ! ton spectacle m'enivre.
Je descends plus bas pour mieux le contempler.
J'ai aux reins ma ceinture de sauvetage
et je puis bien nager, si le désir m'en prend,
dans cette tendre et fraîche mer de feu.
Qui donc a pu d'un souffle anéantir
les continents de pourpre et les pelotes de lions
        liquéfiées ?

Lentement hors des blessures pantelantes
des vagues, émergent les quilles monstrueuses
de trois cuirassés noirs, mâchés et remâchés,
que l'insolence des profondeurs sous-marines
a rejetés sans doute à la surface.
Lentement, un à un, les trois vaisseaux de guerre
recommencent à vivre avec de longs frissons.
Ils nouent leurs membres morts, redressent leur
        mâture,
tout en s'équilibrant... Et leurs chaudières qui
        s'allument
mettent en branle les larges tours d'acier.

Un mal de mer empoigne aux entrailles les canons
qui tressaillent avec un continu vomissement de
        plomb.
Ce sont des hures hérissées d'étincelles

qui grognent en crachant par bordées acharnées
des silicates, des cristaux et des blocs vitreux
sur les ébats rieurs et les chassés-croisés
des torpilleurs et des requins.

Ceux-ci se muent bizarrement en îles fragiles
intermittentes, tôt apparues, tôt disparues
qui luttent contre la succion des flots !
Et cependant un cuirassé s'éventre et coule
en faisant éclater les soutes de son cœur
qui s'épanouit en brasier mugissant contre le ciel.
Ce n'est déjà plus qu'un vagabond arrosoir
d'azur liquide, éventail de fraîcheur.

Je suis enfin au paradis des arbres violets
qui se lamentent sous le poids
des trop larges étoiles en fleur
et de trop lourds éclairs, papillons acharnés
qui sucent la lumière.
Ce paradis est enlacé de tous côtés
par de rondes cascades d'émeraudes coulantes.
Est-ce ton âme, ô Volcan, qui s'élance au milieu
avec un énorme jet de vif-argent poudroyant
dont la force verticale résiste
aux coups redoublés de la rafale ?

O Volcan, j'entends depuis longtemps
le roulement continu de ta voix turbulente
qui frémit dans la rauque cheminée de ta gorge.
Je m'oublie tellement à contempler
l'éruption de tes paroles chauffées à blanc
que je n'ai pas encore démêlé l'écheveau
fulgurant de ta pensée !

Oh ! la maîtrise et l'inspiration
que le tonnerre éclatant de ta voix manifeste
sur les torrides parois de ton atelier !...
Tu sculptes avec ces masses de craie fumante

des monstres symboliques et de grands bas-reliefs
aveuglants de clarté qui pourraient déployer
à l'improviste, ainsi que les comètes,
un feuillage de rayons sur l'insomnie de l'océan !...

Enfin j'entends un mot ! Un formidable mot
se gonfle et saute hors de ta bouche,
en plein ciel, tout au bout d'un long tuyau
de fumée noire,
comme ces globes mous de verre en fusion
que les verriers soufflent à pleines joues
parmi la rage incandescente d'une verrerie !

LE VOLCAN

Je n'ai jamais dormi. Je travaille sans fin
pour enrichir l'espace de chefs-d'œuvres
      éphémères !
Je veille à la cuisson des roches ciselées
à la vitrification polichrôme des sables,
si bien qu'entre mes doigts les argiles
se métamorphosent
en d'idéales porcelaines roses
que je brise avec mes chiquenaudes de vapeur !...

Je suis incessamment mêlé à mes scories.
Ma vie est la fusion perpétuelle de mes débris.
Je détruis pour créer et je détruis encore
pour modeler de tonnantes statues
que j'émiette aussitôt dans l'horreur de durer.

Le soleil pesant d'or que les ténèbres désenchaînent
chaque matin et qui se hisse à grand'peine
sur les montagnes de Calabre
a beau projeter le cône de mon ombre accablante
jusqu'au centre de la Sicile,
pour semer à la ronde l'effroi et la prudence.
Chacun nourrit l'espoir de me savoir dompté

comme une grosse bête morphinisée.
Ma toison d'hermine et ma crinière blanche
leur sont des gages d'innocence et de lente agonie.

J'ai pour complice le détroit de Messine
qui sommeille à l'aube, allongé blanc et lisse
comme un chat d'Angora...
J'ai pour complice le détroit de Messine
avec ses airs las de matelas de soie turquoise,
et les doux mots arabes brodés par les sillages
des nuages et des voiles paresseuses
qu'on a tissés, je pense, en silence,
d'un beau fil argenté, sur la robe de la mer...

J'ai pour complice la lune mensongère,
la plus fardée des courtisanes sidérales,
qui nulle part ailleurs n'est aussi câlineuse,
entraînante et persuasive.

Nulle part ailleurs la lune n'est aussi attentive
à séduire les rouges fanaux durs des paquebots
passants bourrus qui s'en vont,
un gros cigare entre les dents,
en crachant leur fumée contre l'azur.

Nulle part ailleurs la lune ne verse une aussi tendre
et molle cendre violette
pour assoupir la lave ossifiée
des maisons noires accrochées à mes flancs.
Nulle part ailleurs la lune n'a d'aussi poignantes
inondations de lumière et d'extase
sur les entailles des sentiers
creusés par mon feu chirurgien.

Malheur à ceux qui suivent la lumière bêlante
de la lune et les clarines plaintives des troupeaux
et les flûtes amères des bergers qui perdent dans
            l'azur
les très longs filaments de leurs sons nostalgiques !...

Malheur à ceux qui refusèrent d'accorder le galop
de leur sang au galop de mon sang dévastateur !...

Malheur à ceux qui veulent enraciner
leurs cœurs, leurs pieds et leurs maisons
avec un ladre espoir d'éternité !
Il ne faut point bâtir, mais se camper.
N'ai-je pas la forme d'une tente
dont le sommet tronqué aère mes colères ?
Je n'aime que les astres, sveltes équilibristes
qui se tiennent debout sur les sphères roulantes
de mes fumées jongleuses !...

MOI

Je sais danser comme eux, et jongler en plein ciel,
et couvrir de mon chant le fracas retentissant
de tes orages qui se propagent
aux profonds souterrains !...
Et je descends
pour écouter les polyèdres de ta voix.
Espace donc les décharges électriques de tes bronches
qui disloquent là-bas les roches sousjacentes !
Impose le silence à tes grottes loquaces
qui s'ébranlent d'émoi interminablement !...
Bâillonne de cendres épaisses
les échos basaltiques qui t'applaudissent en chœur !

Je n'ai que faire des bombes volcaniques
dont tu ponctues le grondement de ton discours !
Que m'importent les jets rutilants
de ta salive agressive ?
Tes déluges de boue ont sali mes ailes blanches,
mais ne m'arrêtent pas ! Je résiste aux avalanches
de tes scories, et je descends doré, auréolé
par tes pulvérulences d'or émerveillé.

LE VOLCAN

Je ravage à la ronde tous les jardins
des sentiments en fleur
et leurs ombrages, guitares et mandolines
qui pleurent aux doigts des vents,
donneurs de sérénades.

Je bouleverse les sages potagers
et les salades bien peignées,
mais je contourne avec délicatesse
les forêts aux gros troncs téméraires
dont les branches musclées ont horreur de la terre,
et tendent leurs poings carbonisés
contre les astres, fragiles et pépiants moineaux
qui voudraient s'y poser !...

Gare à ceux qui s'endorment
en adorant la trace des ancêtres
sous les calmes feuillages de la Paix !
Je ne respecte rien, ni les ruines de la pierre,
ni les ruines de la chair.
Mon souffle pousse au hasard par pelletées
les vaincus et les lâches dans leurs tombeaux,
seuls sillons que leurs pieds ont creusés,
pioches méthodiques !
Guerre ou révolte, vous n'avez qu'à choisir !...
Grandes fêtes du feu, dont s'honore le monde !

Quel est donc l'oiseau présomptueux
ou la chaloupe aérienne,
qui rame sur ma tête ?
Tu es sans doute un des mes enfants dégénérés !...
Italien, fils refroidi des Laves millénaires !

Toi et tes frères, ah ! que je puisse enfin
vous contempler debout sur le pont véloce
des torpilleurs nocturnes
parmi la haine atroce des bourrasques,

à la merci des rafales d'un cyclone,
et guettant néanmoins les masses d'ébène
plus noires que la nuit,
que tasseront dans le noir les escadres ennemies !...
Que je puisse vous voir devenus tout à coup
des brûlots, des îlots ou des vaisseaux,
en éruption continue d'héroïsme
contre les nues !...

Je sucerai les pierres et la terre
sous les pieds des Italiens,
planteurs de chênes et de palais.
Il vous faut dépasser ma fureur ou périr !
Je briserai vos nids, oiseaux niais d'Italie,
pour que vous appreniez à voler sur la vie !
Avec les crayons bondissants de mes laves
je bifferai du monde les formes géographiques
que ne colore pas l'allégresse du sang !

MOI

Hourrah ! Hourrah ! Je crache comme toi, avec toi,
ô Volcan,
sur tous les usuriers de notre sang conquérant !
C'est pour te plaire que j'ai crié
sur les cimes rugissantes de l'énergie humaine :
« Glorifions la guerre, seule hygiène du monde ! »
C'est pour te plaire que violemment
je débarrasse de la paix parasite
l'Italie, liane puissante
qui doit bientôt grimper en espalier
sur les constellations !...

Oh ! crachons sur la Paix, immonde Raflésie
de l'île de Java,
vaste fleur colossale, aux feuilles pourrissantes
dont le cœur évidé est plein d'une eau puante
où nagent et se nourrissent les insectes gluants
qui colonisent la pulpe infâme des cadavres !

LE VOLCAN

Oh ! que tous les échos attentifs de la terre
embrassent ta voix rouge plus chaude que ma voix !...
Je reconnais en toi mon fils régénéré.
Reçois, mon fils, sur tes joues rayonnantes
ma double et triple accolade de feu !
Mais où donc s'est nichée la meute de mes laves ?
Entendez-vous mon sifflement de vapeur
        étranglée ?...
Chiennes rouges aux longues dents corrosives,
vite à mes pieds ! Couchez-vous
devant cet Homme en feu,
et léchez les deux roues de son beau monoplan !...

Zang Toumb Toumb

Correction
d'épreuves désirs

Pas de poésie avant nous avec notre imagination sans fils et mots en liberté **VIII**ve le **FUTURISME** enfin enfin enfin enfin enfin enfin enfin

ENFIN

PoÉSIE **NAITRE**

mon train train **tron tron tron tron** (pont de fer: **tatatlantlein**) **sssssiii ssiissii ssisssssssiii** train train train fièvre de mon train express-express-express-expressssssss press-press-press-press-press-press-press-presssssss press-press-press press-presssssss picoté par le sel marin arooomaaatisé par les orangers chercher mer mer mer **boNdir BONdir BONBONDIIR** rails rrrails frétiiiillement (*GOUR-MAND SALÉ POURPRÉ FALOT INÉVITABLE IN-CLINÉ IMPONDÉRABLE FRAGILE DANSANT AIMANTÉ*) j'expliquerai ces mots je veux dire que ciel détroit montagnes sont gourmands salés pourprés etc. et que moi aussi je suis gourmand salé pourpré

etc. tout cela hors de moi **mais aussi en moi** totalité simultanéité synthèse absolue = supériorité de ma poésie sur toutes les autres STOP
                    Villa San Giovanni
capture + pêche + avalement du train-requin l'emmailler le pou-pou-pou-pousser dans ferry-boat-baleine   gare flottante
                soliddtté de la mer en chêne varlopé   indigo   ventila-tion (*INSENSIBLE QUOTIDIEN MÉTHODIQUE ÉTOFFÉ MÉTALLIQUE TRRRRÉPIDANT DÉCOUPÉ EMPAQUETÉ CISELÉ NEUF*)   allu-mage d'un voilier = lampe à pétrole + 12 abat-jours blancs + tapis vert + cercle de solitude sérénité familiale méthode d'un second voilier proue façon-ner au tour le métal de la mer copeaux d'écume abaissement de la tem-pérature = 3 éventails par-dessus les Monts Calabres (*BLEU LENT INDULGENT SCEPTIQUE*)
        décoooombres de Messine dans le dé-troit   tremblements de terres presque liquides   sentir la mer comme une somme de poids différents   naviguer = additionner 200.000 blocs poutres cordages barils **(plouououm)** + million sacs bleus plafonds pourris portes vertes fiacres jaunes + 2.000 grossesses à

vapeur **tataploumploum flac flac**
contre la prrroue-ventre   tenir dans
la bouche toute la mer RONDE ⹀ nageur
jongleur ╈ assiette de porcelaine (diamètre
6 Km.) entre les dents

LUNE (*JAUNE VIEUX*)

à

pic

sursauts blancheur bourrrrrdonnements naisssss-
sance exassssssspérée de 4 glooobes élec-
triques suspendus sur mon train arrêté en
gare flo-flo-flottante du ferry-boat

LUNE (*LAIT SALE*)

à

pic

éclairage suffisant pour corriger les épreuves
de mon livre sur Andrinople   *x*
nausée   présence de la ville as-
siégée dans le détroit tourner le dos à
Messine-Mustapha-Pacha   entassement
gradué de Villa-San-Giovanni dégringolade de
8 lampes électriques dans la mer   à
droite 2me cascade de feux blancs Reggio
          sous mes pieds-cale-quille 1000
m. profondeur centre du détroit grand égout
volcanique ouvert il y a 5 ans   pos-
sibles tiraillements de l'intestin terrestre
          Villa-San-Giovanni ⹀ agitation de 300
lampes électriques secouées par 18 épais-
seurs différentes de vent-vent-vent courant

danse de poissons amusés devant la
rampe d'acétylène d'une barque   Reg-
gio ⹀ agitation de 800 lampes électriques
(**BRANDI FURIEUX ENRAGÉ**) secouées par 20
épaisseurs différentes de vent courant
          haine universelle pour la lune
glisssssssade du train hors du filet-ferry-boat

MESSINE

Messine improvisation répétition générale d'une
ville-qui-va-se-jouer indifférence de l'auteur su-
cres et joies de l'atmosphère   es-
carpolette de sérénades (3 barytons 2 ténors)
acharnement frileux du lierre sur les baraques
souplesse du ciment armé en équilibre sur
les espiègleries de la lave FASTE d'un ap-
partement ⹀ alcove ╈ baldaquin ╈ ga-
lerie de tableaux ╈ cuisine engoncé dans
une baraque (8 m. carrés)
          impossibilité d'opposer des façades
altières au vent du détroit pas plus de
10 m. de hauteur AMBITION TRONquée
des propriétaires   préoccupation des
maisons ⹀ se tenir à 4 pattes en lut-
teurs pour ne pas être culbutées rixe
prochaine **PRÉSENCE** du trem-
blement de terre lutteur fatigué dormant
sur le seuil   fumée du volcan
chamade lancée aux vésuves strombolis
          perfidie des végétations ⹀ trav-
estis du tremblement de terre menace d'un
jardin trop parfumé bouffées poivrées du
danger   poudrière ╈ volonté ╈
trrrrrravail ╈ comfort ╈ insouciance de
la fécondation nocturne ⹀ Messine
vitesse d'automobiles vers Catane

70 Km.
à l'heure
trrrrrrrrrrrrrr

{ le **chauffeur couché à la ren-**
verse sous le volant énOrme qui
tourne comme un monde
patiner sur les vitesses lavées par
les virages virages prairies jardins
plages décor calabrais cône de
l'Etna indigo échancrures
promontoires cactus

torréfaction explosive ✛ vitesse ✛ férr-
rrrocité des pneus poussière charbon de la
route soif soif du caoutchouc cactus

futurisme		fé		boyaux
hérissement	des	ro		se tordre
sobriété héroïsme	cactus	ce		torrents
épppaisssseur résistance	**Soldats nègres**	ment		cahots
solidité	qui offrent	nés		courir
métallisme	des fruits	entre		spasmes
antivégétal	jûteux	entre		crier
300.000 solitudes midis	de rose	**SUR**		fumeer
embrasement sables embuscades	comme	dans		de
ghibli bouches yeux brûlés	des lampes	contre		**LAVE**
conquêtes africaines	électriques	(*NOIR*		**PÉTRIFIÉE**
Saharas concentrés		*DUR*		sous
		TORDU)		vastes
				ouates
				gelées de
				l'atmosphère

80 Km.
à l'heure
TRrrrrrrrrrrr

{ vitesse sédentaire du chauffeur couché à la renverse dans son vOlant Saturne dans son anneau tourner tourner faire du pied au lointain pied bleu des plus folles vitesses **glou glou glou** d'air en bouteilles-oreilles vent ventriloque

95 Km.
à l'heure
TRRRRRR

{ nonchalOir musical du chauffeur tenir la pédale à l'orgue ronflante des Kilomètres respirés d'un souffle et ressoufflés au loin

100 Km.
à l'heure
TRRRRRR

{ refouler avec le pied droit accélérateur très loin distances $+$ 1000 profondeurs $+$ 3000 résistances de la terre aux frottantes vitesses qui s'Offrent **pan-pan-traaak tatatraaak**

toung   toungzangCHAAK   panache

Stop

(freinage   instinctif   sursaut   agonie   du   chauffeur) $^1|_3$ d'auto   3   roues   brouter brouter   brouter   blondeurs   fourrages   ironies d'un   village   306   ans   stupidité   du paysage   montagneux   prendre   mon   auto   pour les   ruines   de   Girgenti   les   serrer   dans   les bras   de   ses   vallées   ruisseaux   arbres   herbes   corriger   épreuves   non   non   voici

TENEZ

mes   epreuves   telles   quelles   pour   **NETTOYER** mon   **CHER**   carburateur   survivant

38 bis

CARTE SYNCHRONIQUE
des sons bruits couleurs images odeurs espoirs volontés énergies nostalgies tracée par l'aviateur Y. M.

GAUCHE   matelas élastique vert jaune blanc de bruits fracas d'où sort un long son floconneux = ANDRINOPLE + jardins + 27 forts   DROITE

double ligne droite longue de bruits durs = mitrailleuse

œuf de silence doré = **ballon** captif femme enceinte en étoffes légères bord de la mer prise et reprise par le vent pelage vert tigré de bruits plaine + batterie

jaune **fracas** globulaire = village + fourrages

porte-épingles de bruits jaunes = shrapnel éclaté sur village

5 étoiles argentées de bruits = 5 shrapnels

30 sons **rouges** dégingandés = échos de boulets

ressac écumant de sons liquides = vallon 200 m. profondeur

cascade de sons verdoyants = vallon 300 m. profondeur

parabole lasse de sons bleus = boulet de 150

écroulement de fracas caqués en marche = ligne horizon

400 500 600 700 800 900 1000

shrapnel éclaté

100 200 300 400 500 600 700 800 900 1000

scie de bruits = auto

pelage vert tigré de bruits = plaine + batterie

Nœud de sons roses et de bruits violets = carrefour

tresse azurée de sons moelleux = nostalgie de Paulette Quartier Latin

jet de sons glacés = village

bruit en forme de poire = camp

flaque de bruits salée = carrefour

escarpolette rose de sons languissants = route ondulée + vent du nord

caravane de sons bleus verts roses = Maritza

MONTS RHODOPES

3000 bruits qui se débattent sous un éventail d'échos frais =

chaudière noirâtre de bruits + va-et-vient d'un son trompette piston = MUSTAPHA-PACHA

Hadirlik
quartier général turc

enthousiasme des nizamiés traî-nassement débraillement des mustafiz redif barbe cheveux blancs ihtyats musulmans et non musulmans Grecs Bulgares Macédoniens Israélites Arméniens appelés sous les drapeaux turcs

PENDAISON
1 2 3 4 5

traîtres espions déserteurs professeurs Bulgares

cadavres sandwiches portant sur le ventre affichée la sentence-réclame pêle-mêle officiers et bestiaux Ismaïl-Pacha commandant la citadelle Fuad-Bey officier d'état-major chevaux mulets chars talikas ordre de se ravitailler pour 2 mois ne plus circuler à partir de 7 heures soir population d'Andrinople (55.000 Turcs + 20.000 Grecs + 10.000 Bulgares + 6.000 Arméniens + 20.000 Israélites = 120.000 bouches soif **eau coupée**) 240.000 oreilles pleines du

tatatatatatata des mitriaze aux avampostes Akbounar Kadikeuy tonnerrrrre continuuuu de roues dans la rue de Stamboul-Yolou

DÉFAITE DE KIRKILISSE

communications avec Constantinople coupées débordement de l'armée bulgare sur Babaësky et Lule-Burgas défilé de 300 Turcs déserteurs poings liés entre baïonnettes turques vite enfourner dans les caves de Hadirlik papiers et archives des chemins de fer

jugements turcs sur les Bulgares

{ mauvais soldats que les officiers ramènent au feu à coups de fouet et de plat de sabre goût pour l'embuscade adopter le fez arborer drapeau blanc utiliser ténèbres et pluie embrocher vieillards enfants éventrer femmes enceintes violer fillettes manger oignons courges frites orge grillé etc.

INDIFFÉRENCE

DE 2 ROTONDITÉS SUSPENDUES

SOLEIL + BALLON

CAPTIFS

flammes géantes   colonnes de fumée   spirales d'étincelles

villages   turcs   incendiés

grand **T**

rrrrronronnnnant   d'un   monoplan   bulgare   +
neige   de   manifestes

Nous, Bulgares, nous faisons la guerre au gouvernement ottoman qui est inapte à gouverner convenablement. Nous ne sommes pas contre la population musulmane. Vous devez savoir que nous ne désirons pas verser le sang. Nous voulons vous sauver des hommes du gouvernement ottoman, qui sont cruels, perfides et sans cœur. Nous voulons avoir une garantie sur cette presqu'île des Balkans. En quel état vous ont réduits vos gouvernements vous le savez. Vos voisins les quatre Etats ont occupé votre territoire de tous côtés. Kirk-Kilisse est depuis longtemps entre les mains des Bulgares. Baba-Esky, Lule-Burgas, Domotika, Uskub, Britchtina, Nevrokop, Komanovo, Elasona et bien d'autres villes sont aussi, depuis longtemps entre nos mains. Andrinople est cernée de tous les côtés; la route de Constantinople est aussi coupée. Vous devez savoir que la ville d'Andrinople ne peut plus recevoir du secours de nulle part. Dans ces conditions, à quoi bon verser du sang? A quoi servirait-il? Serait-ce pour la justice ou pour nos gouvernants qui sont des brigands et des tyrans? 1000 pièces de canon sont dirigées sur Andrinople. Si elle ne se rend pas, elle sera détruite et entièrement dévastée. N'est-ce pas regrettable pour la population?

(Avis jeté par l'aéroplane bulgare le 18–31 Octobre 328 à 6 h. 20 du soir)

longs   convois   de   mohadjirs   musulmans   chas-
sés   par   les   flammes   de   leurs   villages-brasiers
vers   Andrinople   6000   Arabas   (hardes
ustensiles   de   ménage   grabats   nattes)

puanteur   rance   et   mielleuse   +   sueur
+   haleines   sifflantes   de   35   mohadjirs   épeler
mot   à   mot   bulletin   affiché

. . . .

Nous espérons fermement qu'avec l'aide de Dieu l'ennemi sera sous peu repoussé. Le Commandant de la place attend des habitants du calme et de la fermeté.

CHOUKRI-PACHA

Commandant   de   la   place.

5   m.   plus   haut   vibration   des   vitres   blocs
de   voix   +   gesticulations   de   Choukri   rage
insultes   pesanteur   de   son   mépris   sur   Khalil-
bey   coupable   d'avoir   laissé   entrer   20.000
mohadjirs   =   20.000   bouches   inutiles

pas   de   charbon   de   bois   pétrole   à   22
piastres   le   bidon   les   marchands   majorent
les   prix   malgré   municipalité   pas   d'éclairage
nocturne

allô   allô   téléphone
Hakky-bey   a   gagné   2   Kilomètres   (du   1er
au   2me retranchement   bulgare)

espoir
d'être secourus
par les armées de {
Nazim-Pacha
(à Tcherkeskeuy 150.000 hommes)
ou Doghrout-Pacha
ou Mouchtar-Pacha
ou Abdullah-Pacha à la rescousse

télégraphe rétabli entre Andrinople et Ouzun-Keupru   ordre du ministre des finances au Defterdar du vilayet verser recettes de postes télégraphes douanes régie dette publique à l'armée   voix nasillarde de 2 garçons de recette répéter répéter les chiffres chiffres chiffres chiffres   obliquité du kalpak d'astrakan sur le front large dur bombé de Choukri double broussaille grise des sourcils   yeux durs aigus nez aquilin droit épaisseur grissonnante de moustache et barbe résistance musculaire huilée par 60 ans de volonté petite tenue vert-kaki souplesse des épaules pattes d'épaulettes agilité des jambes bottées nuit et jour roulement de 3 batteries dans la rue gaîté d'un commandement mordillé avec la cigarette par un jeune officer à cheval petite pluie

PLUIE
GRÊLE

sur les avampostes attaque contre-attaque bivouaquer sur la route   épuisés à jeûn maladies traînards disparus désertions   pluie pluie pluie pluie pluie tatatatatatatata pluie brutalité d'une averse inondation des tranchées bains de pieds-genoux-ventre-poitrine **pic-pac-pan** pluie pluie vaches maraudées départ d'un régiment plutôt

mourir que pourrir en avant en avant contre Bulgares mais Bulgares éloignés disparus

pluie pluie averse torrent de pluie rentrer suive qui peut   village zig-zags de cahutes **patapoum-praak** embuscade tatatatatatata pluie sauve qui peut sergent manchot Bulgares en fuite bivouaquer sur la route s'endormir dans les flammes et la fumée la tête sur le sac pluie (*TORRENTIEL SYSTÉMATIQUE PÉNÉTRANT SINISTRE SOLITAIRE ÉTERNEL ROUGE NOIR FUMEUX ROUGE DANSANT RUISSELANT ACIDE*)

Choukri-Pacha se promener avant arrière derrière ses vitres la tête sur la poitrine   ordre de marche général malgré la pluie sortie de 3 divisions pesanteur des pieds bataillons fondus ténèbres (*FLASQUE MONOTONE SOMNAMBULIQUE AUTOMATIQUE ONDULATOIRE*) boue boue boue boue boue plaines inondées cliquetis cliquetis cliquetis cliquetis   chavirement de soldats masses rompues de fatigue fossés ornières marcher 4 heures pour faire une lieue halte pluie soldats-éponges silence tambours tambouououours pluvieux   ordre de rompre les faisceaux murmures refus cris d'officiers Choukri Choukri Choukri Choukri Choukri circulation magnétique d'un mot dans les rangs **pic-tac-tam** des Bulgares l'ennemi l'ennemi tous debout calmes pluie distances pluie rangs serrés en avant pluie bidons vidés bouteilles jetées Comitadjis patrouilles bulgares à cheval rails enlevés fils télégraphiques coupés pluie explosioooon (pont sauté) détente ballottement de masses d'air halte brouhaha dans les rangs désertion d'une centaine de Bulgares incorporés vent vent vent vent vent balayage des nuages frisson ✛ aigreur d'aube violette

embuscade de T. S. F. bulgares
vibbbbrrrrrrrrer
enchevêtrrrrrrrrer communications turques
Choukri-Pacha - Constantinople

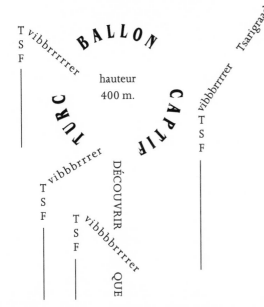

l'attaque contre Seyloglou masquait attaque important contre Marasch point faible objectif bulgare

par télégraphie sans fils { ministre de la guerre renseigné par l'Ambassade turque à Paris informer que armée serbe renforcer Bulgares devant Andrinople pouvoir usurpé par Jeunes Turcs voleurs assassins démembrement de la Turquie

impassibilité solaire de Choukri-Pacha aux supplications de 3.000 affamées **toumtoumtoum tza-tzou** coups de hâche assaut aux boulangeries magasins vidés

prix augmentés du 300 % { sucre 20 frs. le Kg.
riz 2 frs. 50 » »
pétrole 25 frs. le bidon
sel 18 frs. le Kg.

fusiller sur-le-champ

TOUS (100) TOUS (300) TOUS (2000)

les soldats qui ont donné l'assaut à la régie des tabacs

BOOOOMBAAAARDEMENT
BOOOOMBOOOOOOMBAAARDEEEEEMENT

24 Mars
25 Mars { **BOUM BOUM BOUM**
26 Mars

faim détresse terreur des Turcs se réplier sur les forts Kavkaz Aïvaz Bata vendre les armes pour morceau de pain défoncer les boutiques Choukri Choukri Choukri

UBIQUITÉ DE CHOUKRI

ration des habitants réduite à 75 gr. de pain (millet paille sorgo poussière)

3 OBUS

5   obus

2   obus

4   obus   3   obus   **8 OBUS**   **bilan**   21 octobre blocus
sur   Stamboul-Youlou   sur   jardin   Réchadie   **du siège**   15 novembre Andrinople cerné
        sur   Institut   des   sœurs   d'Agram   30 attaques 45 combats
(bâtisse   +   solidité   =   écumoire)   52 duels d'artillerie
démenagements   affolés   de   Khalil-bey   2500 obus
7   heures   du   matin   entrée   de   la   cavalerie   destruction de 430 bâtisses
bulgare   du   côté   de   Kaïk   perdu 15.000 hommes

DRAPEAU
BLANC
S
U
R

Quartier   général   Hadirlik   général   Wasoff   à
la   tête   de   la   2me division   d'infanterie   lour-
deur   barbe   longue   saleté   sauvagerie
férocité   peaux   tannées   par   les   souffles   ex-
plosifs   shrapnels   +   danger

EXÉCUTIONS   EN   MASSE

500   prisonniers
à bas le fez

Pont

300 POUTRES $+$ 180 TONNEAUX $+$ 28 CABLES $+$ 900 BOULONS $<$ PRESSION 150.000 MC. $+$ 190 TURCS

Plouff plouff corps tombé dans l'eau ou porte-à-tourniquet café 2 $+$ 2 $+$ 3 $+$ 2 clients plongeons paletots fourrures dans les ressacs ricochets des lumières électriques miroirs marbres clapotement fièvre d'un journal grands TITRES capitales belliqueuses Balkans tac-tac-télégraphique fleuve torrents ruisseaux lacs d'imprévu ALBANIE NANCY MARITZA ce miroir 5 mètres de profondeur sous le pont construit par les Bulgares cette nuit aube d'il y a 6 mois ou d'hier 15 dégrés sous zéro ennui frissons gare de Kadakeuy déferlement d'un même vent dans les journaux brandis par les camelots à Stamboul Belgrade Sophia Athènes et dans ces drapeaux attente continuité de haine Bulgares Serbes moi-même là-bas pieds glacés cœur chaud ce soir pieds chauds cœur glacé à 10 mètres du pont villa turque

jardin (*RAVAGÉ NOIR VIOLET NOIR VIOLET HUMIDE LENT*) 6 réservistes pansements blancs tachés de rouge odeur-sucrée-de-cadavre
ammoniaque éther chou-pourri se chauffer à un aloès-de-flammes-courge-rôtie pain-de-seigle cuiller-de-bois à la ronde savourer lenteur (*VIOLET VIOLET VIOLET BLEU BLEU*) 2 ronflements réserviste $+$ biplan
(en haut) **HHRRRAAAaaa**

hrrrrrrr (en bas)

voilà sur nos têtes un Farman coup d'oeil distrait béatitude des lèvres meditation de la langue maladresse de l'âme vitalité de l'estomac rouler bien chaque bouchée ventre chaud dos glacé

$$\text{journal} = \begin{cases} \text{déformation} \\ \text{concision} \\ \text{caricature} \end{cases} \begin{cases} \text{distance} \\ \text{angoisse} \\ \text{présence} \end{cases} \begin{cases} \text{résumé} \\ \text{de} \\ \text{l'ITALIE} \end{cases}$$

que fait-on que disent-ils pluie (*VIOLET VERT-TREMBLOTANT*) pont terrifié ruissellement claquement des dents aïe aïe aïe aïe chair cartilages du bois poutres barils clous soffrance laaaasse des fibres (*DUR GLACÉ SERRÉ COLLÉ VERDÂTRE TRÈS LENT*) bas-ventre-du-ciel accouchement de corbeaux lourds bourrés de cadavres

craa-craa tatatatatatata

mettre à point les mitrailleuses ou bien roulement de chariots Halles de Paris avez-vous une cigarette   officier serbe accent français silhouette féminine entre ses cils branle-bas chaud de Montmartre lumières en dentelles âmes retroussées miroirs excités sueur bidet castagnettes hors d'haleine étalage de seins jambes routinières criiiiis

invasion de bruits amers cuisson de souvenirs-désirs blonde   brouillard azuré de ses yeux pâleur électrique de ses joues lèvres blessées sortie de théâtre en charmeuse bleu Nattier ornée de bouillonnés et d'un collier de plumes teintes en bleu   chaleur et malice d'un autre sourire las lourdeur de deux yeux noirs manteau-cape de satin noir brodé de jais roublardise de scepticismes parisiens puits de détresse dans la chair rampement de lassitudes dans les nerfs cri des puanteurs en bataille   hoquets du pont grelottement du bois gémissements des fibres *donnez-nous-5-degrés-de-chaleur-pour-nous—dilater*

craaaaa

3 corbeaux vol de corbeaux (longueur 2 Km.) défaite de la nuit gonflement argenté de nuages vibrant-fuselage-de-l'âme dénouement d'espoirs et de voix 1ère fermentation d'échos bousculade de reflets (*BLEU BLEU MOU GRIS RAPIDE*) délivrance

conquête   oser   or béril périr digérer corbeaux corbeaux construction d'un plafond noir noir 10 km². déjà plus grand 20 km². branlant gonflé de pas de maçons corbeaux démolition de l'horizon-cheminée [200 KM. DE DIAMÈTRE] flocons de suie avalanche de charbon il neige (*BLANC NOIR ÉTERNEL*) vis grincement poulies-rouillées corbeaux inondation d'encre de chine capitonnage fuligineux de l'atmosphère

qu'est-ce qu'on attend l'artillerie **hue hue kring-kring** mares étangs flic-flac rosses canons-gris-perle-Creusot-dernier-modèle **hue hue** fouets clac-clac frénésie des chevaux-martyrs-squelettes solennité des artilleurs montagnards 2 mètres 120 kilos jambes rembourrées laine boue pieds d'éléphants manteau-boa roulé en bandoulière   rosaires de cartouches gros pain sous le bras cabrements vociférations bafouillage d'ordres cris boue pluie

on patauge rien n'avance

qu'est-ce qu'on attend pour passer le pont **craa-craa** après les corbeaux viendront les Turcs **craa-craa** ne tire pas nom-de-dieu faut pas éveiller les sentinelles turques abattre un corbeau manger enfin tirer plutôt dans ce plastron avaleur de reflets et vomisseur de sottises à ma table   ne le tue pas tu pourras causer avec lui quand tu chercheras nuit route défoncée par les roues des canons ta ligne de mort dans le milliard de lignes projectiles des 800.000 fusils ennemis   à la frontière Individu et Patrie vivez ensemble sans vous chamailler   tuer ce corbeau manger du Bulgare ils viennent de Kir-Kilisse lent battement d'ailes   corbeau d'un kilo digestion de gourmet en plein vol 100 1.000 300.000 kilos de pourriture volante **craa-craa** hoquets nausées criaillement d'enfants après le repas savourer lambeau de cadavre turc au bec nez de Bulgare creusé goulûment toute la nuit truffes épices poivre rouge cannelle faudra manger force blé pour se rafraîchir tiens tiens

    voici Mustapha-Pacha sous nos pattes **craa-craa** (*DÉBRAILLÉ DÉBRAILLÉ DÉBRAILLÉ MÉCANIQUE*) ça sentait plus bon à Kir-Kilisse arrêtons-nous de la farine sacs un minaret au rond balconnet désert où le soleil ne parle plus   cimetière

    aller au nord au nord

    vite avant que l'air n'éclate en morceaux voilà le ventre du soleil hisser sur les collines ce cher rôtisseur de cadavres filer filer digérer en paix labours de Stara Zagora **craa-craa** éviter les routes cornes mugissements et roues **craa-craa pet-na-noïe en avant**   baïonettes vers le pont tous les hommes debout se ranger **pet-na-noïe**   solennité inexplicable de 11 bataillons sur les chemins onduleux hérisser les hauteurs de Jourouk   l'air d'être au spectacle   officiers à cheval énormes qu'on fasse couler l'armée sur le pont   tiendra-t-il pendant 3 heures pont construit trop vite la nuit dernière 300 Bulgares à la hâte ligoter pousser enchaîner malgré le courant plongeons vase remous clouer barques tonneaux poutres chut moins de bruit possible il pleuvait heureusement câbles radeaux hissa-hoo hissa-hoo la Maritza gentille à la poitrine dure tumulte de ses mamelles contre le pont vite 2 mitrailleuses pointées contre la rive turque   voilà les Turcs Turcs là là près du fort Kazal-Tépé

au pas de course en masse courir bondir sur le pont siiiifflements balles **pim-pam-pack** nom-de-dieu trop tard 5 10 15 yeux tous les yeux des forts clignements battements **fracas** de leurs paupières en batterie flammes flammes flammes sifflements **strrrrr** sur nos têtes 12 kilomètres de vol **zang-toumb-toumb** 3 échos fracassés ricochet de 4 échos lawn-tennis-de-bruits   vague sonore ovoïdale qui s'en va lentement caresser 3 collines et se coucher sur le ventre vert de la Maritza élasticité 150 km. monotonie vers la mer = 600.000 émeraudes   dents molles du soleil grignoter 4 minarets Selim Pacha et ce grouillement au bout du pont les Turcs à coups de hache éclairs bleus **tsa tsou tsa tsou** vite vite tirez dessus un bon pointeur (*ORANGE ROUGE OR VERDISSANT INDIGO VIOLET INCANDESCENT PÉRISSABLE*) horizon = vrille du soleil + 5 fragments de colline + 30 colonnes de fumée + 23 flammes   vous trois équilibrez vos mitrailleuses c'est ça assis baissez la tête derrière vos 3 appareils à photographier la mort avez-vous compris tintamarre piaillement je sais le turc les entendez-vous crier une scie une scie paille brûler brûler   gros câble crisser craquer **crrrr** la scie **tatatatatatatata** viser bien **plouff** turc 80 kg. dans l'eau   **plouff** un autre 120 Kg. au moins **tatatatatata** très bien 2 3 5 turcs 600 kg. **plouff**   **plouff**

    grappe de turcs **pataplouff-plouff** pour te rassasier chère Maritza éblouissement **zang-toumb-toumb** fichue-la-mitrailleuse 2 autres continuer continuer **tatatatatata** arrosoirs de balles machines à recoudre l'atmosphère déchirée par les hâches **tsa-tsou-tsa-tsou-tsou** le pont **criiiissse** craquement de ses côtes très long long **rrrrrronflement** du câble Maritza pression de 120.000 mc. contre le pont à le fendre **tsa-tsou-tsa-tsou tatatatatata cring-striadiiiiiiooooz** turcs rage furie sanglots

prières je t'en supplie je t'en supplie pont chéri casse-toi en deux ouvre-toi pour enfanter notre victoire les forts les forts ouvrir cligner cligner multiplication de leurs regards (*FORANT RÉPÉTÉ ACHARNÉ IMPLACABLE DUR DUR DUR*) **pata-traaaak boum zoumb-toumb** obus turc sur le pont tourbillon poussière-fange-bois-haine-effroi-sang-viande-en-mitraille-intestins-corridas-hâchis-graisse fracassement des mitrailleuses masques de bouesanglante (*ROUGE ROUGE ROUGE FORT FORT FOU FOU GRAND GROS*) voir **tsou-tsang tsang-tsang** hâches pétillement du fer splendeur des visages en sueur boue lumineuse roue véloce des muscles-anguilles sur la tête éclaboussement solaire hâches câble vite **sciiiiier sciiiiier sciiiiier sciiiiier sciiiiiier** encore 3 boulons **pet-na-noïe pet-na-noïe en avant** suspension élastique de la victoire il faut d'autres mitrailleuses allons vite vous la réglerez après baisse la tête imbécile et tire sur ces 3 géants près du fourneau sous le câble **tatatatata crii-iiiii** (*LONG LONG LONG*) le pont veut se défaire s'effondrer allons vite frapper frapper frapper frapper **tsou-tsa** ouff sépare-toi de moi fibre de 3 millimètres s'ouvrir bonheur (*PETIT PETIT MENU*) se multiplier ivresse en 20 30 fibrilles 400 filaments et 600 pailles chaud trop chaud voici le tranchant **tsou-tsa** allons-nous-mouiller fraîcheur du fleuve vivre libre toutes les pointes tournées au dehors je suis trop épaisse se désagréger

s'émietter ô ma fibre de 6 millimètres si tu t'é-cartes un peu je m'ouvre en deux si tu éclates merci enfin je respire-par-3-trous ah 6 trous odeur de résine moisi fer-brûlé aigre rouille-du-boulon grosses mains calleuses serrant la tenaille tirer tirer tandis que les hâches frapper frapper **tsa-tsou** 2 gros Turcs sur le boulon qui résiste le dernier le dernier **tatatatatata** courageuse résistance du bois **crrrrrrr zang-toumb-toumb tsa-tsou-tsa-tsou** fracassssssement du soleil en pièces 1000 blocs solaires **tourbillonnants** sur les collines 20 shrapnels-gamins (*GOUAILLEUR DÉGINGANDÉ DÉSŒUVRÉ*) trâiner leurs jambes sonores siffler **zang-toumb** effondrement d'un plafond de bronze tous les forts **ouvrir fermer ouvrir fermer ouvrir fermer ouvrir ouvrir ouvrir** leurs yeux-bouches feu-plomb éventail de flammes ampleur 30 km. sur les 15 pointeurs tombés sur le nez l'air de dormir autour des 2 mitrailleuses-chiens-de-garde-gueules-tendues pousse-moi à gauche fibre de 2 millimètres je veux me trancher en trois ne plie pas saute pam casse-toi scie scie tiens voici ma sciure **crrrrr** câble **pet-na-noïe** 3 nouveaux pointeurs second arrosage de plomb sur le câble avant qu'on ne le brûle vite rigolade flasque des remous pilotis drapés d'eau verte rouge **tsa-tsou tatatatatata** câble puer fumer **crrrrrrraaaak** trop tard enfer malheur au diable le pont angle obtus arc tendu bombe son ventre **s'ouvrrriiir aaaaïe patapoumpatatraaack**

malédiction canailles canailles crier crier hurler mugir **joie joie délire les turcs** à tue-tête **hourrrrrraaaah** tatatatatata **hourrrrrraaaah** tatatatatatata POUM PAM-PAM PLOUFF **zang-toumb-toumb-**

toumb-toumb hourrrrraaah tatatatatatata
hourrrrraaaah

HACHÉ ROUGE ROUGE STRIÉ SACCADÉ ÉTERNEL
hourrrrrrrraaaaah hourrrrrraaaaah
vaincre vaincre joie joie vengeance massacrer continuer
tatatatatatatatatatatatata
FIN DÉSESPOIR PERDU RIEN-À-FAIRE INUTILE
plonger fraîcheur se dilater s'ouvrir s'amollir se dilater
ploum plamplam plouff plouff frrrrrrr
crottin urine bidet ammoniaque odeur-typographique

SOLEIL À RÉPÉTITION 20.000 BALLES À LA MINUTE
hourrrrrrrraaaaaaaaaah
joie joie joie joie encore encore vengeance
tatatatatatatatatatatata
RECOMMENCER INUTILE INUTILE PAS MOYEN
veux-tu nager fibre de 2 millimètres
plouff plaff plaff gottgott glouglou
ammoniaque odeur de femme mûre aisselles tubéreuse cadavre

il fait frais il fait vert il fait bleu il fait lisse
dans l'eau j'ai perdu ma tête on nage mieux moi
je n'ai pas de ventre j'ai un trou filtre-tamis par
où laisser passer 1000 gouttes d'eau par seconde

Train de soldats malades

Choukri Pacha par Allah l'outrecuidance de ces grands seigneurs m'exaspère nous n'avons pas besoin d'eux ici tu feras emprisonner Abdul Pacha pour avoir fait détacher une locomotive sans mon ordre il faut que tous ces malades soient enfournés dans une heure au plus tard

gare de Karagatch claquement des panneaux qui s'abattent à chaque extrémité des wagons médecins infirmiers majors civières brancardiers brise lancinante comme les entrailles de ce capitaine Anatolien entérite dysentérie tremblement de sa main décharnée porter aux lèvres la bouteille de lait *fourmillement insurrection fournaise des microbes de la putréfaction dans le tube intestinal s'installer vite se multiplier entamer pourrir parois*

avalanche de lait 6000 ferments lactiques à l'assaut tumulte de la bataille viscérale agglutination de 31 bataillons de microbes fragmentation de 6 microbes-généraux indécision de la victoire $=$ santé $+$ mort *fraîcheur espoir de vivre ébauches de sourire sur les levres tiraillées par l'agonie contre-attaque des microbes*

sapeurs

pioches marteaux tenailles baïonnettes écartellement toute la colère balkanique dans le ventre potion du médecin douche de levure de bière $+$ *touraillons d'orge*

        3000 principes énergiques contre les armées microbiennes fracas assourdissant de la douleur secousses brouhaha du départ santé des vitesses et du plein air rapetissement du corps maigre assis dans le sens du mouvement *chocs contre la peau* vers l'extérieur 30 Km. à l'heure vers Stamboul mon frère guérir guérir guérir (*CONTRE-COUP VISCÉRAL DES ONO-MATOPÉES LYRIQUES DU TRAIN*)

tlactlac ii ii guiiii

trrrrrrtrrrrrr

tatatatôo-tatatatatôo

(*ROUES*)

currrrrr

cuhrrrr

gurrrrrrr

(*LOCOMOTIVE*)

fuufufufuufufu

fafafafafa

zazazazazaza

tzatzatzatzatza

40 Km. à l'heure 45 Km. $=$ *pression gran-*

222

dissante sur les viscères qui vont encore à la vitesse de 30 Km. armée des ferments lactiques + *armée de levure de bière* < 900000 microbes *bataille dans un pays secoué par un tremblement de terre (**TUBULAIRE GRANDISSANT ACHARNÉ FÉROCE MÉTICULEUX ÉTERNEL NUAGEUX DÉVASTÉ**)* arrêt changement de locomotive tirer maintenant le train par la queue et le malade par les épaules assis en sens inverse *chocs agissant sur les terminaisons nerveuses du côté du tronc irritation du système central nerveux* à droite à gauche ralentissement des 2 paysages pivotants = 2 roues dentées horizontales tournant en sens inverse du trainbarre-horizontale chaque arbre-dent des 2 roues-paysages s'encastrer vibrer 3 secondes entre 2 wagons-dents et fuir 3 Km. en arrière entre dents et dents les viscères anatoliens du capitaine pleins de branches aiguës et de ciels verdâtres sur l'impossible Bosphore

POIDS + lenteur du train ralentissement gradué des 2 paysages pivotants (***VELOUTÉ SINISTRE UNIVERSEL***)

rêve

de 1500

malades

{ oisiveté élégances voyages vitesse des trains-bistouris montagnesventres élan des volumes de l'espace agilité des trains-anguilles filets de pluie   brosses du soleil trainsaiguilles coudre montagnes de velours soieries des plaines moires des lacs mouvante étoffe des voyages vitesse prairies-théorèmes mamelles des collines lait de l'aube dans la bouche fraîcheur   gare   lit draps frais   orangeade   glacée

rixe superposition des odeurs de toutes les maladies enfournées dans le train *feuillage vibrant de l'odorat* odeur fécale de la dysentérie puanteur mielleuse des sueurs de la peste relent ammoniacal des cholériques fétidité sucrée des gangrènes pulmoniques odeur acidulée des fiévreux odeur de cave urine de chat huile-chaude moisissure encens paille-pourrie marécage friture vinasse odeur de souris tubéreuse ail chou-pourri **zang-toum-toumb** tatatatatata **stop huhuhuhu huhurlement** des malades dans la **crrrrrrrépitation** des **balles** sifflements **fracas** de vitres cassées portières-cibles Andrinople entièrement cerné train abandonné par mécaniciens et soldats rage des shrapnels bulgares   faim et rapacité volantes mordre minarets-nougats de Sélim-Pacha urgence d'exploser sur les marbres ors toucher toucher les pierreries mystère pouvoir surnaturel faucher arbres hommes et colonnes comme blé   tête cadavéreuse du capitaine anatolien penché hors de la portière = appareil photographique fixer une batterie turque abandonnée   pointeur tête fracassée couvrir le canon de son corps en bouillie putréfaction mouches derrière lui le servant un shrapnel en mains embrasser le caisson ouvert plein d'ors coffre-fort   autour des 3 pièces 12 servants réséda morts trajectoires différentes clouées sur place humour des immobilités 3 chevaux assis sur l'unique compôte de leurs 3 croupes fondues tirer tirer tirer toute la terre entrailles interminables par leurs 3 encolures allongées d'1 m. **heeeeeennissements** très haut vers le ciel implorer flairer lécher cette 1ère étoile Vénus chair pierreries richesse

printemps chatoiement devanture électrique Rue
de la Paix

huhuhuhurlement

de 1500 malades aux portières **fermées à
clef** devant 6 chevaux harnachés morts 24
pattes en l'air écheveau enragé de longes
et roues éclats de shrapnels sacs uniformes
bouleversement du sol entonnoirs trous béants
boues gluantes

huhuhuhurlement

de 1500 malades aux portières **fermées à
clef** devant 18 artilleurs turcs foudroyés
loques   lambeaux
            capotes   officiers   jetés
sur les réseaux de fil de fer passer passer
à tout prix angoisse tordre avec la courte
baïonnette arracher les mailles rage **SOURICIERE**
            ralentissement de la fusillade sous
le poids des nuages $(= 3$ JOURS DE
PLUIE) tremblottement aigrelet d'une musette
venir de loin vent arrière   danser
le koros   fermentation de bivouacs-
plaies dans les premières ténèbres (*ROUGE
NOIR MOU ONDULÉ INDÉTERMINÉ INDULGENT
SPASMODIQUE*) fourmillement d'ombres ram-
pement des postes avancés uniformes couleur
d'ocre se terrer
            ramper patience   des chats
            déplacement de 84 pièces
lourdes tonnerrrrrrrrrre de rrrroues et nuages

Bombardement

1 2 3 4 5 secondes canons de siège éventrer le silence par un accord **zang-toomb** aussitôt échos échos tous les échos s'en emparer vite l'émietter l'éparpiller au loin infini au diable   Dans le centre centre de ces **zang-toomb** aplatis ampleur 50 kilomètres carrés bondir 2 3 6 8 éclats massues coups de poing coups de tête batteries à tir rapide Violence férocité régularité jeu de pendule fatalité

Mes oreilles   mes yeux   narines   ouvertes attention quelle joie que la vôtre ô mon peuple de sens voir ouïr flairer boire tout tout tout **taratatatatata** les mitrailleuses crier se tordre sous 1000 morsures gifles **traak-traak** coups de trinque coups de fouet **pic-pac-poum-toumb** jongleries bonds de clowns en plein ciel hauteur 200 m. c'est la fusillade En contrebas esclaffements de marécages   rires buffles chariots aiguillons piaffe de cheveaux caissons flic flac **zang-zang-chaaak-chaaak** cabrements pirou-

ettes **patatraak** éclaboussements crinières hennissements **iiiiiiiiii** tohu-tohuu tintements 3 bataillons bulgares en marche **croooc-craaac** (*LENTEMENT MESURE À DEUX TEMPS*) Choumi Maritza o Karvavena cris d'officiers s'entréchoquer plats de cuivre **pam** ici (*VITE*) **pac** là-bas **boum-pam-pam-pam-pam** ici là là plus loin tout autour très haut attention nom-de-dieu sur la tête **chaaak** épatant   flammes

flammes

flammes   flammes

flammes   flammes

flammes   rampe des forts là-bas

flammes

flammes

Choukri-Pacha téléphone ses ordres à 27 forts en turc en allemand allô **Ibrahim Rudolf allô allô** acteurs rôles   échos-souffleurs   décors de fumée forêts applaudissements odeur-foin-boue-crottin je ne sens plus mes pieds glacés odeur de moisi   pourriture gongs flûtes clarines pipeaux partout en haut en bas oiseaux gazouiller béatitude ombrages verdeur cip-cip zzip-zzip troupeaux pâturages dong-dang-dong-ding-bééé **zang-toumb-toumb-toumb-toumb-toumb-toumb-toumb**

2000 shrapnels gesticulation explosion **zang-toumb** mouchoirs blancs pleins d'or **toumb-toumb** 2000 grenades tonnerre d'applaudissements Vite vite quel enthousiasme s'arracher tignasses chevelures ténèbres **zang-toumb-toumb** orchestre des bruits de guerre se gonfler sous une note de silence suspendue en plein ciel ballon captif doré contrôlant le tir

BILAN   DES   ANALOGIES

(1re SOMME)

Marche de la canonnade futuriste colosse-leit-motif-pilon-génie novateur-optimisme-faim-ambition (*TERRIFIANT ABSOLU SOLENNEL HÉROÏQUE LOURD IMPLACABLE FÉ CONDANT*) **zang** **toumb** **toumb** **toumb** **toumb** **toumb** tatatatatatatatata picpacpacpanpacpac-panpanpan ouououououm ouououououm

(2me SOMME)

défense d'Andrinople passéisme minarets du scepticisme coupoles-ventres de l'indolence lâcheté nous-y-penserons-demain pas-de-danger pas-possible à-quoi-bon après-tout-je-m'en-fiche livraison de tout le stock en gare unique = cimetière

(3me SOMME)

autour de chaque obus-pas du colosse-note-chute du pilon-création du génie-commandement-courir ronde galopante de coups

de fusil mitrailleuses violons gamins caniches ironies de critiques roues engrenages cris gestes regrets (*GAI GAI GAI GAI SCEPTIQUE FOLÂTRE JOLI AÉRIEN CORROSIF VOLUPTUEUX*)

(4me SOMME)

autour d'Andrinople + bombardement + orchestre + promenade-du-colosse + usine s'élargir cercles-concentriques reflets plagiats échos rires fillettes fleurs sifflement-de-vapeur attente plumages parfums puanteurs angoisse (*INFINI MONOTONE PERSUASIF NOSTALGIQUE*) Ces poids épaisseurs bruits odeurs tourbillons moléculaires chaînes filets et couloirs d'analogies concurrences et synchronismes à mes amis poètes peintres et musiciens futuristes

zang-toumb-toumb **zang-toumb toumb** **tatatatatatatatatata** **picpacpampacpacpicpampam** ououououououououou

MANIFESTE TECHNIQUE

de la

Littérature futuriste

(11 Mai 1912)

héritée de Homère. Besoin furieux de délivrer les mots en les tirant du cachot de la période latine. Elle a naturellement, comme tout imbécile, une tête prévoyante, un ventre, deux jambes et deux pieds plats, mais n'aura jamais deux ailes. De quoi marcher, courir quelques instants et s'arrêter presqu'aussitôt en soufflant !.... Voilà ce que m'a dit l'hélice tourbillonnante, tandis que je filais à deux cents mètres, sur les puissantes cheminées milanaises. Et l'hélice ajouta :

1. — **Il faut détruire la syntaxe en disposant les substantifs au hasard de leur naissance.**

2. — **Il faut employer le verbe à l'infinitif,** pour qu'il s'adapte élastiquement au substantif et ne le soumette pas au *moi* de l'écrivain qui observe ou imagine. Le verbe à l'infinitif peut seul donner le sens du continu de la vie et l'elasticité de l'intuition qui la perçoit.

3. — **Il faut abolir l'adjectif** pour que le substantif nu garde sa couleur essentielle. L'adjectif portant en lui un principe de nuance est incompatible avec notre vision dynamique, puisqu'il suppose un arrêt, une méditation.

4. — **Il faut abolir l'adverbe,** vieille agrafe qui tient attachés les mots ensemble. L'adverbe conserve à la phrase une fastidieuse unité de ton.

5. — **Chaque substantif doit avoir son double,** c'est-à-dire le substantif doit être suivi, sans locution conjonctive, du substantif auquel il est lié par analogie. Exemple : homme-torpilleur, femme-rade, place-entonnoir, porte-robinet.

La vitesse aérienne ayant multiplié notre connaissance du monde, la perception par analogie devient de plus en plus naturelle à l'homme. Il faut donc supprimer les *comme, tel que, ainsi que, semblable à,* etc. Mieux encore, il faut fondre directement l'objet avec l'image qu'il évoque en donnant l'image en raccourci par un seul mot essentiel.

6. — **Plus de ponctuation.**

Les adjectifs, les adverbes et les locutions conjonctives étant supprimés, la ponctuation s'annule naturellement, dans la continuité variée d'un style vivant qui se crée lui-même, sans les arrêts absurdes des virgules et des points. Pour accentuer certains mouvements et indiquer leurs directions, on emploiera les signes mathématiques $\times + : - = > <$, et les signes musicaux.

7. — Les écrivains se sont abandonnés jusqu'ici à l'analogie immédiate. Ils ont comparé par exemple un animal à l'homme ou à un autre animal, ce qui est encore presque de la photographie. Ils ont comparé par exemple un fox-terrier à un tout petit pur-sang. D'autres, plus avancés, pourraient comparer ce même fox-terrier trépidant à une petite machine Morse. Je le compare, moi, à une eau bouillonnante. Il y a là **une gradation d'analogies de plus en plus vastes,** des rapports de plus en plus profonds bien que très éloignés.

L'analogie n'est que l'amour immense qui rattache les choses distantes, apparemment différentes et hostiles. C'est moyennant des analogies très vastes que ce style orchestral, à la fois polychrome, polyphonique et polymorphe, peut embrasser la vie de la matière.

Quand, dans ma *Bataille de Tripoli*, j'ai comparé une tranchée hérissée de baïonnettes à un orchestre, une mitrailleuse à une femme fatale, j'ai introduit intuitivement une grande partie de l'univers dans un court épisode de bataille africaine.

Les images ne sont pas des fleurs à choisir et à cueillir avec parcimonie, comme le disait Voltaire. Elles constituent le sang même de la poésie. La poésie doit être une suite ininterrompue d'images neuves, sans quoi elle n'est qu'anémie et chlorose.

Plus les images contiennent de rapports vastes, plus elles gardent longtemps leur force ahurissante. Il faut ménager, dit-on, la stupeur du lecteur. Ah ! bah ! Soucions-nous plutôt de la fatale corrosion du temps qui détruit non seulement la valeur expressive d'un chef-d'œuvre, mais aussi sa force ahurissante. Nos oreilles trop de fois enthousiastes n'ont-elles pas usé Beethoven et Wagner ? Il faut donc abolir dans la langue ce qu'elle contient d'images-clichés, de métaphores decolorées, c'est-à-dire presque tout.

8. — **Il n'y a pas des catégories d'images,**

nobles ou grossières, élégantes ou basses, excentriques ou naturelles. L'intuition qui les perçoit n'a pas de préférences ni de parti-pris. Le style analogique est donc le maître absolu de toute la matière et de sa vie intense.

9. — Pour donner les mouvements successifs d'un objet il faut donner la **chaîne des analogies** qu'il évoque, chacune condensée, ramassée en un mot essentiel.

Voici un exemple frappant d'une chaîne d'analogies encore masquées et alourdies par la syntaxe traditionelle :

« *Mais oui, vous êtes, mignonne mitrailleuse, une femme charmante, et sinistre, et divine, au volant d'une invisible cent-chevaux qui renâcle et rugit d'impatience…Et vous allez bientôt bondir dans le circuit de la mort, vers le panache écrabouillant ou la victoire ! En voulez-vous, des madrigaux pleins de grâce et de couleur ? A votre choix, madame ! Je vous trouve semblable aussi à un tribun gesticulant dont la langue éloquente, infatigable, frappe au cœur le cercle ému des auditeurs. Vous êtes en ce moment un trépan tout-puissant qui perce en rond le crâne trop solide de cette nuit obstinée. Vous êtes aussi un laminoir d'acier, un tour électrique, et quoi encore ?….un grand chalumeau oxydrique qui brûle, cisèle et fait fondre peu à peu les pointes métalliques des dernières étoiles.* » (« Bataille de Tripoli »).

Dans certains cas il faudra enchaîner les images deux à deux à la manière des boulets ramés qui peuvent trancher dans leur vol un bouquet d'arbres.

Pour envelopper et saisir tout ce qu'il y a de plus fuyant et insaisissable dans la matière, il faut former **des filets serrés d'images ou analogies** qu'on lancera dans la mer mystérieuse des phénomènes. Sauf la forme traditionnelle, cette phrase de mon *Mafarka le futuriste* est un filet serré d'images : « *Toute l'âcre douceur de sa jeunesse montait de sa gorge, comme de la cour des écoles montent les cris des enfants, vers leurs vieux maîtres penchés aux parapets des terrasses d'où l'on voit fuir les bateaux sur la mer.* »

Voilà trois filets serrés d'images :

« *Autour des puits de la Bumeliana, sous les oliviers touffus, trois chameaux, confortablement couchés dans le sable, se gargarisaient de* joie comme de vieilles gargouilles, en mêlant leur crachottement au teuf-teuf de la pompe à vapeur qui abreuve la ville.

« Stridences et dissonances futuristes dans l'orchestre profond des tranchées aux pertuis sinueux et aux caves sonores, parmi le va-et-vient des baïonnettes, archets de violons, que la baguette rouge du couchant-directeur enflamme d'enthousiasme.

« C'est lui qui, d'un geste vaste, ramasse les flûtes éparses des oiseaux dans les arbres et les harpes plaintives des insectes, le craquement des branches, les crissements des pierres.... C'est lui qui arrête net les tympans des gamelles et des fusils entrechoqués, pour laisser chanter à pleine voix sur l'orchestre en sourdine toutes les étoiles en habits d'or, les bras ouverts, debout sur la rampe du ciel. Et voilà une dame au spectacle : en grand décolleté, le désert étale, en effet, sa gorge vaste aux mille courbes liquéfiées, toutes vernies de fard rose sous les pierreries croulantes de la nuit prodigue. » (« Bataille de Tripoli »).

10. — Tout ordre étant fatalement un produit de l'intelligence cauteleuse, il faut orchestrer les images en les disposant suivant un **maximum de désordre.**

11. — **Détruire le « Je » dans la littérature,** c'est-à-dire toute la psychologie. L'homme complètement avarié par la bibliothèque et le musée, soumis à une logique et à une sagesse effroyables, n'a absolument plus d'intérêt. Donc, l'abolir en littérature. Le remplacer enfin par la matière, dont il faut atteindre l'essence à coups d'intuition, ce que les physiciens et les chimistes ne pourront jamais faire.

Ausculter à travers les objets en liberté et les moteurs capricieux la respiration, la sensibilité et les instincts des métaux, des pierres et du bois etc. Remplacer la psychologie de l'homme, désormais épuisée, par l'**obsession lyrique de la matière.**

Gardez-vous de prêter des sentiments humains à la matière, mais devinez plutôt ses différentes poussées directives, ses forces de compression, de dilatation, de cohésion et de disgrégation, ses ruées de molécules en masse ou ses tourbillons d'électrons. Il ne faut pas donner les drames de la matière humanisée. C'est la solidité d'une plaque d'acier qui nous intéresse par elle-même, c'est-à-dire l'alliance incompréhensible et inhumaine de ses molécules et de ses électrons, qui s'opposent par exemple à la pénétration d'un obus. La chaleur d'un morceau de fer ou de bois est désormais plus passionnante pour nous que le sourire ou les larmes d'une femme.

Nous voulons donner en littérature la vie du moteur, cette nouvelle bête instinctive dont nous connaîtrons l'instinct général quand nous aurons connu les instincts des différentes forces qui le composent.

Rien de plus intéressant, pour le poète futuriste, que l'agitation d'un clavier dans un piano mécanique. Le cinématographe nous offre la danse d'un objet qui se divise et se récompose sans intervention humaine. Il nous offre l'élan à rebours d'un plongeur dont les pieds sortent de la mer et rebondissent violemment sur le tremplin. Il nous offre la course d'un homme à 200 kilomètres à l'heure. Autant de mouvements de la matière hors des lois de l'intelligence, et partant d'une essence plus significative.

Il faut introduire dans la littérature trois éléments que l'on a négligés jusqu'ici :

1. — **Le bruit** (manifestation du dynamisme des objets) ;

2. — **Le poids** (faculté de vol des objets) ;

3. — **L'odeur** (faculté d'éparpillement des objets).

S'efforcer de rendre, par exemple, le paysage d'odeurs que perçoit un chien. Ecouter les moteurs et reproduire leurs discours.

La matière a été toujours contemplée par un moi distrait, froid, trop préoccupé de lui-même, plein de préjugés de sagesse et d'obsessions humaines.

L'homme tend à salir de sa joie jeune ou de sa douleur vieillissante la matière qui n'est ni jeune ni vieille, mais qui possède une admirable continuité d'élan vers plus d'ardeur, de mouvement et d'éparpillement. La matière n'est ni triste ni joyeuse. Elle a pour essence le courage, la volonté et la force absolue.

Elle appartient toute entière au poète divinateur qui saura se délivrer de la syntaxe traditionnelle, lourde, étroite, attachée au sol, sans bras et sans ailes parce qu'elle est seulement intelligente. Seul le poète asyntaxique et aux mots déliés pourra pénétrer l'essence de la matière et détruire la sourde hostilité qui la sépare de nous.

La période latine qui nous a servi jusqu'ici était un geste prétentieux par lequel l'intelligence outrecuidante et myope s'efforçait de dompter la vie multiforme et mystérieuse de la matière. La période latine était donc morte-née.

Les intuitions profondes de la vie juxtaposées mot à mot, suivant leur naissance illogique nous donneront les lignes générales d'une **physicologie intuitive de la matière.** Elle s'est révélée à mon esprit du haut d'un aéroplane. En regardant les objets d'un nouveau point de vue, non plus de face ou de dos, mais à pic, c'est-à-dire en raccourci, j'ai pu rompre les vieilles entraves logiques et les fils à plomb de l'antique compréhension.

Vous tous qui m'avez aimé et suivi jusqu'ici, poètes futuristes, vous fûtes comme moi de frénétiques constructeurs d'images et de courageux explorateurs d'analogies. Mais vos filets serrés de métaphores sont malheureusement trop alourdis de plomb logique. Je vous conseille de les alléger, pour que votre geste immensifié puisse les lancer au loin, deployés sur un plus vaste océan.

Nous inventerons ensemble ce que j'appelle **l'imagination sans fils.** Nous parviendrons un jour à un art encore plus essentiel, quand nous oserons supprimer tous les premiers termes de nos analogies pour ne donner que la suite ininterrompue des seconds termes. Il faudra pour cela renoncer à être compris. Être compris n'est pas nécessaire. Nous nous en sommes d'ailleurs bien passés quand nous exprimions des fragments de la sensibilité futuriste au moyen de la syntaxe traditionnelle et intellective.

La syntaxe était une sorte de chiffre abstrait qui a servi aux poètes pour renseigner les foules sur l'état coloré, musical, plastique et architectural de l'univers. La syntaxe était une sorte d'interprète et de cicérone monotone. Il faut supprimer cet intermédiaire pour que la littérature entre directement dans l'univers et fasse corps avec lui.

Il est indiscutable que mon œuvre se distingue nettement de toutes les autres par son effrayante puissance d'analogie. Son étonnante richesse d'images égale presque son désordre de ponctuation logique. Elle aboutit au premier manifeste futuriste, synthèse d'une cent-chevaux lancée aux plus folles vitesses terrestres.

A quoi bon se servir encore de quatre roues exaspérées qui s'ennuient, du moment qu'on peut se détacher du sol ? Délivrance des mots, ailes planantes de l'imagination, synthèse analogique de la terre embrassée d'un seul regard, ramassée toute entière en des mots essentiels.

On nous crie : « Ce ne sera pas beau ! Nous n'aurons plus la symphonie verbale aux balancements harmonieux et aux cadences apaisantes. » Bien entendu. Et quelle chance ! Nous utilisons au contraire tous les sons brutaux, tous les cris expressifs de la vie violente qui nous entoure.

Faisons crânement du « laid » en littérature et tuons partout la solennité. Et ne prenez donc pas ces airs de grands-prêtres en m'écoutant. Il faut cracher chaque jour sur l'*Autel de l'Art.* Nous entrons dans les domaines illimités de la libre intuition. Après le vers libre, voici enfin **les mots en liberté.**

Il n'y a là rien d'absolu ni de systématique. Le génie a des rafales impétueuses et des torrents boueux. Il impose parfois des lenteurs analytiques et explicatives. On ne peut guère rénover sa sensibilité d'un seul coup. Les cellules mortes sont mêlées aux vivantes. L'art est un besoin de se détruire et de s'éparpiller, grand arrosoir d'héroïsme inondant le monde. Les microbes, ne l'oubliez pas, sont nécessaires au sang, aussi bien qu'à l'Art, ce prolongement de la forêt de nos veines, qui se déploie hors du corps dans l'infini de l'espace et du temps.

Poètes futuristes ! Je vous ai enseigné à haïr les bibliothèques et les musées. C'était pour vous préparer à **haïr l'intelligence,** en éveillant en vous la divine intuition, don caractéristique des races latines.

Par l'intuition, nous romprons l'hostilité apparemment irréductible qui sépare notre chair humaine du métal des moteurs. Après le règne animal, voici le règne mécanique qui commence ! Par la connaissance et l'amitié de la matière, dont les savants ne peuvent connaître que les réactions physico-chimiques, nous préparons la création de l'**homme mécanique aux parties remplaçables.** Nous le délivrerons de l'idée de la mort, et partant de la mort elle-même, cette suprême définition de l'intelligence logique.

F. T. Marinetti.

Milan, le 11 Mai 1912.

BATAILLE

POIDS + ODEUR

Midi 3/4 flûtes glapissement embrasement **toumb-toumb** alarme Gargaresch craquement crépitation marche Cliquetis sacs fusils sabots clous canons crinières roues caissons juifs beignets pains-a-l'huile cantilènes échoppes bouffées chatoiement chassie puanteur cannelle fadeurs flux reflux poivre rixe vermine tourbillon orangers-en-fleur filigrane misère dés échecs cartes jasmin $+$ muscade $+$ rose arabesque mosaïque charogne hérissement savates mitrailleuses $=$ galets $+$ ressac $+$ grenouilles Cliquetis sacs fusils canons ferraille atmosphère $=$ plomb $+$ lave $+$ 300 puanteurs $+$ 50 parfums pavé-matelas détritus crottin charognes flic-flac entassement chameaux bourricots tohubohu cloaque Souk-des-argentiers dédale soie azur galabieh pourpre oranges moucharabieh arches enjambement bifurcation placette pullulement tannerie cireurs gandouras burnous grouillement couler suinter bariolage enveloppement excroissances fissures tanières gravats démolition

acide-phénique chaux pouillerie Cliquetis sacs fusils sabots clous canons caissons coups-de-fouet drap-de-soldat suint impasse à-gauche entonnoir à-droite carrefour clair-obscur étuves fritures musc jonquilles fleur-d'oranger ecœrement essence-de-rose-piège ammoniaque griffes excrément-morsures viande $+$ 1000 mouches fruits-secs carroubes pois-chiches pistaches amandes régimes-bananes dattes **toumb-toumb** bouc cousscouss-moisi aromates safran goudron œuf-pourri chien-mouillé jasmin cassie santal œillets faisandage intensité bouillonnement fermenter tubéreuse Pourrir s'éparpiller furie mourir se désagréger morceaux miettes poussière héroïsme elminthes fusillade **pic pac pun pan pan** menthe mandarine laine-fauve mitrailleuses-cliquets-de-bois-léproserie plaies en-avant chair-moite crasse suavité éther Cliquetis sacs fusils canons caissons roues benjoin tabac encens anis village ruines brûlé ambre jasmin maisons-éventrements abandon gargoulette **toumb toumb** violettes ombrages puits ânon ânesse cadavre-écrabouillement-sexe-exhibition ail bromes

anisette brise poisson sapin-neuf romarin
charcuteries palmiers sable cannelle
        Soleil or balance plateaux plomb
ciel soie chaleur rembourrage pourpre azur
torréfaction Soleil $=$ volcan $+$ 3000 dra-
peaux atmosphère-précision corrida furie
chirurgie lampes
            rayons-bistouris étincellement-linges
désert-clinique $\times$ 20.000 bras 20.000 pieds
10.000 yeux-mire scintillation attente opéra-
tion sables-chaufferies Italiens Arabes: 4.000
mètres bataillons-chaudières commandements-
pistons sueur bouches fournaises crénomde-
nom en-avant huile ammoniaque $>$ cassies
violettes fientes roses sables miroitement tout
marcher arithmétique traces obéir ironie en-
thousiasme   bourdonnement courdre
dunes-oreillers zigzags repriser pieds-meules-
crissement sable inutilité mitrailleuses $=$
galets $+$ ressac $+$ grenouilles
        Avant-gardes: 200 mètres chargez-
à-la-baïonnette en-avant Artères gonflement
chaleur fermentation-cheveux-aisselles chignon-
rousseur blondeur haleines $+$ sac 30 ki-
los prudence $=$ bascule ferrailles tire-lire
mollesse: 3 frissons commandements-pierres
rage ennemi-aimant légèreté gloire
        héroïsme Avant-gardes : 100 mètres
mitrailleuses fusillade éruption violons cuivre
pim poum pac pac tim toum mitrailleuses
tatarataratarata

        Avant-gardes : 20 mètres bataillons-
fourmis cavalerie-araignées routes-gués général-
îlot estafettes-sauterelles sables-révolution
obus-tribuns nuages-grils fusils-martyrs shrap-
nels-auréoles multiplication addition division obus-
soustraction grenade-rature ruisseler couler éboule-
ment blocs avalanche

        Avant-gardes : 3 mètres mélange
va-et-vient collage décollage déchirement feu
déraciner chantiers éboulement carrières in-
cendie panique aveuglement écraser entrer
sortir courir   éclaboussement Vies-
fusées cœurs-friandises baïonettes-fourchettes
mordre dépécer puer valser bondir rage
curée explosions obus-gymnastes fracas trapèzes
explosion rose joie ventres-arrosoirs têtes-foot-
ball éparpillement   Canon-149 éléphant
artilleurs-cornacs hissa-hoo colère leviers lenteur
lourdeur centre gargoussejockey méthode mo-
notonie trainers distance grand-prix gueule
parabole x lumière tonnerre massue infini Mer
$=$ dentelles - émeraudes - fraîcheur - élasticité -
abandon mollesse cuirassés-acier-conclusion-ordre
Drapeau-de-combat (prairies-ciel-blanc-de-chaleur
sang) $=$ Italie force orgueil-italien frères
femmes mère insomnie brouhaha-de-camelots
gloire domination cafés récits-de-guerre
        Tours canons-virilité-volées érec-
tion télémètre extase **toumb-toumb** 3 sec-
ondes **toumb-toumb** flots sourires rires
plaff plouff glouglouglouglou cache-cache
cristaux vierges chair bijoux perles iodes
sels bromes jupons gaz liqueurs bulles 3
secondes   **toumb-toumb** officier
blancheur télémètre croix feu mégaphone la-
hausse-à-4-mille-mètres tous-les-hommes-à-gauche
assez chacun-à-son-poste inclinaison-7-degrés
érection splendeur jet percer immensité azur-
femelle dépucelage   acharnement
couloirs cris labyrinthe matelas sanglots dé-
foncement désert lit précision télémètre mono-
plan   poulailler-de-théâtre applaudissements
        monoplan $=$ balcon-rose-roue-
tambour trépan-taon $>$ déroute arabes bœufs
sanguinolence abattoir blessures refuge oasis
humidité éventail fraîcheur

sieste rampement germination ef-
fort dilatation-végétale je-serai-plus-vert-demain
restons-mouillés conserve-cette-goutte-d'eau faut-
grimper-3-centimètres-en-6-jours colle-ta-
tige-pour-résister-contre-20-grammes-de-sable-et-
300-grammes-de-ténèbres voie-lactée-cocotier
étoiles-noix-de-coco lait ruisseler jus délices

F. T. MARINETTI.

Les mots en liberté futuristes

Le futurisme, né à Milan il y a onze ans, a influencé tout l'univers, par des milliers d'expositions, de conférences et de concerts, et a créé d'innombrables futurismes différents, selon les exigences des milieux. Chaque milieu a un passéisme particulier, un passéisme encombrant et pernicieux qu'il faut détruire. Le futurisme a été compris dans toutes les capitales d'Europe et d'Amérique et est devenu partout le point de départ d'importantes révolutions spirituelles. En Italie il a été longtemps calomnié et traqué par les forces réactionnaires, cléricales, moralistes, pédantes et conservatrices. Il sort de cette lutte plus puissant que jamais.

Le mouvement futuriste exerça tout d'abord une action artistique, tout en influençant indirectement la vie politique italienne par une propagande de patriotisme révolutionnaire, anticlérical, directement lancé contre la Triple Alliance et qui préparait notre guerre contre l'Autriche. Le futurisme italien, prophète et préparateur de notre guerre, semeur et entraineur de courage et de liberté, a ouvert, il y a onze ans, son premier meeting artistique au Théâtre Lirico de Milan par le cri: *A bas l'Autriche !*

Depuis ce jour, ces mots sont devenus le cri obsédant de toutes nos réunions orageuses.

Les futuristes italiens sont fiers d'avoir organisé les deux premières manifestations populaires contre l'Autriche, le 15 Septembre 1914, à Milan, en pleine neutralité italienne. Ces deux manifestations furent acharnées et retentissantes : huit drapeaux autrichiens furent brûlés dans l'émeute par les futuristes, qui furent enfermés dans la prison de San Vittore.

Les futuristes, toujours au premier rang dans les rues pour exiger à coups de poing la déclaration de guerre à l'Autriche, furent aussi au premier rang sur les champs de bataille, avec un grand nombre de morts, de blessés et de décorés.

Les futuristes ont fondé durant la guerre le parti politique futuriste, qui a pour organe le journal *Roma Futurista*. Aussitôt après notre grande victoire de Vittorio Veneto, se sont formés les Faisceaux politiques futuristes de Milan, Rome, Florence, Ferrare, Tarante, Pérouse, etc.

Le futurisme italien est l'âme de la nouvelle génération qui s'est battue contre l'empire austro-hongrois et l'a victorieusement anéanti.

Le mouvement futuriste artistique qui s'est forcément ralenti durant la guerre, reprend aujourd'hui son dynamisme excitateur et rénovateur.

Durant notre grande guerre victorieuse, les poètes futuristes, combattants en première ligne ont profité de leurs brefs loisirs de tranchée ou d'hôpital pour pousser avec acharnement leur grand travail inspiré pour la rénovation totale du lyrisme, qui après avoir passé par le vers libre atteint aujourd'hui aux mots en liberté.

La victoire des mots en liberté est déjà un fait accompli en Italie et commence à se déterminer aussi dans les milieux intellectuels du monde entier, qui subissent presque tous l'influence du futurisme.

Nous avons aujourd'hui en Italie une centaine de mots-libristes intéressants.

Les mots en liberté sont une expression absolument libre de l'univers en dehors des prosodies et des syntaxes, une nouvelle façon de voir et sentir les choses, une mesuration de l'univers comme addition de forces en mouvement. Ces forces s'entrecroisent dans notre *moi* conscient et créateur qui les note rigoureusement par tous les moyens d'expression possibles.

Les mots-libristes orchestrent ainsi les couleurs, les bruits, les sons, forment des combinaisons suggestives avec les matériaux de la langue et du patois, les formules arithmétiques et géométriques, les vieux mots, les mots déformés et les mots inventés, les cris des animaux et les bruits des moteurs, etc.

La victoire artistique des mots en liberté tranche nettement en deux l'histoire de la poésie humaine, depuis Homère jusqu'au dernier souffle lyrique de la terre.

Les hommes ont jusqu'ici plus ou moins chanté tous comme Homère avec une succession narrative et un catalogue logique d'idées, faits, sentiments, sensations, images. C'est pourquoi on peut affirmer qu'il n'existe aucune différence réelle entre les vers d'Homère et ceux de Gabriele D'Annunzio ou de Verhaeren.

Les mots-libristes se distinguent finalement d'Homère avec netteté parce qu'ils ne se contentent plus de donner la succession narrative, mais ils donnent l'expression intégrale, dynamique et simultanée de l'univers.

[. . .]

La sensibilité futuriste et l'imagination sans fils

[…]

Les mots en liberté.

Sans me soucier des définitions stupides des professeurs, je vous déclare que le lyrisme est la *faculté* très rare *de se griser de la vie et de la griser de nous-mêmes* ; la faculté de transformer en vin l'eau trouble de la vie qui nous enveloppe et nous traverse ; la faculté de colorer le monde avec les couleurs spéciales de notre *moi* changeant. Supposez donc qu'un ami doué de ce don lyrique se trouve dans une zone de vie intense (révolution, guerre, naufrage, tremblement de terre, etc.) et vienne, aussitôt après, vous raconter ses impressions. Savez-vous ce que fera tout instinctivement votre ami en commençant son récit ? Il détruira brutalement la syntaxe en parlant, se gardera bien de perdre du temps à construire ses périodes, abolira la ponctuation et l'ordre des adjectifs et vous jettera à la hâte dans les nerfs toutes ses sensations visuelles, auditives et olfactives, au gré de leur galop affolant. L'impétuosité de la vapeur-émotion fera sauter le tuyau de la période, les soupapes de la ponctuation et les adjectifs qu'on dispose habituellement avec régularité comme des boulons. Vous aurez ainsi des poignées de mots essentiels sans aucun ordre conventionnel, votre ami n'ayant d'autre préoccupation que de rendre toutes les vibrations de son *moi*. Si ce conteur doué de lyrisme possédera en outre une intelligence riche en idées générales, il rattachera involontairement et sans cesse ces dernières sensations à tout ce qu'il a connu, expérimentalement ou intuitivement, de l'univers. Il lancera d'immenses filets d'analogies sur le monde, donnant ainsi le fond analogique et essentiel de la vie télégraphiquement, c'est-à-dire avec la rapidité économique que le télégraphe impose aux reporters et aux correspondants de guerre dans leurs récits superficiels.

Ce besoin de laconisme ne répond pas seulement aux lois de vitesse qui nous gouvernent, mais aussi aux rapports multiséculaires que le poète et le public ont eu ensemble. Ces rapports ressemblent beaucoup à la camaraderie de deux vieux amis qui peuvent s'expliquer par un seul mot, un seul coup d'œil. Voilà comment et pourquoi l'imagination du poète doit lier les choses lointaines *sans fils conducteurs*, moyennant des mots essentiels et absolument *en liberté*.

L'imagination sans fils.

Par l'imagination sans fils j'entends la liberté absolue des images ou analogies exprimées par des mots déliés, sans les fils conducteurs de la syntaxe et *sans aucune ponctuation*.

« Les écrivains se sont abandonnés jusqu'ici à l'analogie immédiate. Ils ont comparé, par ex., un fox-terrier à un tout petit pur-sang. D'autres, plus avancés, pourraient comparer ce même fox-terrier trépidant à une petite machine Morse. Je le compare, moi, à une eau bouillonnante. Il y a là une gradation d'analogies de plus en plus vastes, des rapports de plus en plus profonds, bien que très éloignés. *L'analogie n'est que l'amour immense qui rattache les choses distantes*, apparemment différentes et hostiles. C'est moyennant des analogies très vastes que ce style orchestral, à la fois polychrome, polyphonique et polymorphe, peut embrasser la vie de la matière. Quand, dans ma *Bataille de Tripoli*, j'ai comparé une tranchée hérissée de baïonnettes à un orchestre, une mitrailleuse à une femme fatale, j'ai introduit intuitivement une grande partie de l'univers dans un court épisode de bataille africaine. Les images ne sont pas des fleurs à choisir et à cueillir avec parcimonie,

comme le disait Voltaire. Elles constituent le sang même de la poésie. La poésie doit être une suite ininterrompue d'images neuves, sans quoi elle n'est qu'anémie et chlorose. Plus les images contiennent de rapports vastes, plus elles gardent longtemps leur force ahurissante. » (*Manif. de la Littérature futuriste.*) L'imagination sans fils et les mots en liberté nous introduiront dans l'essence même de la matière. En découvrant de nouvelles analogies entre des choses lointaines et apparemment opposées, nous les évaluerons toujours plus intimement. Au lieu d'*humaniser*, les animaux, les végétaux, les minéraux (ce qu'on fait depuis longtemps) nous pourrons *animaliser, végétaliser, minéraliser, électriser* ou *liquéfier* le style en le faisant vivre de la vie même de la matière. Ex. : un brin d'herbe qui dit : « Je serai plus vert demain ». Nous aurons donc : **Les métaphores condensées. — Les images télégraphiques. — Les sommes de vibrations. — Les nœuds de pensées. — Les éventails tour à tour ouverts et fermés de mouvements. — Les raccourcis des analogies. — Les bilans de couleurs. — Les dimensions, poids, mesure et vitesse, des sensations. — Le plongeon du mot essentiel dans l'eau de la sensibilité sans les cercles concentriques que le mot produit. — Les repos de l'intuition. — Les mouvements à 2, 3, 4, 5 temps. — Les poteaux analytiques explicatifs qui soutiennent les fils de l'intuition.**

[. . .]

Onomatopées et signes mathématiques.

Quand j'ai dit qu'il faut « cracher chaque jour sur l'Autel de l'Art » je poussais les futuristes à délivrer le lyrisme de l'atmosphère pleine de componction et d'encens que l'on a l'habitude d'appeler l'Art avec un grand A. L'Art avec un grand A représente le cléricalisme de l'esprit créateur. Je poussais les futuristes à bafouer les festons, les palmes, les auréoles, les cadres précieux, les étoles, les péplums, toute la défroque historique et le bric-à-brac romantique qui forme la plus grande partie de l'œuvre de tous les poètes jusqu'à nous. Je défendais en revanche un lyrisme très rapide, brutal, violent, immédiat que tous nos prédécesseurs auraient jugé anti-poétique, un lyrisme télégraphique imprégné d'une forte odeur de vie et sans rien de livresque. D'où la nécessité d'introduire courageusement des accords onomatopéiques pour donner tous les sons et tous les bruits, même les plus cacophoniques, de la vie moderne. L'onomatopée qui sert à vivifier le lyrisme par des éléments crus de réalité a été employée avec beaucoup de timidité par les poètes, depuis Aristophane jusqu'à nos jours. Les futuristes ont eu les premiers le courage de se servir de l'onomatopée avec une audace et une continuité anti-académiques. Cette audace et cette continuité ne doivent pas être systématiques. Par exemple mon *Adrianople - Siège - Orchestre* et ma *Bataille Poids* + *Odeur* exigeaient un grand nombre d'accords onomatopéiques. En outre notre souci constant de donner le maximum de vibrations et de profondes synthèses de la vie nous pousse à abolir tous les liens traditionnels du style, toutes les agrafes précieuses, dont les poètes traditionnels se servent pour attacher leurs images dans la période. Nous nous servons au contraire de signes mathématiques et de signes musicaux infiniment plus courts et absolument anonymes. Nous mettons de plus entre parenthèses des indications comme celles-ci: (vite) (plus vite) (ralentissez) (deux temps) pour régler la vitesse du style. Ces parenthèses peuvent aussi couper un mot ou un accord onomatopéique.

Révolution typographique et Orthographe libre expressive

Révolution typographique.

J'entreprends une révolution typographique dirigée surtout contre la conception idiote et nauséeuse du livre de vers passéiste, avec son papier à la main, genre seizième siècle, orné de galères, de minerves, d'apollons, de grandes initiales et de parafes, de légumes mythologiques, de rubans de missel, d'épigraphes et de chiffres romains. Le livre doit être l'expression futuriste de notre pensée futuriste. Mieux encore : ma révolution est dirigée en outre contre ce qu'on appelle harmonie typographique de la page, qui est contraire aux flux et reflux du style qui se déploie dans la page. Nous emploierons aussi, dans une même page 3 ou 4 encres de couleurs différents et 20 caractères différents s'il faut. Par exemple : *italiques* pour une série de sensations semblables et rapides, **gras** pour les onomatopées violentes, etc. Nouvelle conception de la page typographiquement picturale.

Orthographe libre expressive.

La nécessité historique de l'orthographe libre expressive est démontrée par les révolutions successives qui ont peu à peu délivré des entraves et des règles la puissance lyrique de la race humaine.

1. — En effect les poètes commencèrent par canaliser leur ivresse lyrique en une série de respirations égales, avec des accents, des échos, des coups de cloche ou rimes prédisposées à des distances fixes (**Prosodie traditionnelle**). Les poètes alternèrent ensuite avec quelque liberté les différentes respirations mesurées par les poumons des poètes précédents.

2. — Les poètes se persuadèrent plus tard que les différents moments de leur ivresse lyrique devaient créer leurs respirations appropriées, de longueurs imprévues et très différentes avec une absolue liberté d'accentuation. Ils arrivèrent ainsi naturellement au **Vers libre,** mais conservèrent encore l'ordre de la syntaxe pour que leur ivresse lyrique pût couler dans l'esprit de l'auditeur par le canal logique de la période conventionnelle.

3. — Nous voulons aujourd'hui que l'ivresse lyrique ne dispose plus les mots suivant l'ordre de la syntaxe avant de les lancer au moyen de respirations inventées par nous. Nous avons ainsi les **Mots en liberté.** En outre, notre ivresse lyrique doit librement déformer, modeler les mots en les coupant ou en les allongeant, renforçant leur centre ou leurs extrémités, augmentant ou diminuant le nombre des voyelles ou des consonnes. Nous aurons ainsi la nouvelle *orthographe* que j'appelle *libre expressive.* Cette déformation instinctive des mots correspond à notre penchant naturel vers l'onomatopée. Peu importe si le mot déformé deviendra équivoque. Il se fondra mieux avec les accords onomatopéiques ou résumés de bruits et nous permettra d'atteindre bientôt l'*accord onomatopéique psychique,* expression sonore mais abstraite d'une émotion ou d'une pensée pure.

La splendeur géométrique et mécanique

Nous avons déjà bâclé les funérailles grotesques de la Beauté passéiste (romantique, symboliste et décadente) qui avait pour éléments essentiels la Femme Fatale et le Clair de lune, le souvenir, la nostalgie, l'éternité, l'immortalité, le brouillard de légende produit par les distances de temps, le charme exotique produit par les distances d'espace, le pittoresque, l'im-précis, l'agreste, la solitudine sauvage, le désordre bariolé, la pénombre crépusculaire, la corrosion, la patine = crasse du temps, l'effritement des ruines, l'érudition, l'odeur de moisi, le goût de la pourriture, le pessimisme, la phtysie, le suicide, les coquetteries de l'agonie, l'esthétique de l'insuccès, l'adoration de la mort.

Nous dégageons aujourd'hui du chaos des nouvelles sensibilités une nouvelle beauté que nous substituons à la première et que j'appelle **Splendeur géométrique et mécanique.** Elle a pour éléments le Soleil rallumé par la Volonté, l'oubli hygiénique, l'espoir, le désir, le périssable, l'éphémère, la force bridée, la vitesse, la lumière, la volonté, l'ordre, la discipline, la méthode ; l'instinct de l'homme multiplié par le moteur ; le sens de la grande ville ; l'optimisme agressif qu'on obtient par la culture physique et par le sport ; la femme intelligente (plaisir, fécondité, affaires); l'imagination sans fils, l'ubiquité, le laconisme et la simultanéité qui caractérisent le tourisme, les grandes affaires et le journalisme ; la passion pour le succès, le record, l'imitation enthousiaste de l'électricité et de la machine, la concision essentielle et la synthèse ; la précision heureuse des engrenages et des pensées lubrifiées ; la concurrence d'énergies convergentes en une seule trajectoire.

Mes sens futuristes perçurent pour la première fois cette splendeur géométrique sur le pont d'une dreadnought. La vitesse du navire, les distances des tirs fixées du haut de la passerelle dans la ventilation fraîche des probabilités guerrières, la vitalité étrange des ordres transmis par l'amiral et brusquement devenus autonomes et inhumains, à travers les caprices, les impatiences et les maladies de l'acier et du cuivre : tout cela rayonnait de splendeur géométrique et mécanique. Je perçus l'initiative lyrique de l'électricité courant à travers le blindage des tourelles quadruples, et descendant par des tubes blindés jusqu'aux soutes, pour tirer obus et gargousses jusqu'aux culasses, vers les volées émergeantes. Pointage en hauteur, en direction, hausse, flamme, recul automatique, élan personnel du projectile, choc, broyement, fracas, odeur d'œuf pourri, gaz méphitiques, rouille, ammoniaque, etc. Voilà un nouveau drame plein d'imprévu futuriste et de splendeur géométrique, qui a pour nous cent mille fois plus d'intérêt que la psychologie de l'homme avec ses combinaisons limitées.

Les foules peuvent parfois nous donner quelques faibles émotions. Nous préférons les affiches lumineuses, fards et pierreries futuristes, sous lesquels, chaque soir, les villes cachent leurs rides passéistes. Nous aimons la solidarité des moteurs zélés et ordonnés. Rien n'est plus beau qu'une grande centrale électrique bourdonnante, qui contient la pression hydraulique d'une chaîne de montagnes et la force électrique de tout un horizon, synthétisées sur les tableaux de distribution, hérissés de claviers et de commutateurs reluisants. Ces tableaux formidables sont nos seuls modèles en poésie. Nous avons quelques précurseurs et ce sont les gymnastes, les équilibristes et les clowns qui réalisent, dans les développements, les repos et les cadences de leurs musculatures, cette perfection étincelante d'engrenages précis, et cette splendeur géométrique que nous voulons atteindre en poésie par les mots en liberté.

1. — Nous détruisons systématiquement le *Moi* littéraire pour qu'il s'éparpille dans la vibration universelle, et nous exprimons l'infiniment petit et les agitations moléculaires. Ex.: la foudroyante agitation moléculaire dans un trou creusé par un obus (dernière partie du *Fort Cheittam-Tepé* dans mon ZZANG TOUMB-TOUMB). La poésie des forces cosmiques supplante ainsi la poésie de l'humain. **Nous abolissons en conséquence les vieilles proportions** (romantiques, sentimentales et chrétiennes) du récit, suivant lesquelles un blessé dans la bataille avait une importance très exagérée en comparaison des engins destructeurs, des positions stratégiques et des conditions

atmosphériques. Dans mon poème ZZANG TOUMB-TOUMB, je décris brièvement, la mort d'un traître bulgare fusillé, tandis que je prolonge une discussion de deux généraux turcs sur les distances de tir et sur les canons des adversaires. J'ai noté en effet, durant le mois d'Octobre 1911, en vivant avec les artilleurs de la batterie De-Suni, dans les tranchées de Tripoli, combien le spectacle de la chair humaine meurtrie est négligeable en comparaison de la volée luisante et agressive d'un canon torréfiée par le soleil et le feu accéléré.

2. — J'ai plusieurs fois démontré que le substantif, usé par les contacts multiples et par le poids des adjectifs parnassiens et décadents, peut être ramené à sa valeur absolue en le dépouillant de tout adjectif et en l'isolant. Je distingue 2 genres de substantifs nus : le **substantif élémentaire** et le **substantif synthèse-mouvement** (ou nœud de substantifs). Cette distinction n'est pas absolue, car elle se fonde sur des intuitions presque insaisissables. Je vois chaque substantif comme un wagon, ou comme une courroie mise en mouvement par le verbe à l'infinitif.

3. — Sauf des besoins de contraste et de changement de rythmes, les divers modes et temps du verbe doivent être supprimés, parce qu'ils font du verbe une roue disloquée de diligence, qui s'adapte aux aspérités des rampes, mais ne peut guère rouler vélocement sur une route plane. **Le verbe à l'infinitif est le mouvement même du nouveau lyrisme,** car il a la souplesse glissante d'une roue de train ou d'une hélice d'aéroplane. Les divers modes et temps du verbe expriment un pessimisme prudent et rassurant, un égotisme épisodique, accidentel, une hausse et baisse de force et de fatigue, de désir et de désillusion, des arrêts en somme dans l'élan de l'espoir et de la volonté. Le verbe à l'infinitif exprime l'optimisme même, la générosité absolue et la folie du devenir. Quand je dis *courir*, quel est le sujet de ce verbe ? Tous et tout, c'est-à-dire l'irradiation universelle de la vie qui court et dont nous sommes une petite partie consciente. Ex. : fin du poème « *Salon d'Hôtel* » du mot-libriste Folgore. Le verbe à l'infinitif c'est le *moi* passionné qui s'abandonne au devenir du tout, continuité héroïque, désintéressement de l'effort et de la joie d'agir. Verbe à l'infinitif = divinité de l'action.

4. – En plaçant un ou plusieurs adjectifs isolés entre parenthèses, ou bien en marge des mots en liberté, derrière une ligne perpendiculaire (c'est à dire en guise de ton), on peut aisément donner les différentes atmosphères du récit et les différents tons qui le gouvernent. **Ces adjectifs-atmosphère ou adjectifs-ton ne peuvent pas être remplacés par des substantifs.** Ce sont là des convictions intuitives, et que l'on ne peut guère démontrer. Je crois néanmoins qu'en isolant par exemple le substantif *férocité*, (ou en le disposant comme un ton) dans la description d'un carnage, on obtiendra un état d'âme de férocité trop immobile et trop fermé dans un profil trop net. Tandis que si je place entre parenthèses ou en guise de ton l'adjectif *féroce*, je le transforme en un *adjectif-atmosphère* ou en un *adjectif-ton* qui enveloppera toute la description du carnage sans arrêter le courant des mots en liberté.

5. – La syntaxe contenait toujours une perspective scientifique et photographique absolument contraire aux droits de l'émotion. **Dans les mots en liberté, cette perspective photographique disparaît,** et l'on obtient la perspective émotionnelle, qui est multiforme. (Ex.: le poème intitulé « *Homme* + *montagne* + *vallée* » du mot-libriste Boccioni).

Simultanéité
Tables synoptiques de
valeurs lyriques

Dans les mots en liberté nous formons parfois des **tables synoptiques de valeurs lyriques** qui nous permettent de suivre en lisant simultanément plusieurs courants de sensations croisées ou parallèles. Ces tables synoptiques ne doivent pas être le principal objet des recherches mot-libristes, mais un moyen pour augmenter la force expressive du lyrisme. Il faut donc éviter toute préoccupation picturale, et ne pas s'amuser à faire des jeux de lignes bizarres, ni d'étranges disproportions typographiques. Tout ce qui dans les mots en liberté ne concourt pas à exprimer avec une splendeur géométrique et mécanique la fuyante sensibilité futuriste, doit être banni. Le mot-libriste Cangiullo dans son poème « *Fumeurs IIme classe* » fut très habile en donnant par cette **analogie dessinée :**

FUMEER, les rêveries monotones et l'expansion de la fumée, durant un long voyage dans un train. Pour exprimer la vibration universelle avec un maximum de force et de profondeur, les mots en liberté se transforment naturellement en **auto-illustrations** moyennant l'orthographe et la typographie libre expressive, les tables synoptiques de valeurs lyriques et les analogies dessinées. (Ex. : le ballon dessiné typographiquement dans mon poème ZZANG TOUMB-TOUMB). Dès que ce maximum d'expression est atteint, les mots en liberté reprennent leur ruissellement normal. Les tables synoptiques de valeurs sont de plus la base de la critique en mots en liberté. (Ex. : « *Bilan 1910–1914* » du mot-libriste Carrà).

L'orthographe et la typographie libre expressive servent à exprimer la mimique du visage et la gesticulation du conteur. Les mots en liberté utilisent (en l'exprimant intégralement) cette partie d'exubérance communicative et de génie épidermique que les esprits méridionaux ne pouvaient guère exprimer dans les cadres de la prosodie, de la syntaxe et de la typographie traditionnelle. Ces énergies d'accent, de voix et de mimique, trouvent aujourd'hui leur expression naturelle dans les mots déformés et dans les disproportions typographiques correspondant aux grimaces du visage et à la force ciselante des gestes. Les mots en liberté deviennent ainsi le prolongement lyrique et transfiguré de notre magnétisme animal.

Notre amour grandissant de la matière, notre désir de la pénétrer et de connaître ses vibrations, la sympathie physique qui nous attache aux moteurs, nous poussent à nous servir toujours davantage de l'onomatopée. Le bruit étant le résultat du choc des solides ou des gaz en vitesse, l'onomatopée qui reproduit le bruit est nécessairement l'un des éléments les plus dynamiques de la poésie. Comme telle, l'onomatopée peut remplacer le verbe à l'infinitif surtout si on l'oppose à une autre ou à plusieurs autres onomatopées. (Ex. : l'onomatopée *tatatatata* des mitrailleuses, opposée à l'*hourrah* des Turcs à la fin du chapitre « Pont » dans mon ZZANG TOUMB-TOUMB). La brièveté des onomatopées permet dans ce cas de créer des combinaisons très souples de rythmes différents. Ceux-ci perdraient une grande partie de leur vitesse s'ils étaient exprimés d'une façon plus abstraite avec un plus grand développement, c'est-à-dire sans l'onomatopée.

[…]

Sensibilité numérique

Mon amour pour la précision et pour la brièveté essentielle m'a donné naturellement le goût des chiffres qui vivent et respirent sur le papier comme des êtres vivants à travers ma nouvelle **sensibilité numérique.** Ex. : au lieu de dire comme un écrivain traditionnel : *un son de cloches vaste et profond* (notation imprécise et inexpressive) ou bien comme un paysan intelligent : *les habitants de tel ou tel village entendent cette cloche* (notation plus précise et plus expressive) je saisis avec une précision intuitive le son de la cloche et j'en détermine l'ampleur en distant : **don dan** *cloches ampleur du son 20 Km.* [2] Je donne ainsi tout un horizon vibrant et une quantité d'individus lointains qui tendent l'oreille au même son de cloche. Je sors de l'imprécis, je m'empare de la réalité par un acte volontaire qui déforme la vibration même du métal. Les signes mathématiques $+ - \times =$ servent à obtenir de merveilleuses synthèses et concourent par leur simplicité abstraite d'engrenages impersonnels au but final, qui est la **Splendeur géométrique et mécanique.** Il faudrait en effet plus d'une page de description traditionnelle pour donner imparfaitement ce très vaste horizon de bataille compliquée dont voici l'équation lyrique définitive : « *horizon $=$ vrille aiguiiiiiiisée du soleil $+$ 5 ombres triangulaires chaque côté 1 Km. $+$ 3 losanges de lumière rose $+$ 5 fragments de collines $+$ 30 colonnes de fumée $+$ 23 flammes.* » J'emploie l'*x* pour indiquer les arrêts interrogatifs de la pensée. J'élimine ainsi le point d'interrogation qui localise trop arbitrairement sur un seul point de la conscience son atmosphère dubitative. Au moyen de l'*x* mathématique la suspension dubitative se répand sur l'agglomération entière des mots en liberté. En suivant mon intuition, j'introduis parmi les mots en liberté des numéros qui n'ont pas de signification ni de valeur directe, mais qui (s'adressant phoniquement et optiquement à la sensibilité numérique) expriment les différentes intensités transcendantales de la matière et les réponses incontrolables que leur donne la sensibilité ; je crée de véritables théorêmes et des équations lyriques en introduisant des numéros choisis intuitivement et disposés au milieu même d'un mot. Avec une

certaine quantité de $+ - \times =$ je donne l'épaisseur
et la forme des choses que le mot doit exprimer. La dis-
position $+ - + - + + \times$ sert à donner [...] l'en-
tassement de sensations égales. (Ex. : *odeur fécale de la
dyssenterie* $+$ *puanteur mielleuse* etc., dans le « *Train de soldats
malades* » de mon ZZANG TOUMB -TOUMB).

Ainsi par les mots en liberté nous substituons
au *ciel antérieur où fleurit la beauté* de Mallarmé la *Splendeur
géométrique et mécanique et la Sensibilité numérique.*

Après les mots en liberté

~~La poème doit s'imprimer avec les~~
~~lignes de la main sur le papier~~
~~Les mots doivent courir sur les~~
~~lignes de la main imprimées.~~

~~Le poème de mots~~

~~Dopo avere~~

Après les mots en liberté, les motsfondus en liberté.
Après avoir délivré les mots de la
du vers ~~de la~~ et de la syntaxe il faut
les fondre pour porter la pensée
et la sensibilité dans la roue de
la simultanéité.

Former des fusions de 2 3 ou 4 mots
— motssimultanés
— Blocs simultanés
— Motsfondus

Corsaschienagelata
manidiventosueinfaccia
Bludalghedormeschiumarive
Uomoferrodiamantecrema
donnastelocielo
biondaltazzurroventinpoppa

Le poème de motsfondus doit continuer
les lignes de la main sur le papier.

Le poème s'imprimera avec les lignes de la
main sur le papier et les motsfondus
(ou motssimultanés) doivent courir sur
ces lignes de la main reproduites sur le papier.

La droite trouve la perle

une étoile de mer
qui lui ressemble

mais trop
vermeille
ne la sortez pas de l'eau
Elle noircirait

éternité des cigales cricricricricri
calcaire ~~dans les~~/et pins qui me surplombent
à la nage ~~palper le calcaire~~ fraîche palper la falaise
~~des falaises~~ ~~trous~~
Sous vos moustaches de varech bouches
pétrifiées, montrez-moi la perle

clop clop clap clap clop
plipliplibleu pliplipibleu de la mer qui marche ou-
blieuse
                de Vierge Marie naufragée
en poussant ses plisbleus mon ~~Cœur~~ cœur flaire la
perle
Sur l'arc ~~immense~~ de l'horizon porcelaine d'une
~~huître~~ immense
huître entrebaillée   Non, la voici!   Chair de perle

Je la tiens avec les dents dents dents   Intelligence
~~mordante~~ rocailleuse des
rochers qui boivent ~~du~~/le soleil liquide et salé

aiguillons noirs des oursins en guerre veloutée

Santé cuirassée des langoustes rouges sentinelles
Lécher manger la perle bénie avec le sel
de la vague qui bouge
~~Les~~ crabes ronds de cuir aux trous d'algues
mordez ma fesse tandis que je mange
du ciel   Du soleil et de l'eau
du soleil et de l'eau   De bas en haut
Escarpolette plongeon dans la fraîcheur de
son cœur Abîme glouglou
Remonter surface écume gazeuse ciel
gggggggg

La droite trouve la perle

              mots en liberté futuristes
              pour Beny

Une étoile de mer
        qui lui ressemble

mais trop
vermeille
ne la sortez pas de l'eau
elle noircirait

Eternité des cigales cricricricri
cricri calcaires et pins qui me surplombent
à la nage fraîche palper la falaise
Sous vos moustaches de varech bouches
pétrifiées   montrez moi la perle
clop clop gott gatt clop

pliplipibleu de la mer qui marche en poussant ses plis
plis plis plis bleus de Vierge Marie naufragée   mon
cœur flaire
flaire la perle sur l'arc de l'horizon porcelaine d'une
immense huître entrebaillée   Non la voici! Chair de
perle

Je la tiens avec les dents Intelligence
rocailleuse Intelligence des rochers qui boivent
le Soleil salé

Aiguillons noirs des oursins guerre veloutée

Santé cuirassée des langoustes rouges sentinelles
Manger la perle chérie de sa chair avec le sel de la
vague
Crabes ronds-de-cuir aux trous d'algues
Mordez ma fesse tandis que je mange du ciel
Du soleil et de l'eau de bas en haut
Escarpolette dans le ressac de son cœur Abîme
Remonter   Surface écume gazeuse
ciel liquide gggggggggggggggg

                         Août 1928

Poésie à Beny

L'île lance la jetée fort avant dans la mer jusqu'à l'amertume intense

Jetée dure géometrie dans l'abreuvante poésie des horizons liquides

Jetée poignard dans la chair lamentable des voyages

Jetée thermomètre dans la baignoire du golfe ensoleillé

Jetée couperet de guillotine qui tranche flots sanglots mouchoirs lettres et mouettes dans la tempête trop tôt trop tard trop loin jamais

Jetée ligne droite assiégée par des triangles cônes losanges paraphes coupoles et toupies de folie verdâtre

Jetée devoir de pierre imposé au tempérament exubérant de la mer vices noirs passions bleues tout avoir tout manger sucer mordre cracher pomper délirer

Jetée tremplin d'angoisse sur la mer foule houle évasion tohubohu chimie et jeu de boules vertes qui se débraille en manches de chemise écume sensualité dans les dimanches de l'enfer

Sur la jetée debout Beny spirale de tendresse parfumée

Elle est vêtue mais soudain la nudité étincelante de son âme sous la douche d'azur soleil et vent salé

Sa bouche Sa bouche

Je l'embrasse et ses bras autour de mon cou et son cher visage dans ma poitrine

Un long baiser arrachement

Je suis l'une des deux lèvres de la blessure et je m'en vais

L'autre c'est elle debout sur la jetée

Les vagues mouillent ses pieds en riant aux larmes comme des jeunes filles qu'on joue à chatouiller iii aaaaaa ggggggg iiiiii glott glouglouglou plic glang gloutt

Dans l'eau jusqu'au ventre rouge les barques grasses obscènes maternelles sous leurs voiles mamelles dégonflées dont le lait a nourri tout le ciel pur enfantelet

Je danse dans mon canot neurasthénie des vagues et leurs manipulations bousculade rixe assaut de blocs

Boxe de 3 vagues debout puis tous les trémolos des violons des souvenirs

Accouplements de nostalgies plaintives

Tressaillement d'échos

Echafaudage de notes ambitieuses et tout à coup le motif dominant

Déchirant 20 fibre-nerfs et 50 violoncelles avec leurs ritournelles de remords 100 200 1000 clarinettes d'angoisse préhistorique et enfin à l'unisson plain-chant

Ampleur poids des négations totales

Tonnerre pathétique

Sous mon canot qui danse joyeux les gorges chaudes des vagues jasent gazouillent gloussent jappent pouffent de rire tout à coup se chamaillent

Réconciliation et leurs aveux soupirs mots chuchotés dans le creux de l'oreille

La mer veut me séduire par ses orchestres dechirés par trop d'archets aigus dans mon flanc de Christ crucifié sur cette croix Infini

La mer veut me séduire et m'arracher à Beny mélodie pure une unie continue infinie

Oh! descendre aux profondeurs absolvantes

Transparence

Comme un cristal de sentiment parmi les vagues des instincts courant à l'aveuglette

Une autre vague ébouriffée ouvre les ailes tombe et s'éventre entrailles d'émeraude-remords

Mais déjà l'immense éventail horizontal de plumes d'autruche de la haute mer sur le profil suave d'une voile femme pensive

Les vagues s'espacent soudain irritation de cette vague qui se cramponne

A qui? à quoi bon? mon canot s'allonge sur de moelleux coussins ressorts affectueux pessimismes

Pourtant là-haut Volonté à plomb des falaises sous la sagesse dorée de la lumière devant le désespoir sans bornes de la couleur verte

Mais ici près du canot cette eau est bien une porcelaine de lait

Non non des perles des perles et l'extase parfumée de la peau de Beny

Chère présence dans le jaillissement de sang-désir

Reflets misérables du passé ses jardins jasmins jadis jadis joujoux

Debout sur la jetée Beny bénie par le soleil

Beny amie des éléments

La mer veut me séduire danser danser descendre monter escarpolette

Souplesse de tous les tigres et des chats familiers

Plouff plouff trop bas vvvvv du vent ggggg de toutes les écumes du plaisir et de la rage trop haut encore plus haut sur la pointe d'une pyramide

Baleines un troupeau de baleines pour former un pavé sous les pieds de Beny bénie

Ballons du vent et le vide sous mes pieds parachute

Démolition et décombres d'écume bloc bloc bloc bloc poids de trois phoques dans mon canot

Gonfler se dégonfler s'aplatir creusement abîme vers le néant

Mais tous les ressorts repoussent comme une virilité sauvage dans l'immense et si intense chair Sa chair blanche verte de la mer bénie de Beny

Ondulation animale de la vague sommeils clairs éternels de métaux ondulés

Porcelaine bleue huile azurée

Azur gras indigo charnel presque des cuisses de négresses bleues allégresse de fesses nues d'anges bleus déculottés par les ouragans du Paradis

Elle est debout sur la jetée que l'île pousse bien avant dans la mer jusqu'à l'amertume intense

Bénie !

Beny svelte d'ardeur blanche

Son corps moulé sculpté par la passion qui de la haute mer se rue

But des vents en lutte pour la saisir

Déchirements saugrenus des vagues qui à ses pieds se tordent et s'arrachent les cheveux d'écume

C'est donc un cœur un immensurable cœur verdâtre cette mer

Cœur démonté !

Cœur intarissable mer dont les palpitations font danser mon canot

Ce canot dont je suis le bois et la chair criante et les côtes les clous les nerfs

Canot mon sternum qui encage ce cœur débordant devenu aujourd'hui la mer atroce qui m'arrache à Beny

Elle est debout sur la jetée vêtue sculptée par le souffle des distances qui pleurent

Vagues et vos vagues poignards qui cherchez des cœurs à percer

Voici le mien! Mais vous riez dégringolades d'œillades
      noires à jamais perdues
Vous m'arrachez à Elle ! et vous m'emportez vers mon
      enfance quand je ne la connaissais pas et je rêvais
      d'elle

Elle est debout sur la jetée qui subit les coups furieux
      de ce cœur océan océan océan !
Distance distance je ne la vois plus je la revois mieux
      car elle dort près de moi dans son lit comme une
      mer somnolente de nuit d'été
Elle respire
Ses parfums tous les parfums de sa chair cher cœur
Tiède et suave imploration de ses pores enfantins et ses
      cheveux jardins sur la mer en plein soleil napoli-
      tain
Ivresse d'entrer dans la mer douce de ce ventre et tout
      à coup je prends la mer ! J'entre je plonge en Elle
      Infini
Infini chaud brûlant blessure
Blessure qui m'aime s'éveille et sourit gémit revient
      fuit crie appelle veut veut boit tout mon cœur
      océan Méditerranée Gibraltar Idéal

Deux périssoires à Capri

Sur la turquoise chaude du golfe désert
deux rouges périssoires
Seuls...
Mais on tutoie chaque reflet qui bouge
Elle en maillot corail
près de mon torse nu brique cuite
par ce pesant soleil vermeil
qui quitte à regret la mer
Mots complots frissons suçons des flots
Oscillation
des deux périssoires

plateaux d'une balance d'or liquide
qui soupire et salive
pensive
Brusquement une main invisible
dérobe un des deux poids
et je la vois monter au ciel légère
Pour garantir l'honnêteté de la balance
je plonge en groin de Marsouin
dans ses cheveux mouillés
algues molles ou dentelles de sirène
et je mords
jusqu'au sang
son cou rose qui sent
l'huître fraîche éclose

Nos périssoires collent
Lents baisers d'épaves qui se lavent de pleurs
De dépit
et d'envie
le soleil s'est coupé sur le tranchant de l'île
Aussitôt
l'ombre rideau fragile
descend du poulailler pour éteindre
les fauteuils du golfe
Mort d'un théâtre !
Ma loge en feu !
Boiseries dorées et velours écarlate
se noient au bric-à-brac
d'une province morte
Immense et bleu visage assombri de la mer
un canot blanc comme une larme sur sa joue

Vers lui
tendues pointues
nos périssoires
comme deux ongles rouges brûlent
dans un blond
rayon
suprême polissoir du soir

– Veux-tu prendre ton essor
comme une mouette
parfaite
ivre d'écume et déjà prête
à faire la bombe en Paradis !
Tiens mets dans tes cheveux
cette frêle Voie Lactée diadème
ou plutôt ces bijoux phare
avec leurs feux croisés
ravis à la vitrine Rue de la Paix de Dieu

– Je leur préfère un lit
plus uni que la mer
et plus dur
Encore une fois
au moins
gamin !
Plus tard qui sait ?
La mer voudra bien nous boire
un soir
lentes périssoires
ou larmes
qui cherchent
le fond
absolu
nu !

Juin 1929.

Insupportable orgueil des Lavaredo
mots en liberté futuristes

Insupportable orgueil des Lavaredo montagnes pyra-
midales
Sans cesse surgies du rêve opaque de cent mille brumes
patientes serviles et rancunières jouissez jouissez
de l'ampleur stratifiée de vos conquêtes et des rois

ennemis vaincus jadis par vous et par vous dure-
ment maçonnés
Fières volontés d'un cristal où circule une rose
blondeur humaine qui chante
Extase
Avant de reprendre votre solennelle agression de l'hy-
persensible azur amusez-vous à critiquer de haut
le luxe et la mignarde élégance des vertes collines
ornées de sapins aux mains jointes autour de leur
chalet oublié qui somnole
Ils implorent une houppe de brouillard sur le noir cha-
peau pointu de la chapelle forestière
La poudre bleue la crème irisée de frissons de Misurina
pour cette belle chair de Lac parfumée de résine
Fraîche toilette à miroirs qui reflète des brosses d'ar-
gent touffues de joncs
Un îlot flacon de fard jaune
Une truite au bond vif happe des pierreries
Tinte tinte un rien de dindon gluggloung ruisseau de
bijoux sonnailles d'un troupeau de vaches qui
monte tel un nuage noir et blanc sur le souple
flanc charnel d'une montagne d'émeraude
Orgueil des Lavaredo
Triangles de fureur cosmique
Vous ne dompterez jamais l'orgueil sans limites ni ex-
cuses de Benedetta éblouissante cime spiralique
de neige chaude
Pourtant l'excuse existe et s'appelle sans doute Beauté
Beauté spirituelle armée de charme charme
Beauté dont s'attendrit l'espace !
C'est toi qui fais trembler mon âme flamme ou feuille
de sapin en deuil près de l'eau sanglot
Souris vite Benedetta et la première larme aiguisée par-
tira projectile de joie dans l'infini

Août 1935.

Faut-il choisir ces mots un à un avec soin ou les lancer
    au loin au hasard en éventail de parfums sorbets
    étincelles tropicales
Ces mots
Ces mots dont le devoir est de servir ta Beauté et aussi
    certains midis parés de chance et d'avenir le De-
    voir de bercer langoureusement l'ondulation
    riche en éclairs de tes yeux et de tes lèvres rouges
    divans d'orient
Je lance donc au loin des mots combien combien au
    moins une centaine
— Courez fouillez chassez et revenez c'est vite fait aboy-
    ant aboyant aboyant
Ils reviennent en soufflant chacun sa force et sa vitesse
Lourds museaux embrasés de joie solaire bave en pier-
    reries et gibiers sanguinolents
Qu'ils sont beaux ces mots d'amour aux jambes fines
Je veux les applaudir tous et les cajoler de leurs beaux
    noms
Eclat sourire fête splendeur orgueil délicatesse fluidité
    ivresse ardeur profondeur marine exaltation élé-
    gance grâce
— Tous à mes pieds fiers mots de chasse et de voyage
    couchez-vous donc sous la caresse du poète
Pourtant les deux non les trois derniers ont l'air à bout
    d'élan ils s'étalent la langue dans le sable et
    douloureusement soulèvent des prunelles de rêve
    pour m'offrir le suc limpide de leur brûlante ago-
    nie de bêtes verbalisées
Belle Belle Belle
De tous les points de la sensibilité cosmique des nerfs
    certains échos malins répètent
Belle Belle Belle
Pathétique et verdâtre le Crépuscule se hâte de traverser
    le ciel pour les admirer de plus près

La nuit venue voilà que la plus charmante mamelle de
    la Voie Lactée soupire
— Je n'ai pu qu'une fois réussir le miracle d'une si
    fraîche étincelante goutte de lait surnaturelle
Elle est unique
Parfaite
Malheureusement tout le reste s'enténèbre âcre et mor-
    dant charbon à manger ou sale chocolat des dé-
    mons
Je dis à Beny couchée en maillot au soleil devant la villa
    Varano
— Si ces mots en liberté se sauvent c'est qu'ils te ressem-
    blent

Terminillo - Villa Varano - agosto 1938.